Surviving the Research Process in Politics

Surviving the Research Process in Politics

Edited by

Peter Burnham

PINTER
London and Washington

PINTER
A Cassell imprint

Wellington House, 125 Strand, London WC2R 0BB, England
PO Box 605, Herndon, Virginia 20172, USA

First published 1997
© The editor and contributors 1997

British Library Cataloguing-in-Publication Data
A catalogue record for this book is available from the British Library.

ISBN 1–85567–446–7 (hardback)
1–85567–447–5 (paperback)

Typeset by Ben Cracknell Studios
Printed and bound in Great Britain by Bookcraft (Bath) Ltd.

Contents

———

About the Contributors

___

Vered Bartov is a doctoral student in the Department of Politics and International Studies, University of Warwick.

Robert G. Burgess is a Pro-Vice-Chancellor at the University of Warwick. He is also Director of the Centre for Educational Development, Appraisal and Research, and Professor of Sociology at Warwick. He has published widely in the area of social research methodology and is the Founding Chair of the UK Council for Graduate Education and Chair of the ESRC Postgraduate Training Board.

Peter Burnham is Lecturer in Politics and International Studies at the University of Warwick. His publications include *The Political Economy of Postwar Reconstruction* (London: Macmillan, 1990) and (with Werner Bonefeld and Alice Brown) *A Major Crisis? The Politics of Economic Policy in Britain in the 1990s* (Aldershot: Dartmouth, 1995).

Stephen Day is a doctoral student in the Department of Politics and International Studies at the University of Warwick.

Jonathan Gorry completed an MA in International Studies at the University of Warwick, where he is presently finishing his doctoral studies in the Department of Politics and International Studies.

Ray Kiely is Lecturer in Development Studies in the Department of Cultural Studies at the University of East London. His publications include *The Politics of Labour and Development in Trinidad* (Kingston: University of West Indies Press, 1996).

Carla Koen studied at the Universities of Lueven and Malaga before joining the Department of Politics and International Studies at the University of Warwick as a doctoral student.

Nisha Malhan is a Research Fellow in the Institute for German Studies at the University of Birmingham.

Michael O'Neill studied for his doctorate in the Department of Politics and International Studies at the University of Warwick.

Ed Page is a doctoral student in the Department of Politics and International Studies at the University of Warwick.

Nick Robinson is Lecturer in Politics in the School of European Studies at the University of Derby.

Steven Smith is Associate Lecturer at the Open University, Milton Keynes.

Gail Stedward is Lecturer in Politics at the University of Manchester.

Laura Tedesco is Lecturer in Politics at the University of East Anglia in Norwich.

Rhiannon Vickers is Lecturer in Politics at the University of Leeds.

John Williams is Lecturer in International Relations at the University of Aberdeen.

Chris Woodard is at present a doctoral student in the Department of Politics and International Studies at the University of Warwick.

Foreword

_____

During the last ten years the postgraduate sector has been the fastest growing area in higher education. As a consequence, the concept of the lone postgraduate student in a department almost belongs to the past. However, postgraduate research students still need authoritative guides to the major elements involved in the research process: starting research; choosing a methodology; and designing a project. The postgraduate student also requires systematic guidance on the appropriate methods and techniques that can be used.

This volume is, therefore, a welcome addition to the developing literature on postgraduate work in the social sciences. First, this collection of essays caters very specifically for students of politics who come to research for the first time. Second, it provides a series of detailed accounts written by recent postgraduates. Their essays remind us that there is no such person as a 'standard' postgraduate. Instead, we discover the many ways in which the postgraduate role is handled by the full-time student, the teaching assistant, the academic who is completing a doctorate and the overseas student.

Altogether these essays provide a set of insights into the way in which postgraduate work is developed, designed, managed and supervised. In this respect, the volume contains material that will be useful both for the postgraduate student and for the potential supervisor.

Overall, this volume provides a useful guide to all those engaged in postgraduate work. I am sure that it will soon become essential reading on postgraduate training courses and will establish itself as an essential building block in developing the career of the social scientist. In this way, it has the potential to improve the quality and standard of the postgraduate research experience for future generations.

Professor Robert G. Burgess
University of Warwick

1

Introduction: Themes,
Issues and Methods
in Research Training

PETER BURNHAM

> *Methodology can only be self-reflection on the means which have proven to be valuable in actual research. Explicit self-reflection of this sort is no more a condition for fruitful research than is knowledge of anatomy a condition for the ability to walk 'correctly'. In fact, whoever tried to walk by applying his knowledge of anatomy would be in danger of stumbling. The scholar who attempts to base the aims of his research on a foundation of extrinsic methodological considerations is in danger of falling into difficulties of the same sort.* (Max Weber)[1]

In the last decade there has been a significant expansion and restructuring of postgraduate education in the social sciences in Britain. Proliferation of new taught Master's courses (usually with a dissertation component) and growth in the number of new research students have led to renewed interest in the research process and the teaching of research methods. These developments are set to continue and are reinforced by Economic and Social Research Council (ESRC) guidelines which demand structured training in research methods for postgraduates.

The roots of this process of restructuring can be traced back to 1979, when the House of Commons Committee of Public Accounts (House of Commons, 1980) voiced 'serious concern' over the time taken by funded students to submit doctoral theses across the academic spectrum in Britain and drew attention in particular to the low submission rates of ESRC- and DES-funded students (in 1977 the submission rate for social science students was just 17 per cent). Three years later, the government's Working Party on Postgraduate Education chaired by Sir Peter Swinnerton-Dyer recommended that 'a graded sequence of sanctions should be applied to any university at which the submission rate was unacceptably low' (ABRC, 1982, para.270). In response, the ESRC in 1985 introduced a sanctions policy whereby ESRC studentships would not be granted to institutions if their student submission rate was under 10 per cent. While the current ESRC sanctions threshold stands at 50 per cent (in 1996/97), the ESRC has a long-term target of 70 per cent, and the DES recommends that 85 per cent represents 'good value for money' (House of Commons, 1988).

Operating on the assumptions that the submission of a thesis for examination within four years is the main measure of success, and that the broad objective of postgraduate education is to 'meet the nation's future manpower needs' (House of Commons, 1988), the ESRC has become increasingly involved in issues concerning research training. As indicated later in this introduction, changes in 1996 to develop Research Training Master's courses (possibly as another step towards the introduction of the 'training-based' as opposed to the 'knowledge-based' PhD), follow the issuing in 1991 of Postgraduate Training Guidelines which stipulated that formal instruction in methodology should 'account for up to 60% of the total time available to the research student over the 44-week period of their first year' (ESRC, 1991, p. 4). University departments who ignore this recommendation do so at the risk of losing their 'recognition status', thereby becoming ineligible to admit students in receipt of ESRC awards (or to apply for new studentships).

The laudable aim of this process of restructuring, and of the 60 per cent training provision in particular, is to extend the general range of skill and competence acquired by social science researchers, in addition to developing expertise in specialist disciplines. However, as the Winfield Report emphasized, there is a lack of knowledge about postgraduate education in the social sciences in general, and there is relatively little research on the most fundamental aspects of doctoral training, including: the relation between formal training and completion; supervision; acquisition of research skills; the writing process; and the oral examination (Winfield, 1987; Burgess, 1994, p. 9).

The central theme of this book is that if we are to begin to understand what constitutes 'methodology', and thereby assist incoming researchers to avoid some of the standard pitfalls of research, emphasis must be placed on developing a reflexive analysis of *both the formal and informal nature of the research process. In the absence of* a literature addressed to the method of actual research, as opposed to the myths of methodology texts, it is unlikely that departments will be able to impart the general skills demanded by ESRC (or that the quality of completed research projects will be enhanced). This is particularly evident in three areas highlighted as constituting foundational training. It is requested that students are instructed in how to formulate researchable problems and translate these into practicable research designs. Secondly, that students are trained in how to approach research, and finally that they are introduced to the skills of writing and presentation.

Writing a doctoral thesis is unlike any task a student will have performed or is likely to be asked to perform ever again. Although there is no master plan for producing a PhD, first-hand accounts of the research process conveyed by recent recipients of the doctorate (and those at various stages of completion) are of enormous benefit to new researchers. The broad aim of this collection of first-hand accounts is to encourage fellow academics to discard scientistic mystique and reveal 'how it was done' through a discussion of the informal nature of the research process. The rationale for this approach is that if formal academic competence can, to some extent, be assumed among those who successfully register for a research degree, then the role of graduate research training is to go beyond the textbook to help students sort the method from the myth in the practice of research.

Focusing on the research process as a learned social activity, rather than seeing research training solely in terms of the development of competence in specific techniques, invites us to accept some of the central tenets of critical social science, and in particular of the ethnomethodological tradition of sociology. In short, this tradition implores us to view the acquisition of knowledge as a 'contingent accomplishment of socially organised common practices' (Garfinkel, 1967, p. 33), a moment-by-moment determination of meaning in social contexts (Heritage, 1984, p. 2). In this sense there are no terms for which meaning or use is self-evident; nor does meaning accompany a concept as 'a mysterious halo' (Barnes, 1982, p. 26). In other words, knowledge is conventional, through and through, and understanding is developed step by step, in processes involving successions of on-the-spot judgements (Barnes, 1982, p. 30). Seen in this light it is clear why university regulations which stipulate that a PhD should constitute a 'substantial original contribution to knowledge' remain unintelligible to doctoral students. Formal training carried out with standard methodology texts that present a sanitized, idealized image of research mislead new researchers in social science by denying the thoroughly 'conventional' nature of research as a process (it is in this sense that Weber's remarks quoted at the beginning of this introduction are so apposite).

Even within sociology the development of this 'demythologizing' literature has been slow and remains generally unsatisfactory (for an overview, see Burgess, 1984). While, as Bell and Newby (1977, p. 9) point out, 'it is common knowledge that there has always been, perhaps necessarily, considerable divergence between how sociological research has actually been done and what is found in the textbooks', this discrepancy has not produced a sociology of the informal research process much beyond the American studies of Hammond (1964), Vidich *et al.* (1964), Sjoberg (1967) and Lazarsfeld (1967) (although Platt (1976), Bell and Encel (1978), Stanley (1990) and Hobbs and May (1993) have begun the task). If the 'conspiracy of silence' surrounding the research process has begun, albeit falteringly, to break down in sociology, within political science the standard-bearers of formal methodological orthodoxy hold sway. Neither the 'newer philosophies of social science' (Giddens, 1976) nor some of the older writings on the conduct of natural science (Medawar, 1963; Knorr-Cetina, 1981) have done much to dispel the dominance of the 'received model' of formal methodological practice in political science. Almost without exception the main texts on methods in political science fail to indicate that research is a learned social activity, and one which rarely conforms to the neat but sterile typologies and stages so beloved of Marsh (1982), Judd *et al.* (1991), and Manheim and Rich (1991), to mention just some of the better representatives.

This edited volume seeks to remedy some of these deficiencies and break new ground in the field of politics and international studies. Unlike the ethnographic studies in sociology mentioned above, and the recent 'How to do a PhD' cookbooks such as Salmon (1992), Watson (1987), and Phillips and Pugh (1994), the first-hand accounts presented here are orientated specifically to postgraduates in political science. Moreover, the volume has been structured to take into account many of the 'new issues' that face incoming researchers, and in this sense the discussions should also be of value to those charged with the teaching and organization of research methods.

The organization of the volume

In many ways the material gathered together in this volume constitutes a piece of original research in itself. Although all contributors were asked to focus part of their discussion on a specific issue or approach, they were all given the opportunity to reflect more broadly on their experience of the *process* of research. The result is a unique collection of fifteen first-hand accounts of what it is like to be a doctoral student working in the discipline of politics and international studies in the late 1990s. To maintain the integrity of the contributions I resisted the usual editorial temptation to make heavy-handed alterations to the text. If the volume is to meet its stated aim of presenting the research process from the point of view of practitioners (rather than impose my own view or offer the usual sanitized accounts found in methodology textbooks), it was paramount that editorial 'steering' was minimized.

Part 1 consists of nine papers which address increasingly important themes in research training in the 1990s. While some contributors focus on well-known areas of contention (for instance, student–supervisor relations and research design), others explore under-researched issues, including progression through the years, the teaching assistantship scheme, combining a full-time lectureship with PhD research, and PhD research in Britain as an overseas student.

In 1996 the ESRC announced that a formal link would be established between the structured, broadly based training required for Mode A research students (those who had no previous postgraduate research training) and research training undertaken through ESRC-designated Research Training Master's Courses (ESRC,

1996, p. 5). From 1997 onwards, students who successfully complete a research Master's degree which is an ESRC-designated Research Training Advanced Course (that is, has 'RT' rather than Specialist or 'S' status), and the course is in the same subject area as the proposed PhD, may automatically gain exemption from the broadly based training requirements in the first year of their PhD. Whatever the merits of this innovation in the long term, it is clear that MA courses with 'RT' status will henceforth be seen by many as the first year of PhD training. This raises a number of issues concerning the compatibility of MA and PhD research. These issues are taken up in Chapter 2 by Jonathan Gorry, who concludes that despite their similarities, the MA and PhD research processes are qualitatively different endeavours. He suggests that, 'if the protean PhD resembles the solving of a Zen *koan*, my Master's dissertation represented a challenge similar to solving Rubik's Cube'. A PhD, he indicates, is not just a tenuously connected series of literature reviews that eventually amounts to a long essay of 80,000 words. Rather, it is the search for a particular angle, and in empirical research the extensive use of primary sources, that separates fundamentally the endeavours.

In Chapter 3, 'Beginning Research: The First Year', Carla Koen reflects on the difficulties of starting doctoral research and explores what she terms the 'originality paradox' (researchers need to receive feedback on their 'new' ideas but fear either ridicule or theft in public arenas). She also discusses the benefits of establishing contacts outside of your 'home' institution. Although Koen's work on the pharmaceutical industry in Germany and Japan in the 1990s would appear to be different in kind to Gorry's archival analysis of the attitude of the Church of England to nuclear deterrence in the 1950s, their accounts indicate that there are common elements in the research process. In particular, both stress that although the first year involves an arduous struggle to gain familiarity with a broad research area, the most important task is to develop a central research theme. In other words, 'the thesis must have a thesis', and, as Koen states, 'relevance to argument should be the guiding criterion'. Koen concludes by revealing problems encountered in undertaking interviews in Japan. While there is a vast literature on problems of interviewing, Koen breaks new ground with her first-hand account of the importance of 'introductions' and in examining the peculiarities of interviewing in institutions in Japan.

Most new PhD students find the area of 'research design' confusing and somewhat tangential to their research interests. It seems that research design is a topic which should be central, but when perusing standard methodology texts, it is discussed in terms of moving through logical stages (from theory to hypothesis to operationalization, sampling and selection, to the collection and analysis of data, and then back to theory) which seem both abstract and far removed from experience. In Chapter 4, Vered Bartov discusses how much of the literature on research design fails to capture the reality of PhD research. She rejects the step-by-step sequential models of how research *should* be conducted and points out that the PhD project tends to grow and develop and is subject to many unforeseen modifications along the way. Bartov's conclusion is that although the models of the 'perfect way' were useful in part, 'none seemed to take into account factors related to the day to day experience of many first time researchers'. Her solution is not to embrace the doctrine of the 'seamless web' favoured by many ethnographic sociologists, but to emphasize the importance of designing a flexible research frame which accords with the uniqueness of each individual's situation.

The second year is often the forgotten year in the life of a PhD student. Ed Page, in Chapter 5, discusses how feelings of anomie can quickly develop in a context where 'there is still a depressing amount to read but still, apparently, time to waste'. The second year is also the period in which PhD students are liable to be diverted from the research task. Offers of hourly paid teaching and administration, and opportunities to take up exchanges with other institutions will most often materialize in year two. Page offers a 'survival kit' for the second year, advising students to 'get a methodology; don't waste time on unnecessary research trips/on completion of a literature review; home in on a particular problem you think will sustain your interest for some time (then throw away the review and start again); don't teach unless you have to; and don't moonlight unless in serious financial distress'.

The student–supervisor relationship has been described by the ESRC as 'perhaps the single most important variable affecting the success of the research process' (ESRC, 1991, p. 8). However, recent studies on supervision indicate that few supervisors attend training sessions and the level of experience and commitment varies enormously (Burgess, 1994, p. 7). For example, Michael Youngman's work on the role expectations of research supervisors and students found that within his sample of supervisors only 34 per cent had more than two completed PhD supervisions (Youngman, 1994, p. 95). Chapters 6 and 7 focus explicitly on the student–supervisor relationship and attempt to redress the prescriptive bias of much of the secondary literature with a more pragmatic account of the realities of this relationship from the viewpoint of the student. Both contributors point to the pivotal role played by supervisors in defining and directing research. Ray Kiely charts how, once his original supervisor had taken study leave, a replacement supervisor tried to rewrite the entire project. Similarly, Nick Robinson highlights the problems that can result when supervisors change institutions – 'the key problem which I presented to any potential supervisor was that I was over half way into the PhD process. As such, I was neither close enough to the beginning for extensive, proactive involvement or near enough to the end for early, and comparatively stress free submission. The result was that I quickly developed the feeling of being damaged goods'. Ultimate responsibility for the thesis rests with the student. However, it is clear from both contributors that joint (or panel) supervision may be advantageous to the institution, supervisor and research student.

Chapters 8 and 9 focus on the problems of combining full-time research with employment as either a teaching assistant or a temporary lecturer. John Williams, researching the concept of 'legitimacy' in international relations with a case study on Yugoslavia 1945–92, relates how the teaching assistantship scheme helped him to overcome many of the problems associated with isolation faced by most students on a more 'traditional' PhD track. He also suggests how departments can improve life for teaching assistants, particularly in terms of access to information – 'although a member of staff I was never invited to a staff meeting and it took two years before I received departmental memos and circulars, even covering such mundane information as exam arrangements, changes to course options and other procedures'. Williams also raises important issues explored more fully in Part 2 concerning the black box of the viva, drawing attention to the apparent anomaly that after three years of independent research, examiners' reports are binding, and 'simple compliance is not only expected but required'. Nisha Malhan, in Chapter 9, confirms Williams' remarks about the difficulty of juggling roles, 'switching hats from teacher to PhD student, or more precisely from "teaching mode" to "PhD mode", proved to be difficult. By the time one had got into "PhD mode" it was time to write another lecture. One felt like a schizophrenic constantly changing moods'. Malhan's contribution highlights the range of new demands placed upon lecturers who are struggling to submit within four years (the Research Assessment Exercise, conference circuits and staff development).

Part 1 concludes with Laura Tedesco drawing attention to an under-researched area in the secondary literature – the experience of overseas students studying for a PhD in Britain. Her discussion indicates that overseas students face particular difficulties deriving not only from the complexities of the English language but also from unfamiliarity with British educational institutions and British 'culture' in general. Coming from Argentina, Tedesco had no experience of a university campus or a university library (as typically found in Britain). Moreover, she quickly realized that a British PhD places an emphasis on independent study – 'although I was used to research in my previous work, the PhD is something completely different. In Argentina I had deadlines to fulfil; if I did not meet them, I could be sacked. With the PhD you have to organize your time, you are the director, even if your supervisor is very strict with deadlines, you have the last word'.

In Part 2 the focus of the volume shifts from a study of themes and issues to explore the experience of students who have used a range of qualitative research methods in their work to attain a PhD in politics and/or international studies. Although this section cannot claim to offer a comprehensive overview of all qualitative methods employed in political science (this is not the aim of the volume), contributions have been chosen to reflect the most popular approaches (political theory, comparative analysis, interviewing and archival study) and to provide an introduction to some more innovative styles (interdisciplinary work and the use of information technology and 'unusual' sources). In the final chapter I offer an overview and guide to the PhD oral examination.

Almost without exception, secondary literature in the area of research methodology assumes that 'theoretical' or 'abstract' PhDs need not be discussed in the context of the research process. For some undisclosed reason 'library based' research is seen as not 'proper' research and is therefore omitted from most discussions of qualitative empirical analysis. Chris Woodard's contribution, 'The Practice of Political Theory', highlights the limitations of this orthodox view. Recalling Vered Bartov's critical views on textbook models of research design, Woodard notes, 'in my experience, however, this picture could not be much more misleading. It *may* have some relevance to empirical studies, which perhaps do admit of a *certain amount* of straightforward disaggregation (though even here I'm doubtful), but when the research is very abstract I think it is better to picture a spiral, circling round and round the topic, hopefully reaching a better understanding of the issues and a better articulation of the central claims each time'. One of the exciting aspects of theoretical work is that it is possible to take large steps in a very short space of time (and also, of course, to concede ground very quickly). This can intensify the feelings of insecurity experienced by all students. A solution (a defence against despair) proposed by Woodard is to cultivate 'faked nonchalance': 'it is a kind of nonchalance, because once you've realized the nature of the research student's predicament, it would be foolish to pursue all worries about each aspect of the process remorselessly; it is faked, however, since there is of course a need to worry sufficiently to maintain momentum, and to seek out genuine problems with the work'. This ability to highlight the essential and discard the peripheral is in many ways the key to a successful PhD, and Woodard's account of the research process indicates a number of fundamental continuities between research in political philosophy and more empirical studies in social science.

In Chapter 12 Steven Smith brings to bear the views of a part-time PhD student conducting interdisciplinary research which attempts to combine political philosophy and social policy. In Smith's view the advantage of interdisciplinary work is that it enables new lines of communication to be established relatively easily (hence moving towards meeting the 'originality' criterion), but equally it leaves researchers vulnerable to committing errors in both fields. Joint supervision (with supervisors from each discipline) is thus deemed essential to guard against major gaffes. Smith also offers a useful discussion of what could be called the 'magic books' fallacy. Students often panic that they have missed *the* article or book that is crucial in their field and/or the contribution that will expose their ideas and arguments as fraudulent (a variant is the feeling that I cannot begin to write a chapter or draft until I have everything on my topic or have in my possession an article which I have seen referenced but which is not in the library!). As an antidote, and a way of generating a distinctive hypothesis, Smith suggests that skim-reading should be used sparingly, 'I find that it's much more useful to understand one book thoroughly (or even one chapter) than to half understand ten books (or ten chapters).' More specifically, by focusing on one or two commentators it is possible to 'get under the skin' of the arguments and identify where contributions can be made. In this way a thesis can develop a distinctive argument.

Chapters 13 to 15 recount the experiences of researchers employing the comparative method, interviewing and archival analysis. Michael O'Neill argues the case for comparative analysis, reiterating the point that comparative need not mean cross-national and that any number of institutions and sub-national entities and actors can be considered in comparative research. In discussing his work on the 'New Right in Canada and Britain', O'Neill concludes that more time needs to be given in studies on method to the processes of conceptualization – 'you need more than an interesting subject to write a good PhD, you also need well-defined concepts and variables, a method to measure these and a framework that will hold it all together'. You have not gone beyond the stage of simply having a subject to study, he argues, unless you can pass the 'cocktail test', that is, describe the subject of your thesis in five sentences or less without once referring to your case study.

In Chapter 14 Gail Stedward indicates how she carried out her research on 'Anti-Racist Movements and their influence in British and EU Public Policy', utilizing depth- and semi-structured interviews. By including copies of letters of introduction and interview schedules, Stedward offers one of the most complete accounts of interviewing in political science that is available to the PhD student. In addition to discussing how to identify interviewees, the importance of timetabling and the benefit of piloting, she also offers invaluable advice on security and personal safety (particularly but not exclusively for women researchers), and on how to build rapport and bring discussions back to key topics. In many ways, she comments, a successful interview is like a sheep-dog trial, 'it's your task to keep the interviewee on course without worrying him/her too much or snapping at their heels'. Moreover, Stedward points to the limitations of most secondary accounts of interviewing, in particular the assumption that the interviewer is a passive recipient, and notes that 'sexism, racism, homophobia, classism or general patronizing are spanners that can be chucked into the smooth running of your interview machinery at any time'.

The issue of being a 'displaced PhD person' is one of the topics highlighted by Rhiannon Vickers in her account of using archives in political research. Vickers indicates that she suffered displacement in three ways. Firstly, her topic, trade unions and the Marshall Plan, meant that she seemed to have more in common with researchers in history, economics and industrial relations than those in political science. Secondly, as a teaching assistant she was at one level removed from other PhD students, while at the same time not considered a 'proper' member of staff. Finally, when appointed to a lectureship elsewhere in her second year (and thereby forced to reregister as a part-time PhD student), Vickers experienced the phenomenon of 'distance' supervision. Although perseverance is a necessary requirement for all research, archival analysis makes particular demands, given the difficulty involved in obtaining documentation and recording relevant details. Most large archives are messy and poorly catalogued, and as Vickers points out, 'it was not always possible to tell whether the information I sought had ever existed, had been shredded or whether it was kept elsewhere. Also, it was not always obvious that a document was important until I had looked at other files, which meant that I would often have to return to files I had already looked at to reconsider their significance'. It is also important when using archives in political research to avoid producing a straight historical narrative which fails to explain the significance of events. Even if the narrative is distinctive, Vickers advises a strategy of 'hypothesis-framing' to produce a novel interpretation.

In Chapter 16 Stephen Day offers an innovative approach to remedy some of the common problems encountered in the research process. Day discovered (not untypically) that his home department had relatively little expertise in the area of his research, the realignment of the post-communist Left in Poland and Slovakia. He therefore set about building an independent structure outside the confines of his home institution on the basis of networking at conferences, proactive mail shots, the use of new technology resources (in particular the Internet) and alternative media resources such as short-wave radio. He recalls how chance encounters at conferences had a decisive impact on his ability to conduct research and gain full-time funding for his project in the second year. Moreover, Day indicates how the World Wide Web and short-wave radio can be used to good effect with minimum effort and knowledge.

In the contribution by John Williams in Part 1, it was pointed out that at a time when so much attention is being paid to improving the teaching of research methods at the beginning of a PhD, to make it a more professional, effective and faster process, consideration is long overdue at the other end, with regard to the PhD oral examination. Williams' own experience is that 'echoes of a bygone age of a rather cosy club of academics being able to feel in their bones what is and what is not good enough to be a PhD seem to hang over the process'. Open discussion of the oral examination, from the choice of examiners to the criteria used in assessment and the possible recommendations, will increase the credibility of the exercise for all concerned. In the final contribution to the volume, I present an overview and offer a guide for research students to the viva.

There is no short cut to achieving a PhD. Knowledge of the process (as with any) is built up through practice and learning the conventions of this particular form of social activity. It is perhaps ironic, given the ESRC's close involvement in monitoring training, that studies of the informal research process are quite rare. If the current volume contributes to reflexive discussions on research as a process, it will have achieved its objective.

Note

1. Max Weber, *Gesammelte Aufsätze zur Wissenschaftslehre*, 3rd edition, translated and cited by Guy Oakes in Weber (1975, pp. 14–15).

Part 1

The Social Organization of the Research Process

2

Investigating Methodologies: A Comparison of MA and PhD Research Processes

JONATHAN GORRY

Within Zen there is the *koan* system. A *koan* is a puzzle the 'Master' sets his student on the road to self-discovery. The student ponders on the meaning of the riddle until its elements become clear and enlightenment occurs. The path, we are told, is poorly lit, difficult to navigate, with few meaningful directions. The art of solving the *koan* comes not by presenting the correct answer but by asking the right questions. Such a scenario bears more than a passing resemblance to the PhD process. The *koan* stands as a fitting analogy because, like students of Zen, PhD students intuitively understand what is required of them but are not always sure about the questions they should be asking. The most difficult problem facing incoming students is not the actual mechanics of research but rather the initial formulation of a viable project: like a bad joke, the point is appreciated or not, and enfeebled when explained. My experience of both MA and PhD degree processes suggests that preconceived ideas of the nature of research only inhibit the development of a workable project. Government demands for more structured training, through the medium of the Master's, in many ways fail to convey a realistic sense of the research process and also underplay the uniqueness of the PhD challenge. This chapter develops this theme by comparing research experiences and suggests that students give more attention to their 'research attitude' rather than the ESRC's obsession with 'correct' research technique.

My presentation is split into three sections. The first section details my reasons for studying for a Master's, and my experiences with the degree. Second, I explain how I generated a precise PhD topic – arguably the most difficult and certainly the most poorly documented aspect of the research process. Finally, I outline my general research experiences with the hope of making the PhD research process less mysterious for incoming researchers.

Background

I left school at 16 with little interest in formal education and few qualifications, but with a desire to 'comprehend' still intact. School just hadn't helped me study two issues I found most important: political economy – who gets what, how, and why; and religion. I left school thinking of my prospects, as most of my friends did, not in terms of an academic career but a series of jobs that would feed, clothe, house, and fund a need for two-wheeled motorized transport. After a period on the dole, a succession of low-paid jobs, plenty of books, and several scooters, I ended up working as a caretaker in Coventry Cathedral.

The Church fascinated me. Never before, or since, have I met so many political conservatives and radicals assembled in one place! This intriguing state of affairs prompted me to give formal education a second look. In 1988, as a 21-year-old (mature-ish) student, I took up a place at Staffordshire Polytechnic to study for a BA in International Relations. By the beginning of my final year I wanted a job in the academic world. Imagine, I thought, being *paid* to do something I actually enjoyed – can't be bad, and just had to be better than a manual job. I quickly came to the conclusion that if I was to secure an academic job I needed a PhD. In my naivety I thought this would not be as big a problem as it proved.

My referees suggested it would be sensible to apply to the 'old' universities because not only did they offer a better chance of funding, but they would also confirm (or otherwise) my ability. It was sound advice, and I think anybody who can secure funding elsewhere (and this is the crux of the matter) is better off studying in a department other than their undergraduate one. After three years in one place students get a good understanding of how their tutors' minds work, and if they are keen to broaden their intellectual outlook they should study elsewhere.[1] The amount of time and trouble spent in applying for a PhD place and securing funding is not always rewarding. As most of us realize, the offer of a place is not normally a problem: the problem arises in securing funding. Scholarships are rare, and self-funding means borrowing more money on top of existing student loans. None the less, I reasoned, somewhat laterally, that 'where there's a will there's a way', and with a Master's degree I would be better qualified to secure a three-year PhD scholarship. This strategy was a risk, yet one year's debt is preferable to three.

In October 1992 I accepted the offer of a place to study for an MA in International Studies. I borrowed the money to pay my fees (placating my aversion to debt by constantly reminding myself that the best investment we can make is in ourselves) and moved back to my parents' home to cut costs. I also secured a part-time, five-hour-a-week lecturing job at a nearby university to help pay living expenses.

The Master's degree

Increased demand for the Master's qualification has led to a marked proliferation in new courses, most with a dissertation component. Yet it is not clear whether the taught MA should be considered primarily a means to an end, or an end in itself. The question remains whether more systematic training and supervision in MA form better equips students to complete PhD theses.

My MA was assessed by six 6000-word essays and a 15,000-word dissertation. It is not difficult to write long essays (remember how as first-year undergraduates we used to find writing 2000-word essays daunting?), but it is, of course, more difficult to write *decent* long essays. The department's MA training programme sought to ease the transition from BA to MA studies. There were two main aspects of the department's training programme. The first part comprised a general introduction to politics and international studies, research methods, the university, postgraduate life, and to the presentation skills needed to convey the results of research (e.g., word-processing, formatting and presenting dissertations). The emphasis here being what we can call 'research style'. The second part dealt with 'research methods'. This introduced students to the university's research resources, to the basic ways and means of organization required for effective research (e.g., study techniques, designing a piece of research, research tips). Attendance was compulsory for all MA postgraduates. Those taking undergraduate dissertation courses were also invited to attend. More detailed training in method was offered for those registered on research degrees – though MA students thinking of continuing on to an ESRC-funded research degree could also be present.

The 'research style' aspect of this training was practical, rewarding, and brought lasting results. I learned to type and word-process, to footnote in traditional and Harvard style, to create professional bibliographies, and distinguish an 'op. cit.' from a 'loc. cit.'. I discovered the virtues of Kate Turabian's *A Manual for Writers of Research Papers, Theses, and Dissertations*, the usefulness of *The Oxford Dictionary for Writers and Editors*, and how valuable *Fowler's Modern English Usage* could be. Above all, I was introduced to the common sense of Becker's *Writing for Social Scientists*, who surely develops William of Ockham's dictum, 'in argument, when you can do with less, do not posit more', for the benefit of the social sciences. The training in 'research methods' proved less useful. The most memorable experience was an experienced professor's 'research tips' seminar. Besides extolling the virtues of word-processing, time management, why students should avoid annoying staff, and suggesting the relationship with dissertation supervisors as akin to master and apprentice, she presented a strikingly positivistic interpretation of the research process. She argued that student 'bias' must always be combined with scientific objectivity (to avoid polemic) and that research answers must never be presupposed but weighed up in order to reach a reasoned conclusion. Neutrality was essential: values should be put into the question, not the answer. While conceding that it was impossible completely to separate the activity of thinking from writing, her recipe for research success included staging the research task to give the brain time to work. Students should first 'sketch' what they know about their research idea; second, read up on the subject, take notes, then sketch again; third, reflect on their newly acquired knowledge; and, finally, focus on the writing process. Students were urged not to get depressed by being too critical, and to always remember that 'Originality Wins Rewards'.

I took these pointers to heart in the dissertation component of my MA. My dissertation, *Challenging Positivism: Gramsci, Civil Society and International Political Economy*, examined the dominance of positivism in the study of international relations/international political economy (IR/IPE). The thesis contended that positivism is methodologically incapable of capturing the increasing complexity of economic relations because it has failed to move research beyond a structural analysis of the 'international system'. I argued that the work of Antonio Gramsci and 'transhistorical materialist' ideas allowed a holistic means for analysing appropriate concerns while also suggesting a prescription for change. The thesis suggested that Gramsci's ideas on civil society offered substantially more than the mere emphasis of 'ideas and culture' because it called for a research agenda that challenged static applications of 'the state' and 'individual' as basic units of analysis. It was not particularly difficult to write my Master's dissertation. The work was not agonized over, I didn't lose sleep, and its completion took no more than two months. The thesis was not particularly revealing, and, I have to admit, not devastatingly original. I did not get my fingers dirty with primary sources and the dissertation utilized only secondary material. From the beginning I had a clear idea of structure: I believed Gramsci was appropriate to the study of IR/IPE and that all that was needed was to present my argument in a novel way using supporting evidence from the wealth of existing secondary sources. This work however, proved neither methodologically helpful nor theoretically appropriate to my eventual PhD. To mix metaphors once more, if the protean PhD resembles the solving of a *koan*, my Master's dissertation represented a challenge similar to solving Rubik's Cube.

The most important thing to be realized while reading this is that I viewed my Master's purely as a means to an end: the objective being to secure three years' funding for a PhD. My Master's proved to be a worthwhile investment. The MA did lead to PhD funding, and it allowed me to pursue my interests more clearly, and sensitized me to the Marxist methodology so disparaged at my first university. It can, however, be a stressful experience especially when working part-time to pay your way. I remember the experience as something akin to a highly intensive undergraduate third-year. More than once I ended up chewing the carpet in my frustration and feeling that I had taken on board more than I could cope with. In retrospect, a Master's degree is, judged by its own intrinsic merits, something close to an indulgence. Yes, the Master's option (at least as I experienced it) is an intensive and serious form of study. Yes, it results in a valid qualification, while expanding intellectual horizons, and it gives you training in methodology (as do many undergraduate degrees). But what is it for? Is it an end in itself? Is it a necessary prelude to a PhD? I would suggest that most students are unclear about *what* they want from a Master's before they embark on it. If as a result of your MA qualification you are lucky enough to go on and secure PhD funding because you can now write 'long essays' and are now deemed 'methodologically competent', it is worth every penny. Yet if, on the other hand, you think it will prepare you qualitatively for the PhD, you are in for a surprise.

The PhD

In October 1993, after completing the MA and securing three years' funding, I began work for my PhD. There were four main aspects of the department's training programme. First, the induction element. This involved familiarization with supervisory arrangements, departmental procedures and departmental workspaces; introduction to bibliographic searches, CD-ROMs, dissertation abstracts and the university's in-house archives (the Modern Records Centre); the development of word-processing skills and the use of statistical software packages for social scientists. The second aspect was held over three terms. It covered qualitative and quantitative research techniques, focusing on elite interviewing, documentary analysis, questionnaire design, participant observation, surveys, in-depth data analysis (using simple correlation and regression), and an introduction to multivariate analysis. The course covered issues in the philosophy of social science, looking at debates on the nature of 'science', functionalist explanation, interests and the growth of knowledge in politics and international studies, and the historical development of the disciplines. The most valuable element here was that students were encouraged to present papers relevant to their research and to use the sessions to discuss common problems (e.g., preparing for the viva, student–supervisor relations, workshops on the writing process). The third component of the department's research training was the graduate seminar programme. Held fortnightly in the first year, this provided students with the opportunity to develop study skills and discuss issues such as how a hypothesis can be refined, conducting literature reviews, designing a piece of research, time management, research presentation and the ethical and legal problems of research. Finally, the department provided tuition in the areas of political theory and international relations theory, while offering a number of specialist modules including comparative politics and public administration.

The choice of thesis topic

The first and most demanding question presented by the PhD research process is how to formulate a viable research topic. In my case the task was to translate a broad interest in politics and religion into a working hypothesis. This was no mean task, and remained the most difficult part of the entire project. The MA did not prepare me for how hard this exercise would be or suggest how projects, questions or hypotheses could be generated. I had firm ideas regarding the area

I wanted to study, but was not sure what questions I should be asking that would develop into a serious project.

The problem was to translate a broad interest in politics and Christianity into a working hypothesis. I was sympathetic to Alasdair MacIntyre's (1985, p. 263) assertion that shared beliefs and values were necessary to bind a society together (to generate a sense of meaning, purpose and, above all, hope), and interested in the extent to which a critical commitment to orthodox Christianity could lead to a willingness to question the political and moral assumptions of 'capitalist democracy'. By examining the Church as a moral alternative to the authority of the Western state, I thought I could develop an understanding of the Church–state relationship. For the first few months my time was spent producing book reviews on Marx, neo-Marxist accounts on the role of Christianity, and evaluating radical theories of Church and state. The shortcomings of this approach soon revealed themselves. It became clear that I needed to have more than firm ideas about the intellectual debate I wished to join. A PhD was not just a tenuously connected series of literature reviews that eventually amounted to a long essay of 70–80,000 words. Developing a serious project required asking the right questions from the start. For this I needed a particular angle with which to focus my energy. In short, I had a research area but no clear research topic. A theoretical approach was favoured, as in my Master's dissertation, but every time I prepared drafts for my supervisor with what I thought were sound enough ideas, I received valuable comments but I seemed incapable of carrying the ideas forward. With the benefit of hindsight, one of the problems I faced was that I had reflected on religion and politics for many years, read widely in a vast field, and could not bring myself to focus on one particular topic. I had plenty of ideas that involved the Church–state relationship, yet could not think of the appropriate question that would lead me deep into the research process. After two months I was still without a viable topic and began to think I was too 'stupid' to do 'proper' research. I simply couldn't grasp what was required of me. I was thinking, reading and writing (in that order[2]), but every attempt I made at solving the puzzle that would suddenly reveal a doable proposition was frustrated. It should go without saying that every other first-year student was racing ahead and revelling in the thrill of being 'proper' PhD researchers. Everyone else was clearly more clever, more capable, and had been blessed with a revealing vision of what was required. In many ways, my experience was like the child playing 'pass the parcel': I was keen and so much wanted to be a winner, but every time the music stopped the parcel was with someone else!

In my desperation I tried reading (and even buying) both research 'hand-books'(e.g., Watson, 1987) and 'experience-based' accounts (such as Salmon, 1992), which I hoped would make sense of what was required. These accounts made me no wiser. It was only when I proceeded to read as many PhDs as I could manage that things finally began to become clearer. While nirvana was not quite within my grasp, I did now understand what actually made a PhD. It was more than intuition that told me they involved some labour. One thing that struck me was that a number of the more interesting PhDs were based on archival analysis. As a consequence of this, and with my supervisor's backing, in January 1994 I put any idea of a purely theoretical PhD behind me.

Reading PhDs and heeding Kavanagh's (1991) call for a greater use of historical sources in politics brought me to a historical methodology. This led me to three conclusions. First, archives could be a useful source of primary material and, if theoretically informed, a useful way of demonstrating links between the past and the present. Second, the use of church archives would be original and could test the extent to which the Church's responsibility for public life had actually led to the renewal of political struggle. Finally, archives were appealing because it seemed to me that historians did not theorize enough when using them, and political scientists, in the main, were not using them at all. In short, archival analysis presented an opportunity.

I decided to utilize the archives of the British Council of Churches (BCC), a constituent assembly of the World Council of Churches (WCC) and the established vehicle for communicating official non-Catholic approaches to politics. This organization was chosen primarily because no one had attempted to research it within the discipline.

The research process

The BCC archive is found in the Church of England Record Centre, Galleywall Road, Bermondsey, London. Because there is no automatic public access I required a letter of introduction from the General Secretary of the Council of Churches for Britain and Ireland (CCBI).[3] This happily proved to be a formality, and the church authorities were pleased to see records used for PhD purposes. Once past a rather elaborate security door, the archivist furnished me with a copy of 'Transfer and Box Lists' relating to the political activities of the BCC. These indexes gave me some idea of the type of material I could expect to find but presented two immediate limitations: first, closure rules limited access; and second, much material was inadequately indexed.

In the first instance a 30-year closure rule on administrative files (and a 100-year closure on personal files) effectively forced the historical period I could research to before December 1962. This served to discipline me into researching angles that would locate my study in the 1950s or early 1960s. The fact that material was not only inadequately indexed but also incoherently catalogued[4] caused more of a problem. Indexes only gave a vague idea of the contents of particular files. For example, the index suggested that the records for the BCC's 'International Department 1959: Miscellaneous' were located somewhere in the cavernous 'Box 14'. Such limited information was frustrating, and I had little choice but to recall plenty of files before gaining some sense of the nature of the archive. Bearing in mind these limitations, and with the help of the transfer lists, I selected 1962 as a starting-point and worked back chronologically, hoping to appreciate the issues of political significance that had most exercised the interest of the Churches. I found that the material contained in files varied greatly, but most included information on resolutions and reports issued by the Council; correspondence with government and other bodies, particularly the WCC and the American Council of Churches; minutes of the regular meetings of the BCC's Assembly and its various departments (of particular interest to me was the International Department); reports from associated regional church councils; letters and memoranda; reports written by council officials returning from foreign visits; reports on the activities of visiting foreign dignitaries; newspaper cuttings; and transcripts of telephone conversations. This initial perusal revealed two issues that dominated the Churches' attention in the years from 1957 to 1962: nuclear weapons, and decolonization in Central Africa. I favoured researching the politics of the Churches in the formation and dissolution of the Central African Federation 1953 to 1963. This topic seemed more viable to me for the simple reason that I was more interested in development studies than in peace/security studies. On closer inspection, however, and after careful discussion with my supervisor, I decided that the nuclear debate would prove to be a much more interesting proposition. This was partly because the nuclear dilemma is still with us, partly because it is both controversial and highly political, and partly because of the success of movements like the Campaign for Nuclear Disarmament (formed in 1958) in galvanizing opinion in the Churches. The decision to research the Churches' attitudes to nuclear weapons was undoubtedly the correct one, and the prime reason why I managed to submit in just over three years.

These observations lead me to three general conclusions. First, researchers cannot go wrong if they heed the dictum that, on a practical level, the viability of completing a PhD within three years depends fundamentally on ease of access to primary sources (see Burnham, 1992). My example suggests this is so, and that utilizing archival analysis is an intellectually rewarding experience. Second, once this step is taken and archival analysis becomes the preferred methodology, choose an area that is controversial and which allows you to challenge conventional secondary accounts. Seek out obtuse sources, like church archives, remember that you need a good spread of data (supply should be plentiful, sources varied), and that it is better to have plenty of worthy secondary accounts with which to engage. In my case nuclear weapons were a boon but Central Africa would have proved to be a bane because of a comparative lack of archival material and because there are few secondary accounts that deal with the Churches' involvement in the crisis. Finally, it is not necessary to choose a research topic that is an all-embracing passion in your life. Like any labour of love, a PhD takes sensitivity, devotion, patience and the ability to compromise. The PhD is a 'living thing' that evolves and develops according to the effort you put into it and brings its own reward in due course.

Once the decision to research church attitudes to the nuclear arms race was taken, the research process became much easier. I henceforth selected a certain number of files to work with each day in order to become acquainted with my new topic. Interesting information would be entered straight into a laptop computer, to be written up at leisure. While much was learned from studying the official church publications found in the archives, more interesting information was revealed by looking at the way these publications were produced. Draft chapters and correspondence between the writers gave me a good sense of the tension between different attitudes held by church leaders. It is worth noting, however, that these archives, like any others, do not give a complete picture of events. Studying newspapers of the time such as *The Times* became an invaluable additional background research tool. Newspapers were particularly important because there is a serious lack of published information in book form in my particular area (i.e., BCC attitudes in the late 1950s). With such a topic I was free to engage secondary material which dealt with church attitudes to nuclear weapons in a more theoretical manner.

Conclusion

My experience has taught me a number of lessons about MA and PhD training. First, the main difference between the research processes is not quantitative but qualitative. The PhD is not just a longer version of an MA: they are different tasks. My MA did not therefore prepare me methodologically or theoretically for this fact. Second, the PhD requires an original slant, and hence primary material is a useful, if not indispensable, source of inspiration. My MA was based on secondary material, while the PhD is firmly rooted in primary sources. Third, if you are inclined to choose archival analysis as your preferred research method, do not try to develop a precise topic (hypothesis) until knee-deep in the documents. Finally, thesis production is taught, if at all, by trial and error, and in many cases by the arbitrary demands of the supervisor (Reese, 1996). My experience suggests that what is needed is not greater structured training in formal methodology but more sensitivity to 'research attitude'. The three essential requirements for any PhD are therefore: faith, patience, and determination. Advancement is achieved by paying attention to the 'research process' rather than by gaining proficiency in 'technique'. This, like Zen, is something only grasped in the 'doing'.

Notes

1. This advice may prove to have a limited shelf-life. The way things are going, the universities that receive most money will be those that are successful in building up an active research base and/or vibrant postgraduate community. Because of this, it is questionable whether departments will want to encourage their best students to go elsewhere, especially if they rely on postgraduate revenue. In other words, individual institutions will need to hang on to their own graduates. A university 'super-league' would also add to pressures in this direction. See Broers *et al.* (1996).
2. With hindsight, my labour would have been made much easier if I had written more than I read, and read more than I thought.
3. The CCBI succeed the BCC – the name change coincided with the incorporation of the Catholic Church in Britain and Ireland in 1990.
4. A more systematic, coherent and user-friendly system is now in operation.

3

Beginning Research: The First Year

CARLA KOEN

Although most of the research that was carried out to obtain my Master's degree is, in one way or another, related to the topic of my PhD dissertation, and, in fact, constitutes an essential preparation for it, I could hardly wait to start the 'real' doctoral research. I was feeling enthusiastic about the fact that my research topic was original. I was going to carry out empirical work that hadn't been done before. Additionally, I had some ideas to improve an existing theoretical framework in which I could conduct my research. However, after two weeks of enthusiasm and a strong belief in the originality of my work, a book was published which covered, not largely, but, in fact, entirely, my 'original' ideas. Not only did it study the same subject, that is to say, government–industry relationships in the pharmaceutical industry; but it also covered the same countries, Japan and the UK; and, indeed, the same reasons were put forward to legitimize the focus on this particular industry and on these particular countries. In addition, the study used a similar approach, that is, it identified the main actors in the policy arena and the linkages between them. Although I discovered weaknesses in the authors' analysis (it is always easier to find gaps in other studies rather than actually think and write for oneself), if I were to continue with my original research topic this would imply a great deal of repetition and probably frustration. In other words, my originality was gone. Hence, if I wanted to make a contribution to the study of comparative politics, I had to refocus either the empirical or the theoretical part of my research. In view of the efforts that I had made to find a theoretical approach that would enable me not only to explain and understand my research topic, but also to do this in a framework that was consistent with my ideas, beliefs and, perhaps, expectations, I did not want to give up my theory. Despite the strong reasons underlying my empirical focus on the study of government–industry relations in Japan and the UK, I convinced myself of the equally strong reasons for studying the comparison Germany–Japan.

This rather long introduction of the actual topic of my dissertation serves to point to the paradox that is faced by every researcher. Although the above problem is not entirely covered by what I shall call 'the originality paradox', it does reflect the concern for originality that is embodied in this concept. The originality paradox is used here to refer to, on the one hand, the strong need that researchers feel to talk about their research and to get feedback; while, on the other hand, they fear that throwing their ideas in the open might result in others gaining similar thoughts, and, thus, there is an equally strong tendency to keep one's ideas to oneself until they are publishable. In the following sections, I describe some of the difficulties that can be involved in the process of getting started and thereby attempt, on the basis of my own experience, to offer some guidelines. I will point to the importance of carefully considering the choice of supervisor and of establishing a network of contacts inside and outside your department and university and will also emphasize the advantage, at least in the early stages of the PhD, of carrying out doctoral research in the same university where you may have studied for your MA degree. I will conclude by covering the experience of doing fieldwork in Japan.

The originality paradox

Most authors who deal with the concept of originality in relation to PhD dissertations focus on acceptable conventional definitions and thereby attempt to convince PhD students of the relative ease of meeting the criterion of originality (for a discussion, see Phillips and Pugh, 1994). They do not, however, refer to the difficulties and frustration that can arise when, in the course of the research process, studies are being published that cover similar subjects. Indeed, it might not be difficult to find original empirical material or alternative ways to apply and test a theory. Problems can arise, however, when as a result of a publication you have to refocus your empirical work. It might be that you have based the empirical focus of your dissertation on fieldwork that you were to undertake in a foreign country. You might already have made a lot of effort to establish useful contacts or to find sufficient funding. Are you willing to throw these efforts away? If not, what if the author or authors continue to do research and to publish in that field? Are you willing and able to accept this challenge?

Although, obviously, there is no clear-cut answer to this problem, it is important in the first year that you remain flexible. That is to say, be prepared to alter the focus of your research, and have the courage to apply for additional funding once you have established the need to change focus. It is important to realize that you are only one member of an enormous community of researchers, and you should expect that others may have similar ideas. After all, each field has only a limited amount of core literature and core ideas. So it is important from the start to consider alternatives and to give yourself the possibility to change parts of your empirical or theoretical project, at least in the early stages of research. In my case, it turned out that I had wasted a lot of effort in trying to find funding to cover my fieldwork for a period of one year in Japan. The fact that I had now to consider studying the German and Japanese pharmaceutical industries and their relationship to government in a comparative framework, rather than focusing on the British and Japanese industries, implied that I had to spend time in two foreign countries. This inevitably meant that I was not able to stay an entire year in Japan and, thus, had to find short-term funding for Japan. Additionally, I had to establish contacts in Germany and find funding to finance trips to Germany.

Getting started

As a first-year doctoral student you have already chosen the area in which you want to work. Inevitably, the chosen study area and, in particular, the actual dissertation topic to a large extent determine the methodologies that can be used in your research topic. Hence, one of the first steps every PhD student takes, or should take, is to know his or her field of study to full professional standard. As Phillips and Pugh (1994, p. 57) state, it is important to be aware of the present state of the art: what developments, controversies, breakthroughs are currently engaging the leading practitioners and thus pushing forward thinking in your subject. In this respect, I have experienced that, apart from your supervisor, two groups of people can be of importance in making this process easier and more efficient. Obviously, it is important that your supervisor works in the same field or at least has an interest in, and knowledge of, this field. He or she is the first person who can advise you with respect to the core literature and core authors. In my case, this turned out to be very significant. I had studied political theories during my MA year. However, the approaches to my research topic differed substantially from my earlier studies. Moreover, my economics background was not really helpful in selecting the core literature and getting to know the major figures in the area in which I had chosen to work. Hence, particularly in the early stages of my research, I noted how important it was that my supervisor was willing to get to know my area and point me in the right direction. This obviously makes the choice of supervisor crucial.

Additionally, I was fortunate to have enormous support from my peers. During my MA year I met several PhD students in the department who, especially at the beginning of my research, were a source of support and information. They helped me become familiar with published work on my research topic and informed me about the best organizations to join to attend conferences, give papers, and get useful information on academics in my field. Most importantly, however, at a later stage in my research, their criticism of my theoretical approach and the fact that I was not able fully to legitimize my rejection of alternative approaches made me aware of the importance of making an in-depth study of all the relevant approaches to the study of my research field. If I was to defend myself on the day of my viva (which seems a long way ahead, but, nevertheless, has an impact upon the way you carry out your research), I had to know 'my enemies', as one of my peers suggested. Additionally, in some instances, my peers were of help when I was reluctant to disturb my supervisor for certain minor matters. They can also be important at times when you are not willing to admit your ignorance or lack of knowledge to your supervisor. Both the help of my supervisor and the support of my peers made me realize the significance of my decision to carry out doctoral research in the same university department in which I had studied for my Master's degree. In that way, I got to know the department and, most importantly, my supervisor and her field of interest.

Finally, an under-utilized resource worth mentioning are the core authors in your research field. Once you have established which approach you are going to take in your research, it is important to identify the leading figures in that study area. This work not only stimulates research in the area, but is also the essential basis from which to start your own research. Moreover, these authors can provide you with additional information, make useful suggestions, point you in new directions, and will most of the time prove willing to give you feedback on pieces of work that correspond to their interests. Contrary to what most students assume or expect, most academics, although it sometimes seems they are locked up in ivory towers, turn out to be very approachable. If you refuse to contact them or make no effort to introduce yourself, obviously no one will contact you. Although it seems 'pushy', you have to take the first step, even if it means getting a reluctant reply, or no reply at all. One positive answer can be sufficient to improve your research. During the first months of my research, once I had established that I wanted to work within the policy network framework, I started to write letters to leading authors in the field. I asked them how to obtain some of the unpublished articles to which they had referred in some of their publications. The responses I received were overwhelmingly positive and formed a great stimulus for my research. Not only did I get the unpublished studies I asked for, I also obtained additional information. Moreover, one of the professors was kind enough to invite me to join a seminar that particularly focused on my research approach. This seminar enabled me to get in touch with PhD students from other universities working within the same theoretical approach. Although second- and third-year PhD students in our department initiated a postgraduate seminar in which each student has the opportunity to present a piece of their work, and get feedback and critical comments, I nevertheless felt the need for contacts outside the university. In Belgium, where I studied for my undergraduate degree, I already experienced how taking additional courses in different departments and universities improved the richness of my thoughts and work. While studying for my degree as a development economist, I took additional lectures in the politics department of another university. The fact that pure economics, and the models it supports, are not preoccupied with the political feasibility of the well-studied economic programmes led me to embrace alternative thoughts and approaches.

When I came to the UK to study for my postgraduate degree, it became even clearer to me that differences in the way of approaching certain issues, in emphasis, and even in core literature and authors, contribute to acquiring different and perhaps more mature thoughts. This process of maturation inevitably contributes to quality of research. Hence, invitations such as this one to join seminars were more than appreciated. Approaching the major figures in my field has contributed to establishing a whole network of contacts that will prove useful and, indeed, essential to making progress. Working in isolation may have advantages, but it certainly also has limits. Contacts outside your own university and department cannot but contribute to the improvement of your work and does stimulate thinking. It is in this respect that first-year doctoral students should also see conferences.

Although for some of us it is too early at the start of the PhD to write conference papers, it is never too soon to go to conferences and to join relevant associations (Political Studies Association (PSA) and British International Studies Association (BISA) at minimum). Attending conferences should especially be seen in the light of building a network of contacts. Individual contact, inevitably, has more impact than a letter. It also involves getting in touch with PhD students from different backgrounds and different universities. While all this demands time, resources and energy, in my experience there is a high return on investment, not only in academic feedback, information and efficiency, but also in moral and social support. Although it does not really change anything materially, to know that others experience similar problems, difficulties and doubts can sometimes be enough to keep you going. The fact that you can express your doubts and problems and that you can share your euphoric feelings can be a stimulus to continue and to do better. Hence contacts, which inevitably form part of, as well as constitute, the environment in which you work, are as important and influential as good supervision.

The thesis must have a 'thesis'

One of the most important facts of which my supervisor made me aware was the necessity of having a 'thesis' or a central research question from the early stages of the research project. This implies, as Phillips and Pugh state, that your dissertation must argue a position. According to these authors, this means that, at a minimum, the study must have a 'story-line', a coherent thrust which pushes along an argument, an explanation, a systematic set of inferences derived from new data or new ways of viewing current data. The importance of focusing on a central research question from the start of the PhD onwards becomes clear when one has a closer look at the relevant research literature. It is very easy to get lost on side-roads and, as Phillips and Pugh point out, to spread oneself too widely and too thinly. It is impossible in the context of PhD research and its time limit to make an in-depth analysis of several major issues. Moreover, to preserve the coherence of the project, and, indeed, to finish successfully, your 'thesis' has to organize data. Relevance to argument should be the guiding criterion. This became particularly clear when, during the first week of my research, my supervisor asked me to produce a chapter outline.

This seemed at the time both impossible and certainly too early. How was I to produce a chapter outline when I had only started to browse through the literature and to think about how I was going to approach my research topic? The upshot was that it forced me to develop a central research theme. It is very easy to get carried away by interesting and related but, nevertheless, side-issues. A central research question enables you to focus and select and, hence, to work more efficiently. Additionally, because I was asked to produce a chapter outline within the first weeks, and I certainly did not want to disappoint my supervisor, my motivation was reinforced. The work that I had done during my MA study contributed to making the process of reflection and analysis easier and faster. During that year, I concentrated on empirically based description and analysis. I thereby focused on issues that were related to my PhD topic. This strategy enabled me to have well-developed thoughts concerning the empirical part of my PhD. In turn, this facilitated my search for an appropriate and satisfactory theoretical framework. To sum up, a thesis or central research question renders research more focused and hence more efficient and coherent. Additionally, producing a chapter outline at a very early stage of the PhD is a very useful and advisable exercise, even if it is not required. It forces you to focus and think about the thesis as an integrated whole. This, in turn, makes it possible to produce a timetable. On the basis of your chapter outline, even if it is only a first and rough sketch of ideas, and although you are aware that in the course of your research a lot will change, you will be able to plan how much time you can afford to spend on the different aspects of your research. In my case, it enabled me, during the first year, to plan the interviews that I carried out in Germany and Japan. It is always easier to contact individuals or organizations and to ask for their co-operation once you have a timetable in mind. It is advisable to contact them as soon as possible to make sure you can count on their co-operation. If, in addition, you can give an approximate date for the interviews, you are more likely to receive a positive answer. As one of my interviewees told me, 'When someone asks me in January to help him or her in the second half of the year, I almost never refuse. It is a long time ahead, and, almost automatically, I agree.'

The main research technique I used in the first year was elite interviewing. During my MA, I had established some useful contacts in the Japanese pharmaceutical industry and in certain government institutions in Japan. The contacts in the Japanese industry, it turned out, led to further contacts in the German pharmaceutical industry as well as in other German government institutions. By way of conclusion, the rest of this chapter relates my experience of *actual* research in the first year, in contrast to the standard textbook model of research I encountered in methodology training courses.

Elite interviewing: the Japan challenge

The day that I received the news that I had been granted the 1996 Canon Foundation Research Visiting Fellowship was one of great confusion. I had mentally prepared myself for a short-term visit to Japan (one month) and six months to Germany. Also, my research was developing in such a way that I would only need a short-term visit to Japan – at least, this was my plan. However, as my supervisor argued, a longer-term stay in Japan (in my case approximately seven months) would give substantial depth to my research. Also, the substantial financial support from the Canon Foundation was most welcome in view of the high living expenses in Japan. Even a short-term trip to Japan would have meant a major financial burden, as I realized during my first days in Tokyo. Anyway, here I was, in the middle of Tokyo, not being able to speak or read Japanese. Fortunately, as mentioned above, over the preceding two years I had already established a few contacts in the Japanese pharmaceutical industry. I was also extremely privileged in that I was offered logistic support in a pharmaceutical company in Tokyo. This company was in many ways the cornerstone of my research activities. Without the company's support, my task would have been almost impossible. It was the only place where I could use computing and printing facilities, and where I had access to fax, phone and copier without having to spend enormous amounts. My search for e-mail facilities, however, remained unsuccessful. Apparently, at the time of writing, e-mail is still not that commonly used in Japan. The resistance, or should it be hesitance, to using the English language is the main explanation. Japan becomes even more idiosyncratic when you visit libraries. Library searches are still carried out according to old systems. Consequently, do not expect to use a computer too often unless you are in one of the foreign libraries, and even then the computer system is likely to be completely outdated. If you are lucky, you may be allowed to use the copier in the library. Quite often, however, probably due to the age of the copier, the librarian will ask you to fill out a form stating the number of copies required. Library staff will then laboriously make the copies for you. The price reflects the level of labour intensity.

The personnel of the company in which I did my research usually demonstrated a willingness to help me with my project. However, the amount of time, patience, frustration and effort that was involved in making minor progress was enormous. First, it took me approximately four weeks to politely make it clear to different people in the company that, to a large extent, my research in Japan would be based on interviews but that it was not sufficient merely to carry out interviews in the company, no matter how well-informed the people in the company were. Second, I also experienced problems in explaining exactly what kind of information I needed. Most of the people with whom I had contact in the company were either chemists or pharmacists. My inability to speak the Japanese language and their difficulty in understanding the purpose of research in political science considerably slowed down my work. In this respect also, one professor told me, 'Your questions and explanations might be intelligent, but they might not be intelligible to the Japanese.' What complicated the whole matter and made my research even more cumbersome was that in the company it was impossible to talk to, or to meet, a person alone. For a start, everyone seemed to be involved in the work of the department. My efforts were hampered in particular by the open-plan office system. Most often in Japan, it is the case that everyone who works in a specific department of a company shares the same office space, with desks put closely together. Consequently, quite a few people are involved in each issue that is being discussed. This meant that a considerable amount of time was lost deciding how best to gather information. Moreover, everyone wanted to understand what I was doing without necessarily being able to help me any further. Furthermore, every time I visited a person in another department, I was accompanied by someone from my department. This, of course, was to introduce me. However kind this was, quite often it also involved the postponement of a meeting since it had to fit in with the agenda of more people. The difficulties involved in formulating intelligent and intelligible questions and eliciting satisfactory explanations not only applied to my dealings with the people in the company in which I worked, it also applied to most other meetings.

In Western countries, people want precise questions and will give you as precise an answer as possible. In Japan, this did not seem to work. One foreign professor advised me to ask very broad and general questions. Eventually, I would end up getting an answer to the question that I had in mind. Another strategy came from an industry spokesperson. An American executive advised me to ask many precise but similar questions. This involves posing the same question, differently formulated, a number of times. This would eventually produce results.

An additional difficulty in this context, which I have already alluded to, is the necessity of being introduced. Without introduction, it is likely that your request for a meeting will be turned down, and then a subsequent introduction becomes difficult. A professor who was carrying out research at the same time as myself had been refused some crucial interviews by Ministry of Finance (MoF) officials because of his inability to speak Japanese. This professor had interpreters who were working for him and the Japanese officials in question spoke fluent English. The real reason was the risk-averse attitude of Japanese people. The professor had not been introduced. Hence, the MoF officials did not know whether they could trust him. In Japan, the interviewee wants to know you before you meet him. In the West, you get to know each other while meeting and talking. In this context, it is perhaps also useful to relay further advice I received from another foreign professor in Japan.

In Western countries, he said, an interview or meeting between two people is of the kind 1+1=2. Two individuals are meeting, sharing knowledge and opinions, but they remain two individuals. In Japan, he argued, a successful meeting or interview involves 1+1=1. Two individuals become one. There is harmony, understanding, and, especially, trust. As mentioned, this implies that the interviewee will want to know you before you actually meet. I was very fortunate that I had been introduced by a Belgian executive to the president of the company in which I worked in Tokyo. The president, in turn, had prepared my arrival in the company in the sense that he had informed people of my arrival and had asked them to co-operate in so far as it did not hamper them in their work. Consequently, I began by interviewing people in the company. As mentioned, this made me aware of the problem of asking questions that are intelligible to the Japanese. It also, however, demonstrated the necessity of formal introduction and of establishing longer-term relationships built on trust. Japanese executives, especially senior ones, like to get to know your background and your relationship with the company. The fact that I quite often had lunch with some of them in the company's cafeteria, and had repeatedly explained the purpose of my research, made them more co-operative.

However, I still had to wait for an introduction to *former* governmental officials until they had found the time to express their opinions in a formal interview.[1] This takes time, since these senior executives in the company were also very busy. However, as I was told, the Japanese are always busy and occupied even when they are playing golf. Consequently, you have to find the right balance between being polite and attentive, but also, at some stages, being insistent and letting them know that you have a time schedule as well. However, before you get to the stage where you can start pushing people, already a couple of weeks have passed and you are left with the feeling that you are getting nowhere with your research.

It was at this stage that I decided to use three other strategies in an attempt to work faster. First, I contacted some Japanese academics who were working in an area related to mine. Once again it is important to show that you are interested in their work, and that you have read some of it. I had already established some contacts before arriving in Japan. This proved extremely useful. There are two very good reasons for trying to establish contacts in the academic world in Japan. One reason is that experienced researchers can point you to places where you can find information on your topic, thus saving a lot of time and money – since there are many libraries and research centres in Tokyo, and transport is not cheap. Moreover, they might provide you with further contacts, quite often in the government.

A second strategy that I used to speed up my research progress was to fax quite extensive messages, explaining my research, my background, but, especially, emphasizing the support that I had already received from many companies and the relationships that I had established with several Japanese executives and/or officials. In this way, I could obtain interviews without having to wait for a formal introduction by the people from the company in which I was based, yet the potential interviewees could contact the company if they felt it necessary. This also proved an extremely successful and effective strategy.

Lastly, I contacted executives from European and American companies or joint-ventures. These proved to be more approachable since they were interested in the same information and, hence, were quite willing to provide me with introductions since, in a sense, my research would be a source of information for them. Perhaps the best piece of advice that someone could get before taking off to Japan is: expect everything to be different and do not get frustrated by the amount of effort, patience and time that is involved in the process of collecting information.

Note

1. I am emphasizing *former*, since in the company it was felt that it was not appropriate for the industry to introduce me to ministry officials while they were still in office.

4

Research Design – 'A Rough Guide'

VERED BARTOV

This chapter does not attempt to offer a step-by-step guide to the 'best way' in which to design research projects. What it does attempt is to highlight some of the difficulties that can be encountered along the way and compare these to the way in which research is often portrayed in the secondary literature. The chapter is divided into several sections. The first offers a description of my own research agenda. Following on from this is a brief discussion of a sample of the literature on research design. How my project related to this is then highlighted. The chapter then gives a brief, and somewhat general, account of my experience in designing a feasible topic. It also examines how the process itself began. In other words, the chapter will analyse how the literature tallies with the actual experience. Included too are certain problems that were encountered in the first year. These are highlighted in order to show that often the process itself is not always as smooth as the orthodox accounts imply, and indeed may be subject to various 'hiccups' along the way. The process of designing my research came about more by accident than design. All too often the secondary literature advocates a step-by-step approach to designing research projects. In my experience this logical process did not tally with day-to-day practice.

Outline of project and research design

The thesis itself has the rather glamorous title: 'The politics of the life assurance industry in the single market programme with special reference to the UK's life assurance industry'. It aims to research and conceptualize the politics of European market integration and regulation in the life assurance sector and the related national policy process in the UK. The aim of the thesis is then to contribute to an understanding of the role of political authorities and the private sector in the EU's process of market liberalization, illustrating the linkages between domestic and EU policy processes. The primary focus is on the elaboration of the single market programme in life assurance, the detailed negotiations, and the implementation process of EU directives. These are systematically linked to UK national regulatory and policy change. The pressures and constraints in the development of the single market project, the negotiation of EU legislation and how we understand these policy processes is examined from an international political economy perspective. As stated above, the process by which I arrived at the topic was achieved as much by accident as by design.

Starting research and designing a feasible research topic can often be far less of an organized process than most of the literature on 'how to do a PhD' implies. I had originally assumed that reading enough books on research design would offer me such useful insights into the process that progress would naturally flow on from there. Although I could identify with some of the readings, I really could not locate myself easily into the 'models' presented or the steps advocated. The idealized form as presented in some of the literature was of little relevance for me. The process of starting research in the initial stages before you 'find your feet' is comparable to stumbling about in the dark looking for the perfect design technique that can be utilized and then transformed into the thesis that will succeed at the viva, subject to no more than a handful of typographical errors.

One common thread in much of the literature is the assumption that there are certain logical steps that can be followed. Few if any of the authors allow for the sorts of distractions, problems or limitations confronting many first-time researchers. In the end it was my own supervisor's method that was of relevance to me in terms of offering clarity and efficiency. Only a limited number of accounts of the *experience* of research have been produced to date; such studies as there have been are few in number and tend to be related directly to the discipline of sociology, often drawing predominantly on the ethnographic tradition. A number of books on research design seem at first to offer useful models. Ackoff (1953, p. 1), for instance, pursues an aim common to most of the secondary literature, namely showing 'how the best possible investigation can be conducted in the social sciences by using the latest developments in scientific method'. Ackoff attempts 'to make explicit how research *should* be conducted, not necessarily how it is conducted' in the social sciences (1953, p. 25). He also suggests how the various phases of enquiry can be brought under control. Although this is undeniably desirable, one could question whether this is ever possible. Ackoff talks of 'controlling the research procedure' and of a 'process of deliberate anticipation directed toward bringing an expected situation under control' (*ibid.*), implying that we can anticipate most situations. Yet, in practice, unforeseen situations often arise to throw us off track, force us to redirect our studies or even delay them.

Most authors on this topic approach the meaning of 'design' by analogy, comparing the process to that of an architect who 'designs' a building, considering each decision that has to be made in constructing the building before the actual construction begins because he wants a picture of the whole before starting construction of any part. The analogy here is very weak, as it suggests that knowing what the house looks like from its blueprint is the same as knowing what the project will look like. Yet if the purpose is to explore a topic, and carry out serious investigation, then how can you have the final blueprints there in front of you? The need is rather to set the boundaries of the research.

Although some recent books have offered far more useful insights, all too often a step-by-step sequence is prescribed that in reality is difficult, if not impossible, to follow. Judith Bell (1992, p. 11), for example, suggests that what you need to do is 'select a topic, identify the objectives of your study, plan and design a suitable methodology, devise research instruments, negotiate access to institutions, materials and people, collect, analyse and present information and, finally, produce a well-written report or dissertation'. Useful advice is given, although in essence it amounts only to a set of guidelines. Moreover, much of the methodology that is referred to in the book relates directly to sociological approaches. What is supposed to be a guide for first-time researchers in education *and* the social sciences seems to refer exclusively to one discipline, sociology.

Hedrick *et al.* (1993) and Miller (1991) offer similar steps to be followed in the process of designing research. Both also seem to assume a logical progression between the planning and execution stages. In Hedrick *et al.*, for example, you move from stage 1, the research definition, through to stage 2, the research designing and planning stage. The first stage essentially involves understanding the problem, identifying questions and refining and revising those questions. The second stage involves choosing design and data collection approaches and assessing the feasibility of the project (Hedrick *et al.*, 1993, pp. 12–13). Hedrick *et al.* recognize that a process of continual assessment needs to be carried out as to the feasibility of the project at each stage. This approach, although specifically referring to applied research, allows for flexibility as you continuously refine and revise the research questions, determining the enquiry's scope and limitations. This 'cradle to grave' approach is much too simplistic. It is difficult when a project is in its infancy to follow any of the steps prescribed. In presenting the 'Sociological Problem', one must, according to Hedrick *et al.*, describe the relationship of the problem to a theoretical framework, forming a hypothesis and describing the ideal design with particular attention to the control of interfering variables. In my experience, however, the PhD project tends to grow and develop, and is subject to many fundamental modifications along the way.

Writers such as Burgess (1993, p. 1) move away from the traditional approach in some ways, recognizing that the last decade has 'witnessed considerable developments and changes in discussion of research methods'. Once again, however, his work is very much grounded within the discipline of sociology. He acknowledges that methods are no longer 'considered to be a standard set of techniques that can be applied to any project' and recognizes the rigidity of the previous models. Whereas previously there had been an 'ideal type' process of social research (see Table 4.1), where research can be subdivided into a number of discrete steps and stages, science, he argues, 'seldom involves a straightforward logical sequence . . . Instead, it involves some guesswork, competition, rivalry and lucky breaks' (Burgess, 1993, pp. 1, 5–6).

Table 4.1   An Ideal Typical Research Process

Research design	Sampling	Data collection	Data analysis	Report
Establishing the problem Conceptualization Definition	Selecting units of study	Choosing methods of investigation for the problem and units of study	Methods of data analysis and interpretation	Writing and publication of the report

Although Burgess offers a useful critique of the ideal process, the utility of his alternative is difficult to ascertain. How useful, for example, is the idea of viewing research as a seamless web? In this model, we are told there is no beginning and there is no clear order as theory, observation and techniques are brought together. Starting with the premise that there is no order to a process seems to be a less useful approach to take than prescribing an ordered one and yet at the same time recognizing that there has to be flexibility within it.

Research design – 'A perfect model'?

For me, it was important to have a clear idea of what was expected of the research process. Even though the research had not begun, I needed to have at the very least a 'straw man' to help keep me focused and on track.

The secondary literature had little relevance, due to the fact that the early stages of the research process were more comparable to Mosaic wandering in the wilderness. It helped to be given clear guidance from my supervisor, even if I could not immediately make sense of it and the pieces of the jigsaw didn't immediately fall into place. A useful structure which provided some focus and direction and helped 'frame' the thesis was provided in terms of the following model that consisted of a number of sections:

(a) Introduction

This sets out briefly the project outline and the main arguments. In the introduction, locate your work within a particular context.

(b) Focus and scope

This section highlights not only what the research will focus on and what parameters are set for it, but, just as importantly, what it will *not* focus on. It is important to set the boundaries of your research and highlight not only why you feel it is important to concentrate on certain aspects, but why others should be excluded. This is also an insurance policy for the viva. It may be necessary to show you have anticipated the question as to why you have excluded certain topics, as some might attach more significance to them than you do.

(c) General issues

This section focuses on what conceptual issues are raised by the thesis.

(d) Argument

Although it is often difficult to know what your argument will be at the early stages of the research, this should be attempted. Even if you later discard this, it helps establish some boundaries for the project.

(e) Structure of thesis

This section should give a rough indication of how the thesis will be divided. An attempt should be made to divide the work into chapters in order to make the topic more manageable and clarify the structure. A colleague in the law school refused throughout the duration of his research to acknowledge that he was in fact writing a thesis. The word itself seemed so daunting to him that he preferred instead to describe the project in terms of writing a series of short 'essays'. The delusion seemed to have helped him cope with the burden. The thought of writing a work of 80,000–100,000 words of 'publishable quality' seems far more daunting at first than thinking of it as five to eight 'essays' all relating to the same topic.

(f) Plan of study

Research methods

An analysis of the pros and cons of the various methodologies available has to be made. Consideration should also be given to data collection and data analysis techniques. In other words, what methods of investigation will be employed in the research, and what methods of analysing the data will be used? My research, for example, would rely on documentary analysis as the main method. However, given the current dynamic of market integration in European insurance, some use would also be made of elite interviewing. The method of evaluating the influence of the various actors in the policy process would be via a combination of documentary research and analysis and elite interviewing where appropriate. The process would need to rely for much of its information on primary interview material to back up information gleaned from secondary and tertiary sources, and would also rely on cross-referencing of sources.

Timetable

Divide the three years up into manageable slots and then set yourself realistic deadlines. For example, divide the year into quarters or monthly slots and set realistic targets for what you wish to accomplish in the individual time periods.

Bibliography

This need not include all the sources, but indicate what types of documentary sources you intend to consult. This may include not only documentation, but also what contacts you intend to make. For example, I soon realized that several types of sources could be employed. This included insurance associations and firms, scholarly and business journals, government publications and EU documentation. The focus would rest primarily on referring to parliamentary debates and reports and other governmental documents, backed up by elite interviewing for the case study. Time needed to be spent drawing up a list of associations and governmental departments that were involved in the policy network. In many dictionaries on insurance and materials relating to the industry there are lists of the trade associations and contact addresses which could be drawn upon as a starting point. A twin-track approach was needed to find what types of sources were available for my case study and which ones would inform my theoretical framework.

Although I had been given this model to work with in my first week of having registered, it was not until six months later that I managed to have a clearly defined and feasible research proposal. The process seemed at times both long and tedious, as I was asked to review and revise proposal after proposal in order to frame the research in a coherent manner. The transition from Master's level had by no means been smooth. It took me a while to adapt to my new role and find my feet. Although the models on the perfect way in which to design research were useful in parts, none seemed to take into account factors related to the day-to-day experience of many first-time researchers. It was not always easy knowing exactly what was expected of me, or indeed what to expect of the research process itself. No longer was the format as clear cut as in undergraduate or Master's level studies. Despite having a supervisor, the onus was still largely on me to guide and motivate myself. Added to this was the pressure to identify my research interests accurately and locate a fruitful area to research in the shortest time. For me, this was more difficult than I had first imagined. I had, after all, not been born with a burning desire to study insurance markets!

It is commonly thought that a PhD topic should be an extension of a Master's dissertation. Originally this was the path I had chosen to follow. By the end of my Master's programme, however, I had come to the realization that studying how European Free Trade Area (EFTA) and Visegrad countries differed in their approaches to membership of the EU held little appeal. Admittedly, the decision was made easier by virtue of having failed to secure funding for this particular research from the ESRC.

The research itself can begin in several different ways. One may, for example, wish to expand on an area of knowledge or interest gained through one's experiences in academia or the workplace. My interest in insurance, however, was not born of the fruits of undergraduate or postgraduate study. There was no innate urge (at that stage) to study the workings of life assurance markets in the EU. This 'passion' was born more of a process of elimination and a careful assessment of compatibility and feasibility of the options available.

Miller (1991, p. 17) offers some practical advice on the matter of choosing a topic for research, advising that in choosing a field one should consider the following: your interest, your capacity, your potential growth and future career, the ability of your professor, and your ability to work with the professor. Some would argue that interest in the research is far from being a crucial determining factor. Even though you often look on the thesis as your own creation, it does not follow that you have to be enthusiastic about it. If one is analytic in one's approach, then the project can grow in interest. Enthusiasm early on can wane, and indeed by the end of the three years it often does. As for your potential growth and future career, it is not easy to ascertain how taking a mercenary approach to choosing your topic can be beneficial. Often in certain academic circles there is a tendency to research the fashionable areas (globalization in the case of international political economy (IPE) at present). The trouble with this bandwagon effect is that three years hence the same topic can seem terribly dated, the gap in the market having long been filled. It is not necessary, either, to have a supervisor who is an expert in the field. Of more importance is your ability to work effectively with them.

Before launching into the process of designing the research itself, I needed to establish several things. The first was whether there was a suitable supervisor in my proposed field and whether I would have sufficient funding to enable me to carry out the research. I also need to have a clear idea of what was expected of me and, indeed, what was expected of the PhD itself.

Finding out what is expected

When starting out, it is not always made explicit where a PhD starts and an MA ends. In the early stages I was confronted with the problem of not knowing what was expected of me, or indeed what writing a thesis was really all about. There were also the usual insecurities about confidence in my own ability. I started to wonder if I was intelligent enough for the task, for the supervisor and, indeed, for others. At several academic conferences I attended I had witnessed the intellectual mauling others received, and wondered if I would ever have the courage to put myself in front of a firing squad and possibly be shot down in the infant stages of my academic career.

The concept of making an 'original contribution' is one that can cause confusion too. There is pressure to work out the significance of your research before this has in fact begun in earnest. The probable contribution to knowledge is difficult to foresee for research not yet undertaken and tested. It is one thing to be told what is expected of a thesis, and what constitutes a significant contribution to knowledge, but quite another to understand and apply this in the early stages. It is not always easy, without guidance, to know what are the unanswered questions in your chosen field.

Finding a suitable supervisor

One positive outcome of being rejected by the ESRC was that it helped clarify certain matters and put issues into perspective. In particular, I decided that I had no real interest in the topic for which I applied for funding. It also forced me to acknowledge that I had chosen the topic partly in order to be supervised by one of the so-called 'big names' in the field. A 'heavyweight' supervisor, as I discovered, was not necessarily going to increase my chances of securing funding. It is also debatable whether the 'heavyweight in the field' approach has any bearing on future career prospects. The issue of compatibility is far more pertinent than usefulness in those terms. Further to this, it became apparent that I had in fact been steered towards a research topic more suited to the supervisor's research agenda than my own. Having noticed the remarkable similarity in the work that some of his other students were doing, it was not difficult to see a pattern emerging of 'empire building'. The prospect of being little more than an unpaid research assistant for three years held little appeal. The issue of funding dominated almost as much of the first six months of my PhD as did the issue of designing a workable topic.

Funding

Complications are bound to arise if you embark upon research without securing funding beforehand, as I discovered. The mundane 'bread and butter' problem of how to feed, clothe and generally maintain solvency for the next three years or so occupied more of my time at the early stages than I had bargained for. Having failed to secure ESRC funding, it seemed more appropriate to register in January instead of October, thereby allowing me three months in which to seek alternative sources of funding and earn some money. Having registered in January, I then discovered that I was ineligible for any research assistantships as these were not awarded to those already registered at the university. This left me with one internal avenue, that of applying for the central university scholarships and competing on a cross-faculty basis.

It is easy to underestimate how time-consuming the process of attempting to secure funding can be. Although there were only one or two registers of grant-awarding authorities and charities available in the library for reference, it took a considerable amount of time to sift through these to ascertain which grants I was eligible for. I also spent valuable resources phoning, faxing and writing to various grant-awarding authorities. Time and effort were employed in exploring avenues outside the country, such as the EU who have various schemes for funding projects. Despite having taken a three-month break between completing the MA and registering for the PhD, the first four or five months of the research were spent simultaneously trying to find both a focus for the research itself and writing out various proposals to the organizations to whom I was applying.

In the end, after five months, I managed to secure funding from a trade association. Almost by accident I discovered that I was eligible for an award not from an academic or governmental institution, but from a trade organization that represents all the insurance companies in the UK, the Association of British Insurers (ABI). They were running a scheme whereby five students that year would be funded to carry out research on insurance-related work. A fellow student in the department had mentioned in passing that they had seen an advertisement the previous day. As a last resort, I sent off for the application forms, although I held out little hope. Despite these doubts and reservations, the grant was given on the basis of both a written proposal and an interview conducted in front of a panel of three insurance academics, two senior practitioners and one member of the organization's economic and political research department.

In this case perseverance paid off, but the process was very distracting and the outcome far from guaranteed. It is useful to bear in mind, given the intense competition for the usual sources, that it may be worth exploring the less conventional. Do not be intimidated by the fact that you may not seem to fit the profile. It may even play to your advantage in terms of novelty value if you seem to be drawn from an under-represented discipline; international political economy in my case. At my interview I was able to justify to some effect that insurance was heavily under-researched in my field. The panel were also suitably impressed by an approach which seemed to them unusual (i.e., one that combined an analysis of both state and market actors in the political process). The proposal needed to be well marketed. The ones I had sent to the ABI and ESRC, for example, bore little resemblance to one another, despite the fact that in essence the research topic was the same. The one to the ESRC, for example, needed to sound academically rigorous. When applying to a trade association, on the other hand, it was important to make the case that the research would also be of direct relevance to the wider business community at large.

Timing

Although in theory it should make little difference what stage of the year one begins the research, in practice several problems arose. For me there was the feeling of isolation that resulted from the fact that networks seemed to have already been established between the other first-years during the first term. There was also the barrier of entering what is still essentially a male-dominated environment to add to the pressure of being the 'new kid on the block'. This was not so much a problem of direct exclusion as a feeling of isolation. This was felt too on the social level, where it seemed to me that it may have been easier for a male to integrate. The feeling was partly self-imposed, and I soon found that the process went both ways in that the onus was on me to integrate myself into the group and make an added effort not to be excluded. It is all to easy to feel intimidated in a predominantly male environment, but this I found was due in no way to any conscious effort by any of the others to exclude anyone. On a more practical level, there was the setback of having missed out on the first term's methodology course. The classes and discussions may have helped in overcoming the feeling of isolation and reassured me that I was not the only one facing 'teething problems'. They dealt with matters that, by and large, I was left to grapple with in isolation. For example, discussions on designing your research and the writing process had been held within the first two weeks of the autumn term. A forum was provided whereby incoming students could discuss their experiences of the 'research process' and seek collaborative solutions to common problems encountered in research.

Despite the various setbacks or 'teething problems' and distractions of the early stages, I did eventually manage to find a focus and define the scope of my research.

Narrowing the field: making a molehill out of a mountain

The process of focusing my research was far less organized than any of the secondary literature implied it might be. At the start there was enormous pressure from my supervisor to narrow the focus and scope of the research agenda and present a proposal mapping out the precise agenda of my research. Some of the secondary literature on research design (for instance Miller, 1991, p. 17) did at least acknowledge that the selection of a problem represents a substantial commitment of time, money and energy, and that it is not unusual for a researcher to give six months to a year to finding a specific problem and formulating it for research study. It felt that I had been allocated no longer than six days for this purpose! During the first few weeks I felt both disheartened and frustrated at the fact that I still did not seem to have a clear direction and focus. The impression was given, rightly or wrongly, that I had to map out the policy community I was to study and establish a network of contacts almost immediately. I often felt like I was merely muddling through in an *ad hoc* fashion, stumbling from one idea to another, taking on some and disregarding others as I attempted to locate my interest. Having decided not to go for the 'heavyweight in their field' approach with regard to the choice of supervisors, I took the 'gap in the market' one with regard to topic. In other words, I had to decide how my research interests coincided with an area that was both original and topical. My broad research interests lay in both IPE and European integration. The problem then became how to narrow down the focus further, given the infinite number of possible combinations. It should be borne in mind, however, that often a project may be defined too ambitiously at the outset and that the project tends to grow as it is written. The research is a process, not an act. The lines of communication should be open at this stage, not only with one's supervisor but with one's colleagues and peer group too, in order to 'bounce ideas' off as many people as possible.

At this stage I needed to work out not only where my academic interests lay, but what would be a practical and manageable topic. Eventually the focus was narrowed down to the single market programme and financial services. During both undergraduate and graduate studies I had carried out a limited amount of work into the former topic. The latter, however, was new to me, thereby offering the challenge. It was only through the initial literature review that I was able to narrow the focus further.

The literature review

Within the broad area of the single market programme in financial services, I needed to locate a more precise field of investigation. An initial survey of the literature helped in this respect. By carrying out an 'audit' of the literature I was able to find a feasible topic and clarify the focus of my work. This took about four weeks of hibernation in the library, stooped over a computer terminal. The 'audit' itself involved looking through the library's on-line catalogue searching out the secondary sources on insurance. Extensive use was made of CD-ROM networks and Bath Information and Data Service (BIDS) to find what other books and articles were written on the subject. I also looked up what was available in other (often far better equipped and stocked) libraries in the area. This allowed me to locate an issue, find an angle or perspective on it and get a feel for the debate in a particular area. It also provided new materials and ideas for a case study and enabled me to locate my position *vis-à-vis* others. The readings had to be digested and critically analysed in a relatively short period of time. As the onus was on me to locate an area, I often had to carry out an internal dialogue as I debated the pros and cons of any given area and tried to anticipate the potential pitfalls.

Surveying the literature informed me of the gaps in the research. In the case of insurance, paradoxically, there was both too much and too little with respect to writing on the subject. When surveying the IPE literature it was evident that too much research had already been done into banking and too little on insurance. Furthermore, all the literature on insurance and the single market programme seemed to have been written from a neo-liberal position, with many of the authors giving virtually the same type of analysis. After exhausting the conventional sources in the library, I turned to the so-called 'new sources' to see if there was anything of relevance to my subject.

IT and 'new' sources

'Navigating' the World Wide Web (or 'surfing the net') seemed daunting at first, partly due to all the fatuous jargon that surrounds it. The trick for all technophobes is to have the 'net' demystified and to see it as little more than an extension of the library's on-line catalogue (with far better pictures). In practice, it should take no longer than about thirty minutes to become familiar with the system.

Having launched myself into 'cyberspace', the temptation was to head straight for the web sights of my favourite football team, singer, film, etc., before proceeding to the more serious task in hand. The software packages all have some sort of keyword search, which is by far the easiest way of finding what is available if you do not have a particular site in mind. Starting with the most obvious term, 'insurance', I found myself inundated with sites within seconds. The sheer volume of material was overwhelming, until I realized that most of it was irrelevant.

I was able to find a directory of insurance resources on the Internet. This enabled me to see almost straightaway that most of the sites were US-based. The amount of information overload was eased dramatically when I realized that many of the sites were merely companies promoting themselves or trying to sell insurance. Within an hour, I was able to narrow the search down from about 100 sites to one that looked useful, Risknet. This site is an electronic discussion list that allows persons around the world to hold discussions on risk and insurance issues. Topics for discussion included areas such as corporate risk management, underwriting cycles, insurance solvency and regulation, insurance economics, insurance finance, the globalization of insurance markets, etc. Circulation of draft articles for comment and discussion also took place on this site.

I subscribed to Risknet for several weeks, until I realized that out of every 50 to 100 messages I would receive a week, only one or two would ever be of direct interest. Risknet, I discovered also archived all the discussions, classifying them by both author and subject. This turned out to be far more useful than joining the mailing list, as few of the discussions were specifically related to academia. The mailing list was more useful as a reference for contacts, giving you e-mail addresses of all the subscribers along with a brief description of the subscriber's research interests and employment. Such a reference can be useful in enabling you to build a network of contacts. Similar on-line industry forums or newsgroups are available in most academic disciplines.

Using the Internet is cheap in monetary terms. It can also afford you access to US libraries and archives whose information might otherwise be unavailable. However, this has to be weighed against the fact that it can be very time-consuming and tedious to access. It can often take hours to find a site due to the inefficiency of the system itself and the heavy volume of 'traffic' in cyberspace. Much of it remains purely a marketing exercise.

In many ways, the Internet has been rightly described as not so much 'information superhighway but information overload'.[1] That is to say, the 'net' is a 'massive factfile' which is often 'of less use than a thin volume'. Essentially the Internet is still a prototype, and is in its infancy as regards speed and accessibility. As with all things that are hyped, there will eventually be a backlash against its usefulness. This should not detract from the essential truth, that it is useful if you know how to use it properly and ruthlessly prune out all the irrelevant sections. Some question whether communication is taking the place of writing arguing that 'the trouble is there are no writers on the net, only communicators and you don't look on it for information you want to find. You just find on it information somebody wants to tell you'.[2]

Other 'new sources' that were of greater use were the CD-ROM networks. These proved invaluable in finding what had been published in mainstream business and social science journals. BIDS social science section contains abstracts and information on over 3300 journals with a staggering 6000 books per annum added. *Current Research In Britain* (CRIB) allows you to see who is researching what at any particular time. The disadvantage with this, as with other databases, is that it can lull you into a false sense of security. Having seen from the CRIB search that no one was researching my topic, I then, to my shock, found out six months later that someone sponsored by the same organization as myself had chosen the same case study. Other databases on the EU, such as SCAD (prepared by the European Commission Documentation Service), for example, offer bibliographic information on union acts and preparatory documents. SCAD also provides abstracts of periodical articles on union affairs, and statements and opinions from all sides of industry on union policy. They also index key publications originating from the union. ABI-inform is another useful database that offers references to articles from 1000 or so management and business journals. The searches were, however, by no means exhaustive. Most of the specialist insurance journals, for example, were not included. The CD-ROM network consists of regularly updated bibliographic databases. Many of these indexes only begin from 1980 or later and are therefore incomplete. They are also updated on a quarterly basis, so up-to-the-minute information is unavailable. Furthermore, only a limited number of publications are included. As a supplement to a thorough literature review this can very useful; as an alternative, dangerously inadequate.

It may, however, often be quicker to consult a reference book or index directly related to the subject area in which you specialize. The most useful source for my own research proved to be a real (as opposed to a 'virtual') specialist library in the City that gathered insurance publications and little else.[3] The Chartered Insurance Institute (CII) library has what is possibly one of the most extensive collections of insurance materials in Europe, and included practically all the tertiary sources I required. The library contains over 13,000 textbooks on insurance, 2000 journal titles and annual reports on the subject and 100,000 cuttings of journal articles, classified and indexed. It also has access to over 400 on-line databases and can print the full text of relevant articles on request. Having found the closest thing in Europe to an insurance researcher's heaven, I then had to face the more negative aspect of the membership charges. Although consultation is free, access to the library is restricted to CII members. Membership of this body cost around £60 per annum, though I was able to convince the department, that given the enormous savings on interlibrary loans I would be making, it was worthwhile reimbursing the fee.

The initial 'audit', which took little over a month, helped me finally to settle on life insurance liberalization in the single market programme. The reason for this stemmed partly from an interest in how financial markets work and interact with organs of the state; i.e., the states and markets nexus. Insurance in general, and life insurance in particular, was chosen in some ways by a process of elimination. This segment of the insurance industry proved more sensitive to government concerns than non-life or reinsurance. This made the life sector a far more fertile ground than non-life or reinsurance for an investigation that was to deal tentatively with the politics of negotiation. Having worked out some sort of focus and scope, I then proceeded with the final stage of framing the thesis with a consideration of which type of methodology to employ. I also set about establishing which would be my primary methods of gathering data and where my primary sources would lie.

Conclusion: which methodology?

Although I had a wide range of methods to choose from, not all were appropriate. There are several types of methodology that could have been harnessed in the research. I needed not only to assess what these were, but also to offer a critique of their suitability to my research objectives. There was a need to consider both the methodological justification and the contextual justification. Other issues that I needed to take into account were who else in my field had used the methodology, and how useful were the results achieved by those who had used similar approaches to data collection and analysis. Both the advantages and the shortcomings of the methods available needed to be recognized, as did how to overcome the problems of validity.

Due to the nature of my research, I realized early on that access to British documentation would be difficult. Beyond Command papers, parliamentary debates and legislation, it was difficult to see what 'unofficial' documents could be made available for this research. I would therefore need to use elite interviewing to permit the cross-referencing of tertiary and secondary material. A multiple data source, although far from unproblematic, would enable me to attain a fuller understanding of the process of the negotiations.

One of the major problems that I had to resolve was how useful the insights gained would prove. As a method of data collection, interviewing has many drawbacks which can not be discounted. These include whether the selection process would correspond with the reality of the situation. There was also the problem of whether those who were involved in the process would still be in the same positions and whether access to them could be gained. For example, in the ABI only one of the three principal negotiators was still working for the organization. As a 'gatekeeper', she would probably prove the least useful in terms of providing insights. There are various other problems associated with the technique, such as receiving limited and selected data. Research into interviewing techniques and the insurance policy community itself emphasized that a large proportion of companies and governmental departments may not always welcome in-depth interviews, not only because of confidentiality issues, but because they do not have control over the process.

Access was also by no means guaranteed by virtue of being funded by ABI. Despite the fact that the City is one of the most open markets in Europe as far as access for investment goes, when it comes to research access a comparison with Swiss bankers would not be far from the mark. One has to take political culture into account. Mention has already been made of the tradition of Whitehall secrecy. If, for example, you were to make a comparison between the British and French outlook regarding allowing access, you may find that it is more fruitful obtaining documents from European sources. Luckily, the European insurance association (the Comité européen des assurances, CEA) was situated in France, where there is less scepticism towards freedom of information. When in the second year I made a visit to the CEA, I discovered that many of the position papers and documents that were unavailable to me in the UK were there waiting for me to photocopy in Paris.

During the early stages of my research it took a while before I was able to 'find my feet', let alone design the research. Precious time was lost due to having overestimated my ability to be able to juggle teaching, part-time work and research commitments. There were initially limitations on finance, physical resources and administrative back-up, and these had to be taken into account and dealt with. It was crucial to attempt to be organized early on, to establish a routine, and keep open lines of communication with my supervisor as I attempted to narrow the focus and assess the feasibility of the research. By the third month of my PhD I had grown sick of the sight of my research proposal, although the process of constant development and modification in the light of progress was beneficial in the long run. Although the final draft will rarely, if ever, resemble the initial proposal, it is important to design the research well at an early stage in order to avoid unnecessary distractions and unfocused wanderings. The guides presented in the secondary literature on the process of social research can be useful in parts, but only if interpreted in a flexible way and in a manner that takes into account the uniqueness of each individual's PhD and personal situation.

Notes

1. Truss, L. 'Too many words, too little said', *The Times*, 17 April 1996.
2. Truss, *ibid*.
3. The Chartered Insurance Institute, 20 Aldermanbury, London, EC2.

5

The Second Year and How to Survive It

ED PAGE

Taking two years out after my MA, I returned to university, freed from the bondage of one temporary job after another, to do a PhD in political thought. The provisional title of my PhD was, and still is, 'Justice between generations', and, put simply, my research involves investigating and evaluating the strengths and weaknesses of competing political theories, particularly liberal theory, in the light of the question of what obligations the present generation has to future generations.

It was all a bit of a shock. Isolation, being in a new environment and so on contributed to a difficult first term. It was only around spring of the first year that I began to feel more confident, most importantly feeling that I had done the right thing by coming back. On reflection, like most researchers I've spoken to, I would have benefited from a more structured first year of study (developed a series of thesis outlines from an early stage; kept regular writing and studying hours, and so on). However, by the end of the first year I had nevertheless completed a second draft of a literature review on my project, given a few seminar/conference papers (one in Germany), attended the annual national Political Studies Association (PSA) conference, and was on a roll. Or so I thought. The reality was that I had a *thesis to find*.

Finding a thesis

'Thesis finding' can be difficult. So it probably ought to be. After all, what is the use, one might ask, of knowing your way around a large, possibly vast, area of political science or theory if you have no novel idea, approach, or position to defend? I, however, at the start of the second year, was still lost in a sea of constantly expanding reading matter (my topic was not as under-researched as I thought – I'm now convinced that all PhD students come upon this shocking fact sooner or later). 'Neglected research area rules no longer apply,' I tried to tell myself, and others, 'you simply can't read everything.'

Now there are some on the periphery of academic research who might be forgiven for thinking that this development (read less, but in more detail) might be a liberating conclusion to reach. However, choosing a more focused area to research in real depth is, perhaps, more frightening than reading everything related to one's topic (in my case with 'future generations' or 'intergenerational justice' in the title). Thus, what if this more specialized, streamlined, project goes wrong, or fails to provide the interesting results which it promised at the outset?

Nevertheless, as the second year progressed I became increasingly convinced that the processes of specialization and focusing are certainly the only path towards avoiding the trap of writing a thesis which is merely 'a short trot with a cultured mind' (Phillips and Pugh, 1994, p. 42). This may sound rather daunting, but defending a position does not necessarily have to involve creating a new model or approach to one's area (which is another second year trap – overestimating what is required of you). More often than not, in political theory anyway, it involves simplifying what has hitherto been regarded as a complexity, or on the other hand complicating what was regarded as simple (though even this way of thinking about the project can be daunting).

Out of focus?

As I mentioned in the introduction, my thesis is about applying various moral and political theories to the question of obligations to future generations. The corner stone of my early attempts at organizing my thoughts about the project was that, pretty much across the board, traditional theories do not cope very well with questions of intergenerational morality at the *theoretical* level, despite the fact that at the *intuitive* level we often have quite strong feelings that we owe our descendants something by way of natural, cultural, or capital conservation.

One obvious problem I faced was deciding which theory or theories I ought to attack or defend. Another problem was that showing that traditional theories fail is far easier than constructing a theory which doesn't fail. And yet another problem was that there is a massive amount of primary and secondary literature on intergenerational justice (material quite overtly on future generations and a vast amount of material on the ideas of justice, rights and obligations generally).

In fact, early on in my second year I realized that I had been neglecting the latter material in favour of the former throughout the previous year. Though a natural mistake to make (everyone wants to be on top of their literature), this was nevertheless a mistake. Essentially, this was in not recognizing, consciously anyway, that some material is simply better than other material: I was not reading *selectively* enough and, most importantly perhaps, I was not reading *critically* enough. As a result of these twin mistakes, my literature review was enormous (35,000+ words). I had a serious problem of focus.

About the same time as all this was going on, I came across a PhD thesis on intergenerational justice which was then published as a book-length study, which had pretty much the same chapter running order as I was considering (does this happen to everybody?) as well as a lot of arguments and other material that I was planning to present in a similar manner. The bigger irony was that I only came across the book version by 'accident', on a day research trip to another university library, a day which I classed as 'icing on the cake' research (the moral being, there is no such thing!), which also illustrates a point about the way in which the second year often marks the point at which you start reading literature which your supervisor probably has not heard of, or may never read thoroughly. On this last point, in the first year I often thought *'What's the point'* of writing 80,000 words on obligations to future generations when my supervisor appeared able, if asked, to write it in an afternoon (over a packed lunch). The second-year experience shows why this is not the case.

Post-literature review blues

So what *do* you do, having just put the finishing touches to the most comprehensive (you hope) literature review on politics and the widget industry, the political thought of Joe Bloggs, or in my case *intergenerational justice*, in the history of political research? Most probably harbour feelings of hopelessness and dark thoughts about leaving university.

In a sense, in the second year of your PhD there is no light at the end or the beginning of the tunnel. You've just spent a year on the breadline doing research, so you can't really give up now. On the other hand, there is still a depressing amount to read but still, apparently, time to waste. The completion deadline (effectively three years) seems so long away, doesn't it? But pressure is beginning to mount for you to publish something (*anything!*), and attend conferences. In short, you are aware of your ignorance but are nevertheless in search of some ideas to defend.

In my efforts, I came to the following conclusion. Many contributions to my topic, and I suspect many others in political science, can be broken down into those which describe problems and those which offer solutions to, or more broadly approaches to, these problems. Thus in the literature on future generations, for example, some contributions explain and develop the problem, attributed to Addison, of why we should do, or conserve, anything for posterity given that posterity is not in a position to do anything for us. On the other hand, some contributions focus on ways of answering this point, for instance, (1) by developing theories of justice which deny that Addison's claim undermines the case for justice between generations, or (2) by suggesting that future generations can harm us by their control over our reputations and so on.

I decided to hedge my bets somewhat by choosing to concentrate on one problem in the literature (the 'non-identity problem') and one approach or solution to this problem (what I call the 'specific rights approach'). Clearly, for the purposes of this chapter the technicalities are unimportant (for an overview, see Parfit, 1984; Woodward, 1986). What is more important, though, is the claim that at the end of the day a choice or a narrowing of focus has to be made and that this choice is often to be made in the second year of PhD research. These choices – if not better postponed until – are generally best informed if they are made after the completion and digestion of the literature review process.

Now, while I was still grappling with these problems I was also in the process of taking up a visiting research studentship at the European University Institute in Florence, which specializes in postgraduate research in the social sciences. So, in my second year, I was faced with three major problems: finding or re-finding a thesis; concentrating my research in order to develop the thesis; and moving to, adapting to, and making the most of a new research environment. I will now move on to look at the pitfalls of exchange trips in the second year (the most popular time to go) before looking at two additional preoccupations, which are especially interesting to second-year students – the necessity of acquiring teaching or other academic-related experience, and the issue of methodology.

Exchanges/Missions

Towards the end of my first year, I jumped at the opportunity of being a visiting ERASMUS student at the European University Institute in Florence for four months. In EU parlance, this was a 'mission' rather than an 'exchange' because, funnily enough, no one from Florence seemed to want to come to visit our institution! Anyway, what a great opportunity to meet new people and build up research contacts in my field, I thought. What a great opportunity to see Italy, in particular Florence and Tuscany, Venice and Rome. Amazingly, I thought at the time, my supervisor gave the green light – she was after all a self-confessed 'Italophile'. I received some extra money from the ERASMUS programme for travelling expenses, booked a few nights in a cheap Florentine hotel, and I was off.

Anyway, I loved it from the moment I arrived. I had a marvellous time from start to finish, had no problem in finding a super and affordable flat in the historic centre of Florence, succeeded in doing plenty of high quality work without any struggle, had many new fresh ideas, and picked up Italian quite easily, of which I am now a fluent speaker. Most importantly, I had few problems of assimilation. All in all, it was the making of my PhD.

The previous paragraph is almost entirely fiction. Obviously, opportunities to study abroad vary enormously from university to university, and while not advising caution *per se*, my experience tells me that a balance has to be struck between excessive inertia, in other words the offhand rejection of the idea of study trips, and the idea of exchanges for exchange's sake. You could sum up my attitude by saying that the motto 'A change is as good as a rest' may be true of some things but not, generally, of PhD research. A more apt motto might be, from my experience of Florence, 'Don't mend what ain't broke.'

If you're thinking about going on a research trip

One thing I would advise would certainly be to find out *who* will be there to work with, and exactly how you propose to spend your time. I ended up in what struck me as a rather insular academic environment, with the exception of one visiting professor, upon whom lay all the academic hopes of my trip. As for social and academic dealings with other students, I was fairly disappointed by the lack of interchange of ideas. Most importantly, there were few researchers working in the same field as myself. I also think that it is worth remembering that while exchanges or 'missions' will often bring obvious superficial, touristic, payoffs, especially if the destination is somewhere obviously enchanting like Florence, don't underestimate the downside. Don't be swayed into making what should be primarily an academic decision by tales of beautiful churches, cathedrals, and so on. What good are these (unless like one friend of mine, you are studying art history) when trying to write a chapter for a political science thesis?

Of course, everyone who has participated in an exchange will probably glow with stories of sun-drenched balconies and gorgeous views. But ask them about the low moments, the problems about settling in to a new environment, above all, the *opportunity cost* in terms of research time lost in the adaptation process, and you might get a different response. In the current environment, where completing on time and bashing out pre-completion articles is so important, a wasted term or year could be disastrous.

Mission implausible?

Another thing worth mentioning is that if you find yourself applying for any research trip that's going, this might be indicative of other problems which you'd probably better face head on, for instance inadequate supervision, feelings of boredom or frustration, feelings of isolation, or waning motivation to pursue your topic. These are the sorts of problems which will either be replicated during the research visit or only postponed until after you come back (which could be very depressing indeed).

Before I went, a friend told me that another research student had been 'advised' not to go on the same 'mission' by his supervisor on the grounds that it would not be 'productive' for his PhD. How we laughed. 'Sour grapes,' we thought. Perhaps not. The flip side of that old post-grad favourite, 'Never do or believe exactly what your supervisor tells you' is a more obvious truth: 'Sometimes listen to your supervisor, pure chance says they'll give you sound advice from time to time.'

Another problem which you might think is superficial, but which is omnipresent, is the *time lag effect*. Thus the application, interview and setting up process of a foreign exchange or research trip is such that there will inevitably be a considerable period of time between you accepting the place and embarking on the trip. In my case, this period was over seven months. This is fine where your research (and possibly personal) life are more or less the same at both ends of this altogether 'phony war' period. I'm sure that this is the case for many, crucially for those who apply for the exchange for good reasons in the first place. Thus the problem really arises if you do not fully consider why you are taking the opportunity. So, if the main reason for applying for the trip has to do with inadequate supervision or dislike of the home institution, or simply what might be described as the 'second year itch', then you might find yourself committed to an exchange that seems less purposeful than before. It is also worth noting that exchanges, like visits to the dentist, though ultimately fulfilling, as a rule prompt more anxiety the nearer you get to the date of departure. Psychologists, I am told, refer to such trips as bringing on attacks of 'approach–avoid' anxiety.

Exchanges: key points

- Think carefully what you want to get out of it. Devise a schedule of what you want to have done by the end, and stick to it (memories of sun-drenched balconies and espresso bars don't write theses or build academic careers).

- Think about the opportunity cost, opportunity cost, and thrice opportunity cost! Weigh what you will most likely achieve, *all things considered*, if you stay, against what you will be likely to achieve if you go.

- Think about the language issue. Will it be useful for later study, work, play? In any case, make the most of pre-departure language tuition. The English (and Americans) are famous in Italy for being linguistically arrogant and incompetent, with long-time ex-pats having the linguistic skills of young children. If you're the sort of person, like me, who is embarrassed by linguistic incompetence, then try to prove these stereotypes wrong, you'll make many more friends than enemies by doing (or at least trying to do) so.

- Timing is also important. Not just management of time, but when you fit in these research trips. In my case it turned out that arriving later in Florence would have been better for finding accommodation, but arriving earlier would have been better as far as making more contacts. Clearly the person you hope to work with must be there at the same time as you. (This also goes for students who make several necessary fieldwork trips, the bulk of which are often carried out in the second year.)

If you're already committed to going, or you're already at your destination, of course, then you have to make the most of it. In which case:

- Discuss a timetable of reading/writing with your supervisor before you go; organize how you will communicate with him or her, family and friends, and how often; and also plan the dates of departure and return, and stick to them! I found that a lack of a strategy on these issues caused sizeable problems which could have been avoided.

- Go to language classes on arrival. Four or five hours a week might seem to have a high opportunity cost, but they will probably be worth it, you'll meet new people, and, if you're lucky, like me, you might end up in the same class as the Professor you came to study with (and his wife) so he cannot ignore your existence even if he wanted to!

- Prepare for up to a month's quite serious homesickness, and feelings of isolation. Friends in foreign places aren't always quick to find (or the right ones if they are). It took me the best part of two terms properly to settle in to the PhD in England, so doing the same in the context of a 'mission' is truly a feat to be performed, for most research trips only last a few months.

To teach or not to teach?

On moonlighting

You just know you need it. Everyone tells you that your 'real job' is the PhD, but they also insist that you must get teaching experience (useful) and assemble some sort of publication strategy (indispensable) in order to get an academic job on completion. I remember, as a first-year researcher, getting quite frustrated by all the talk of doom and gloom associated with the 1996 Research Assessment Exercise, and remarking to my disgruntled second- and third-year comrades, 'Why not just concentrate on writing a good PhD – the publications will sort themselves out.' But now comments of this sort seem to me just plain wishful thinking: trade-offs have to be made.

In fact, the balance between pursuing one's PhD research and gaining 'on the job' experience is compounded in the second year, as now your face is known around the department, and you must expect to be habitually press-ganged into teaching and other administrative jobs, e.g., photocopying, compilation of bibliographies, indexing of books. Moreover, as the third year appears quite a long way off, it is easy to get carried away with senior staff members' apparent sudden interest and confidence in your ability to teach or, in some cases, to organize undergraduate courses.

The $64,000 question, then, is: 'When is a suggestion of some work on the side *an offer, a threat* or, in theoretical parlance, *a throffer* (a threat which is also an offer)?' For non-staff researchers these offers and acceptances are often a nightmare of doublethink. Clearly doing photocopying for the resident expert in your field at £3.50/hour is not worth the opportunity cost of time lost on your PhD. But what if you get a few articles copied for your trouble or, more interestingly, some 'Brownie points' with a valued staff-member who might introduce you to the right person at the PSA, the British International Studies Association (BISA), and so on?[1] Obviously you don't particularly want to get a reputation for being easy prey for unscrupulous 'delegators' of routine chores. On the other hand, you don't want to be labelled uncooperative.

Squaring the circle

How then does one begin to square this circle: of getting CV-filling experience and making real research progress on the PhD, of becoming known as a potentially valuable and cooperative colleague while not becoming a dogsbody? Speaking as someone who has a persistent, possibly congenital, problem saying no, the following are a few tips to have your cake and eat it. Clearly offering your services (even in the bar to an apparently worse for wear Prof. Bloggs) will probably get you work. However the trick is to get them to ask you. Don't be ashamed of asking how much you will be paid and try to find out how much others get: are there any dodgy deals being made in the background? Then ask yourself what you can get out of the task 'unofficially'; a 'one for Prof. Bloggs one for me' type of photocopying strategy might make the paltry hourly fee look like time better spent. Then, if you think that the delegator is abusing his or her authority (putting you in a 'straw that broke the camel's back' position), decline gracefully, using the 'working on a crucial chapter/conference paper at the moment' line (which is probably in any case true, as it is your second year). They'll soon move on to ask someone else to 'help'.

Publish or be damned?

As I mentioned earlier, the second year is usually when people come under pressure to publish their work. Towards the end of my first year, I wrote a collaborative paper with a second-year colleague, travelled to Berlin to present the paper with him at a large conference, and later it was edited (with much help) and made into a departmental working paper. Working papers (the PSA has a separate scheme for graduate members) are a very good outlet for getting your ideas 'out there', and if, as in my department, they are carefully looked at by senior staff, can be a legitimate addition to your CV.

Most graduate researchers in major university departments are more or less expected to give papers at, or at least attend, the PSA or other relevant professional conferences once in their three years (often the second year). These conferences are excellent venues for making contacts, meeting possible external examiners informally, and often the papers presented are made into conference volumes, meaning that you'll get a publication for your trouble.

Most important in the second year, though, is to get a publications strategy. Thus while you may not yet be ready to send manuscripts to the refereed journals in your field, it is still worthwhile discussing with your supervisor, or other colleagues, where your ideas are heading and which 'target journals' it will be worth contacting in the future. Moreover, consider non-standard outlets for your ideas, particularly when these ideas may not be destined for the thesis proper, for example books on research methodology(!). . . it all counts.

Premature lecturing?

Finally, as for the occasional bout of premature job temptation: *resist it*! There's nothing like doing other people's work for little obvious reward or living on a paltry research grant to inspire job fever. Finding yourself sneaking into the common room in order to leaf through departmental copies of Tuesday's *Guardian* or the *The Times Higher* while nobody is looking is reminiscent of recent government anti-drugs initiatives ('It's OK, I can handle it, I've got it under control') and a classic symptom of 'second year itch'.

The gist of this is that, while a few weeks into the second year you may feel vaguely confident in your teaching/research skills and sick of the fact that you're still stuck at the bottom of the ladder, and say 'It can't be that difficult to finish while lecturing a few hours a week', resist the temptation. Some second-year PhDs I've known have been interviewed, and others have actually got the jobs they went for. But the pressure of teaching, course design, lecturing and miscellaneous (and contractually necessary) administrative work has its own nightmare side. The conclusion must be, I think, that it is best to shrug off the temptation of applying for jobs until you are further along in the thesis process (i.e., the third year).

Methodology: the forgotten concept

Methodology as a distinctively second-year problem, *surely not*? Methodological paranoia dogs all academics from studentship to professorship, as anyone knows who has ever been asked (or has posed) at a seminar, conference, departmental coffee lounge, or university bar, the following question: 'So Mr Page, what is your methodology?' Cue the sweat glands, memories of that dentist scene in *Marathon Man*, and general panic.

One aspect of the methodological question which is distinctive to the second year is invariably that you either haven't got one (is this possible?) or more precisely it is under-developed, implicit, and in need of some serious elaboration. It's now all too apparent to me at the end of my second year that the demands of writing a literature review are not the demands of showing explicitly one's allegiance to a specific and defensible methodology.

Running the risk of seeming rather behind the ball, it was quite early in my second year that I began to think seriously about methodology, prompted in large part by the necessity of giving a short talk about my research topic and its methodological underpinnings to other researchers at a research methodology 'self-help' group. Despite my comical impression of some of these meetings, the opportunity to look again at the way I was conducting my research and to consider some problems with this was highly rewarding. The irony I stumbled upon in my preparation for this talk was that it is not just political scientists who have a problem with methodology; and it is not just those doing primarily empirical research, elite interviewing, archive research, and so on, who, when challenged, often appear to be baffled by what their (or anybody else's) methodology is. The fact is that many political theorists or philosophers, whom you would think would be quite sensitive to methodological questions, take research methodology pretty much for granted. 'It is how a good political philosopher or theorist goes about their research,' would probably be the best way of summing up this view.

Not only is this sort of posturing extremely unhelpful when it comes to a student of political theory attempting to uncover what sort of methodological approach is best suited for their project, but it also mystifies the research process. Now I cannot honestly say that I have now developed a methodological approach which is immune from criticism, still less that I have mastered all the theoretical techniques at the political theorist's disposal. However, I have come to believe that methodological questions are central to my particular project, indeed to political theory in general, and not just to empirical projects (see Griffin, 1993; Heyd, 1992). In short, with the start of my third year beckoning, *I'm working on it.*

In summing up what I take to be the most salient points I have made about pursuing doctoral research in the second year, it's worth recapping on how I think it differs from the first and third years. Unlike the first year, there is serious publication, conference/seminar paper pressure, and extended opportunities (pitfalls) of teaching, and other academic-related experience. Unlike the third year, there is still time to make serious changes to the PhD without risking a submission overshoot, and again there are possibilities for research exchanges or 'missions'. In common with both is the ever-present methodological 'sword of Damocles', the problem of financial support and the problem of a way of life peculiarly subject to isolation. In short, if I have any checklist to help 'survive the second year' it's this: get a methodology; don't waste time on unnecessary research trips; on completion of a literature review, home in on a particular problem you think will sustain your interest for some time (then throw away the review and start again); don't teach unless you have to; and don't moonlight unless in serious financial distress.

Note

1. Both the PSA (Political Studies Association) and BISA organize annual 'to be seen, and be seen to be seen' conferences.

6

Changing Locations, Supervisors and Strategies

RAY KIELY

This chapter relates my three-year experience as a PhD student from 1988 to 1991. I was a recipient of an ESRC grant, and my research topic was 'The Politics of Labour and Development in Trinidad, 1937–90'. Happily, I was awarded my PhD in October 1991, and this was eventually published as a book five years later (Kiely, 1991; 1996). The successful completion of the thesis in a three-year period tells a number of stories, and this chapter is a reflection on some of the central issues faced in those years.

In particular, I want to focus on how the research process may be changed by unforeseen factors – in this case a temporary change of supervisor and a period of study overseas. My research involved a period of study in Trinidad in the first six months of the second year, in 1990. In this time my research methods, and with it the thesis as a whole, underwent a profound change. This transformation was partly a product of due consideration given to what research methods were appropriate to my particular thesis, but it was as much a response to the wider social and political situation in Trinidad at the time. This changing strategy was complicated by events that occurred before I visited Trinidad, which related to the (temporary) change of supervisor. To fully understand my changing research agenda then, it is necessary to start with my arrival for PhD study in October 1988.

The first nine months

The period from October 1988 to June 1989 was, I now see, quite typical for a PhD student. I was unsure about what was required of a PhD, and at the start was even more clueless about what I was actually going to do in my thesis. Initially, my research topic had proposed an account of economic and social development in Trinidad since 1962, but I had some idea that labour should be a core component of the research. My supervisor was more than happy with this, as he is a 'specialist' on 'international labour studies'.

On my first day, I informed my supervisor that I had never used a computer in my life. He immediately set me the task of finding 20 relevant references and word-processing them by the following week. He showed me how to word-process, but within two minutes I had forgotten. After three days of painful trial and error, I stumbled on the (more or less) correct method and typed up my 20 references. Learning basic word-processing skills probably saved me one year of time spent on my PhD. It was all the more important because my supervisor insisted on a strategy of writing up as I went along, with the option of editing as new pieces of material were found. After hearing the horror stories of people aimlessly collecting data and thus taking far too long to complete their thesis, I readily agreed with this approach (and now recommend it strongly to my own PhD students).

There was, however, still the problem of what was required from a student studying for a PhD. All the research students in the department were required to attend a fortnightly class where this very issue was discussed. However, this was a very frustrating experience which simply confused me even more. I quickly took the view that there was too much agonizing over the mechanics of a PhD, and not enough time spent 'getting on with it'. In fairness to the course tutor, I think that was one of the points she was trying to get across.

Far more productive, however, was my attendance at an MA class in comparative labour studies. Along with weekly discussions with my supervisor, these classes convinced me that I should adopt a 'labour studies' approach. It was this issue which became such a problem, both with my substitute supervisor and when I arrived in Trinidad. My initial – and indeed final – approach was strongly influenced by macro-studies of labour in the so-called Third World, and so it was one that combined an analysis of labour and development studies. It has been called the 'new international labour studies', and it addresses a selection of the following questions:

> *What is the shape and character of the working class in different areas? Where do its parameters begin and end, especially when dealing with allied and cognate groups like child labourers, women, domestic, household and agricultural workers, migrants or the peasantry? What is the relationship between these different segments of the working class, at home and at work, in the street, at the voting booth, in the markets and public squares? How do these different sections articulate with the political parties of left and right and with public institutions? What forms of consciousness can the working class develop* vis-à-vis *rival ideological appeals like nationalism, religion, race or ethnicity?* (Cohen, 1987, p. 23; see Munck, 1988)

It was precisely these questions that my thesis addressed. Given that my research covered a 50-year period (and it actually went back further to explain divisions based on 'race' and gender), large-scale questionnaires hardly seemed appropriate. This became a major issue in my second year.

Nevertheless, the period from October 1988 to June 1989 was particularly constructive. Relying on secondary sources, I wrote a long draft theoretical chapter on the relationship between labour and development, with particular reference to the Caribbean, and a historical chapter on labour in Trinidad before 1937. In this time I adopted an instrumental approach to my work, basically treating it as a nine-to-five job rather than a way of life. I also gained a sense of perspective about what a PhD involved – it did not mean finding out everything about Trinidad from 1937 onwards, but simply focusing on a small number of key issues. In my view many postgraduate students become too precious about their research, and all too easily allow it to take them over.

Preparing for 'fieldwork'

At the end of June 1989 I moved down to London and undertook research at the Institute of Commonwealth Studies. I continued my historical account of the development of trade unions and political parties in the pre-independence period (1937–62). At the Institute I had access to a wide range of trade union documents, including primary material from the Colonial Office and the British TUC. This gave me the basis for my third chapter.

In this period I also worked on planning my later chapters. Here my research strategy for the period in Trinidad was crucial. At this point I envisaged relying on historical material such as trade union documents, political party pamphlets, parliamentary papers and newspapers. I was unsure as to the precise shape that later chapters would take, but I did envisage a chapter on the Black Power rebellion of 1970 (which became chapter 4), and the formation of the main labour party in Trinidadian history, the United Labour Front (chapter 5). I was most unsure about the research for the current period. Although some plans were made for interviews, these were of secondary importance. The main interviewees would be trade union leaders and the focus of the semi-structured interviews would be the impact of retrenchment on the labour movement.

By this time, however, I was effectively without a supervisor. My original supervisor had gone abroad on study leave. A basic strategy for research in Trinidad had been agreed, and so far the research had gone well. I had certainly got over my fears concerning the requirements of a PhD, and the relationship with my supervisor was excellent. Nevertheless, there was a nagging doubt about the specifics of the research in Trinidad, which increased when I returned to my home institution in October 1989.

This short period up to leaving for Trinidad in January 1990 was not very productive. By this time I had virtually exhausted the research possibilities that existed in Britain. Even the secondary material for the period after 1970 was poor. But more problematic was the relationship with my new supervisor. A substitute for the period from October to January had been agreed, and I would return to my original supervisor after the trip to Trinidad. This was a very uncomfortable few months, as I felt that the replacement effectively tried to rewrite the project. He read the opening two chapters and was very dismissive of them (my original supervisor had read them and was very enthusiastic). He was keen for me to substantially rewrite the early chapters, and more significantly to undertake a substantial reworking of my research agenda in Trinidad. (I was later told that the replacement had criticized my research heavily and reported this to my original supervisor. When asked by the latter (who informed me of the incident) what was wrong with the work, the former failed to give a coherent reply.)

After some consideration, I decided largely to ignore his advice concerning the early chapters. I had the original approval of my supervisor, and so felt confident that the drafts were more or less satisfactory. Moreover, my first supervisor was more firmly integrated into a 'new international labour studies' approach, which was not really true of his replacement. This was really the nub of the issue – my first supervisor saw the work as part of this tradition, while the replacement saw it as a more standard (albeit still radical) industrial relations approach. Unfortunately, at the time I failed to realize this and relented on the issue of reworking my research agenda in Trinidad.

At this point, an 'industrial relations' and interview specialist was called in to assist in the formation of a series of detailed and highly structured interviews. I went along with this, albeit reluctantly, because unlike my early chapters I did not have the confidence of supervisor approval for my planned agenda. It was envisaged that I would undertake at least 50 interviews with trade unionists, and that this would form the basis for at least two, possibly three chapters in the thesis. Where this would fit into a work of labour history was entirely unclear, but of course there was no agreement with my replacement about the earlier work. What was at issue, then, was the heart of the project – was it to be a standard, albeit Marxist approach to industrial relations, or was it to be a Marxist-influenced approach based on longer-term historical and macro-sociological questions? As I began to realize in Trinidad, if I continued with the strategy of structured interviews with trade unionists, then most of what I had written was virtually useless. The thesis would become an account of contemporary trade unionism in Trinidad.

I did not realize this at the time, and therefore embarked on my trip with the thesis at a point of great uncertainty.

Changing location: researching in Trinidad

In the first few weeks I became used to my new surroundings and familiarized myself with the library at the University of West Indies. I consolidated my earlier research by using documents and pamphlets which were unavailable in Britain, and began to structure my fourth chapter, on the Black Power revolt of 1970. At the same time I made contact with academics working in related fields, and wrote to trade unions informing them of my research and requesting material, and possibly interviews. I was still unsure about the kind of interviews I would carry out, and particularly the problem of gaining access. At this point, I was relying on my contacts with academics and potential new contacts in the national trade union movement.

It was these contacts that convinced me that a strategy of structured interviews in trade union branches was not viable. At the time, political and social tensions were very high. The International Monetary Fund (IMF) and World Bank had both been involved in the granting of loans on condition that the economy was restructured. This restructuring entailed the granting of incentives to the private sector and 'rolling back' state intervention in the economy. As I argued in my thesis, the effect of such a programme was to undermine long-term economic prospects by undermining investment in infrastructure, subjecting weak local capital to unequal competition from cheap imports, and moreover made the export of capital to the 'First World' even easier. 'Restructuring' also brought social costs which were just as devastating, as subsidies for the poor were cut, and employment in the state sector reduced. The political and social climate was therefore very tense, as unemployment and crime soared. Given that the IMF (which came to stand for It's Massa [slavery] Forever) and World Bank were seen as foreign organizations who took much of the responsibility for the problems, it was not surprising that there was some suspicion of foreign officials and researchers throughout the country.

This was not necessarily a problem, as my research (and political) sympathies were clearly 'with labour'. However, two Trinidadian colleagues who were studying labour then confirmed that researching trade unions at branch level was not advisable. In their own research, based on around 80 interviews with trade unionists, they had faced considerable obstacles. After the Trinidadian government had announced an agreement with the IMF that would result in widespread dismissals in the public sector, these hindrances reached a peak. Trade unionists refused to be interviewed, and one of the interviewers was threatened with physical violence. When told, I responded that this was probably a one-off and unlikely to occur again. My colleagues said that in fact this hostility was quite typical, and that most trade unionists believed that the interviewers were in fact working for the IMF. They indicated that this remained the case despite constant attempts to inform the interviewees of their own political sympathies for labour. Given that I was a white 'outsider', it was likely that the suspicion and hostility that I would meet would be far greater. It was at this point that I abandoned any attempt to carry out interviews with trade unionists at branch level.

On reflection, I probably could have gone ahead and taken risks. This story was a deterrent, but on its own was not sufficient to deter me from my research agenda. It convinced me that six (or by this time, five) months was not sufficient to gain access to, and more importantly the trust of, trade union members. But also important was the fact that I was unconvinced that such research methods were of use to the kind of thesis I was trying to produce. I therefore resolved to fall back on my original approach, which involved primarily relying on documentary sources. Somewhat fortuitously, this switch back to the original methodology probably saved the thesis, as it meant that I could reactivate the 'new international labour studies' approach.

The next few months were very productive. I relied on documentary material from libraries at the University of West Indies and various trade unions, some of which had excellent collections of materials. I also established contacts with key trade union and political party officials, some of whom gave me access to confidential material. They often told me anecdotes about corruption which unfortunately could not be used in the thesis, but which gave me a 'feel' for the political divisions within the trade union movement. I also interviewed trade union and political party leaders. In retrospect, these loosely structured interviews were more important as a means of access to important documentary sources than as material in themselves. Some of the interviews were also important as insights into the way individuals worked. For example, the content of one interview with a senior (and highly egotistical) politician was predictable and told me nothing I did not already know from other sources. However, the *way* in which he told me the information gave me an insight into how he worked as an opportunist, more intent of course on winning office than on sticking to political principles.

By the end of May I had collected enough information and began to structure the rest of the thesis. Chapter 5 was to be a case study of the United Labour Front in the 1970s, and chapter 6 was to be a detailed analysis of the state of the labour movement in the 1980s. My research in the 1980s had also shown that the historical divisions within the trade union movement, based around the issue of the relationship between trade unionism and politics, had been undermined by the fact that the 'anti-political', conservative trade unions had been forced to recognize that trade unions had to be political in order to secure their very survival. I therefore had a 'running theme' throughout the work, which focused on conflicting political ideologies among trade unions, and the labour movement more generally.

The final year

The final year of the research was a hard slog. My one regret on my visit to Trinidad was that I did not take a computer with me. I had collected a lot of information for the final three chapters, as well as new material for the earlier chapters, but had not yet begun to write this up. After arriving back, there was an enormous sense of anti-climax, a feeling that I had nothing to look forward to in this particular project, and that it was therefore time to move on. This is always a problem for a comparative political sociologist (as opposed to a Caribbean specialist, something I never intended to be) eager to research new material, and still today I remain easily distracted by work that is not of direct relevance to my research. The tedium of the task of writing these chapters was such that in the last year I sometimes went three weeks without writing anything. On reflection, I think that I could have finished my thesis by March 1991. Once again, I think that this experience shows that it is counter-productive to collect all your information before writing up – although I recognize that the kind of work that I carried out was perhaps more conducive to writing up as I went along than theses based on other methodologies.

At the same time, there were positive factors. My original supervisor was back after study leave and I had no more contact with his replacement. I had already written around half of my project. In addition, and perhaps just as important, I resolved that the completion stage would not dominate my life and so I continued with my instrumental approach to the thesis – although sometimes I took this too far, and my thesis became a very low priority. Nevertheless, I would still avoid at all costs doing a thesis that takes over your life.

By August 1991 I had completed and submitted the work to my examiners. A viva was arranged for October. I am sorry to say that the two hours that made up the viva are a complete blank, except for the part (at the end) where I was told that I had passed.

Reflections and possible lessons for others

Looking back on my PhD, I realize just what a small piece of research it involved. When I started, I thought that it involved studying the world, the universe and everything else, or at the very least it involved me knowing absolutely everything about Trinidad. In fact it involved nothing of the sort. Probably around two-thirds of the thesis involved summarizing secondary material, although admittedly with a slightly different slant than existing literature. The other third involved collecting and analysing new material, but this actually amounted to around only 20,000 words. I think that this is the most important lesson that I can pass on to other PhD students – make the project simple and manageable. As a development sociologist, I am very critical of the maxim that 'small is beautiful', but would happily apply it to a PhD thesis.

To finish off this brief chapter, I want to point to the lessons that *may* be learned from my own experience as a postgraduate. Of course I realize that there are no hard-and-fast rules (a lesson in itself), and that lessons learned will depend on particular experiences. My points are therefore no more than suggestive.

1. Do not let the research dominate your life. I have met many postgraduate researchers who have let the research take them over. Often they have started with over-ambitious projects and have researched for a number of years without

putting pen to paper (or fingers to word-processor). They are left with a mass of material and no real idea of what to do with it. Thus, once again, the *manageability* of a research project is crucial.

2. It is vital to utilize the correct and appropriate research methods. This follows from the first point. If appropriate methods are used, then it is possible to *focus* a PhD, rather than aimlessly reading around a subject.

3. At the same time, it needs to be recognized that using the correct methods is a matter of trial and error. In my own research, I gradually came to realize that certain methods were neither very safe (given the social conditions in Trinidad), nor appropriate (given the kind of approach that I was taking).

4. Given that the use of certain research methods is a matter of trial and error, it seems useful to stress that a research student should expect the unexpected. This is even more likely if one is researching overseas, particularly in developing (or former 'socialist') countries, where social and political conditions are likely to be unstable and you may face distrust as an outsider. Establishing key informants is particularly important in this respect, but so too is the ever-recurring question of manageability. If, as is likely, you are visiting a country for a relatively short period, such as six months, then it is simply not practical to expect to carry out major projects based on surveys, questionnaires and so on – unless of course you have already established access.

5. A good relationship with your supervisor is important. I had a good relationship with my original supervisor, although this could easily have been undermined by the actions of his temporary replacement. Lacking full approval for my original research plans, I temporarily allowed myself to be talked into an inappropriate research agenda which could have destroyed my original research project. Fortunately external circumstances, my own resistance and the fact that I knew that I was returning to my original supervisor meant that I ultimately ignored this advice and thereby produced the thesis I had intended.

7

The Student–Supervisor Relationship

NICK ROBINSON

Unlike many of the topics covered within this volume, an extensive literature already exists on the student–supervisor relationship (Youngman, 1994; Phillips and Pugh, 1994). This literature tends to be written by 'experts' in the field (i.e., established supervisors of doctoral students) and tends to make a series of prescriptive suggestions as to tactics and strategies for the management or control of the student in the interest of good supervision.

This chapter, while acknowledging the role, and contribution, of such literature, takes a different tack and attempts to redress the prescriptive bias of the literature with a more pragmatic and realistic account of the practical realities of this relationship. A power asymmetry, it is true, must necessarily exist, but I hope to show that this asymmetry need not result in a feeling of frustration for the student. It can, in fact, be utilized positively, with highly productive results. The second contrast between this and the prescriptive orthodoxy is that I wish to emphasize the imprecise nature of the first stage of the process (i.e., selecting a supervisor and securing funding). This process is frequently governed by a curious combination of luck and the personal lobbying and commitment of the potential supervisor. As such, working with a supervisor is a process which often begins months before you arrive with trepidation to enroll. The potential supervisor, by helping with the development of the research proposal and by networking around the university to identify potential sources of funding plays a crucial role in determining whether a student is able to begin the process at all. The importance of the supervisor, in this respect, is a factor which many orthodox accounts of the student–supervisor relationship fail to emphasize.

In order to attend to the key deficiencies which I have identified within the literature, I will present a structured personal reflection ordered under a series of thematic headings: establishing the boundaries of research; deciding on a topic; selecting a supervisor; from supervisor selection to realization; the day-to-day relationship; changing supervisors; and some underlying themes.

The boundaries of my research

The development of my PhD and the changing nature of the scope of my research is a theme which I will return to on a number of occasions throughout this chapter. The most important point I wish to stress is that research design cannot be set too rigidly. My project has been allowed to react pragmatically to practical constraints (such as time and word count) and to changes which have resulted from the process of research itself. As such, some blind alleys have been followed, but some apparent blind alleys have resulted in the restoration of vision.

It is important to emphasize that while the scope of the project changed, the central theoretical and methodological tools did not. My research remains a piece concerned with subjecting the conflicting models of the agenda-setting process to empirical evaluation via a case study of the politics of transport policy in the Major era. In order to facilitate this task, four characterizations of the agenda-setting process were constructed by classifying apparently disparate models under different headings. These models focus on the actions of :

(a) an identifiable actor which raises an issue on to the agenda (actor-centred models);
(b) a specific property of an issue which results in its rise to prominence (problem-centred models);
(c) an external or exogenous shock which destabilizes the policy sector and causes a change in the agenda (systems-level models);
(d) the role of ideology and of structurally located interests in constraining the scope of political debate via a process of policy internalization (non-agenda setting models).

Originally the scope of the research was broader than its present form. The PhD aimed to subject these models to cross-national comparison by evaluating why Britain and the Netherlands had a very different political priority in the relative prominence of public and private solutions to transport. Constraints of time and word count resulted in the removal of the Netherlands as a source of comparison, thankfully before any substantive research had been undertaken. With the removal of the Netherlands the depth of the research has necessarily been increased. However – and this is the issue which I feel may make the work which I produce less readily classifiable – the scope of the research has remained broad. By this I mean that I have tried to resist any micro case studies, such as the decision to cancel the proposed widening of the M25, and have focused the analysis in the broadest possible sense. As such the case study is the road–rail split in general and anecdotal illustrations have been used to illustrate what is largely a theoretical piece of work.

The central methodological tools (largely keeping in step with my supervision) have been to combine use of *Hansard*, pressure group papers (such as reports by environmental groups, the CBI and pro-roads organizations), and developments as reported by the news media, with a series of in-depth interviews with actors in the political process (such as anti-roads campaigners from environmental groups, traffic safety experts, members of the pro-roads groups, civil servants, local government officials and MPs), interviewing both those who are centrally concerned and those who are on the margins of the process. This combination of broad-based case study to examine the utility of this fourfold typology of agenda models enabled me to reveal a series of inadequacies with the actor- and problem-centred models. In the case of agenda-setting models, it is not merely a case of bringing the state back in but of attempting to bring in the global economy as well!

Deciding on a topic: a bus stop guide to PhD research

The process of selecting a supervisor began for me after my exams in the second year of my undergraduate degree. Two years earlier I had selected a four-year degree entitled 'Politics and East Asian Studies'. After two years studying Mandarin Chinese and Asian politics (among other subjects), I was about to commence a year in Beijing at a cultural and language institute. My primary concern at this time was that a degree largely centred upon the study of Asia would not stand me in good stead for my perceived area of research, which was Western Europe.

It was at this point that the first decision which I took had an important effect on my ability to undertake a PhD. I decided, much to the dismay of my department, not to go to China and to transfer my registration to single honours politics. At this stage I witnessed the first example of the conflict of interest between a personal tutor as a friend and confidant and as a departmental (i.e., institutional) representative.[1] At a psychological level I was subjected to a variety of persuasive sentiments. 'I would be the first person who had never arrived. I would upset the relationship between my university and their Chinese partners. I knew how sensitive the Chinese were to matters of honour . . . Didn't I care that I might cause offence?' To say that I was a little unhappy with this approach was an understatement. I am sure that a number of less forthright students may well have consented to the year abroad despite being fully aware of the detrimental effect it was likely to have on their future. At this point it is important to emphasize that I did not know, with any certainty, which topic area I wished to research. My motivation was driven by a knowledge of the area I did not want to research! I was fully aware at this time that I did not want to become an expert in the study of the politics of China, and as such changing to a degree in politics was inspired by a desire to keep my options open, rather than to foreclose them. By November of my final year I was becoming increasingly aware of three issues. Firstly, I was certain that I wished to do a PhD. Secondly, I was aware that securing some form of financial assistance would play an important role in the selection of my proposed institution and supervisor. Finally, I was aware that discovering my research topic was as elusive as the proverbial needle in the haystack. This was not helped by the fact that the expertise which I needed was not in my home institution.

The initial tentative steps towards developing a research proposal occurred in the most unconventional of circumstances. My uncle and I were standing at a bus stop on a main arterial route into Leeds at 4.30pm. He began discussing the irrationality of a modern Western society having such an infrequent and primitive public transport system and of the impending eco-catastrophe which faced us all unless we stopped relying so heavily on the private motor car. Half an hour later the queue at the bus stop was growing so long there was a very real danger that not every one would get on the bus, if, and when, it did finally arrive. We did, but our irritation was compounded by the inability of the driver to give us any change! The impact of this and similar events led me to concentrate the focus of my research on the low political salience of the transport issue in general terms and on discerning an explanation for the relative prominence of private as opposed to public forms of transport provision. This rather curious tale serves an important function. It illustrates the imprecise way in which ideas are generated by PhD students at the start of the process and the openness of the student's mind to the impact of external input.

Selecting a supervisor

My initial moves to select a supervisor were haphazard, to say the least. I, like many other potential PhD students, did not treat the task, initially, at least, with great seriousness. I sent off for prospectuses from a wide variety of institutions whose only common theme was geographical location (reflecting my desire to stay in the North). After receiving the prospectuses I attempted to isolate potential supervisors from their sketchy profiles. The first confusion arose almost immediately. No one in any of the fifteen or so prospectuses I perused seemed to have any interest in transport policy. At this time, I was obsessed with the notion of expertise and my immediate reaction was that my project would be untenable as no one was able to supervise it. The letters I sent off became much more speculative as a result. They were targeted at individuals with interests in policy-making, British politics and/or pressure groups. Enthusiastic responses came back from York, Hull and Strathclyde, and only after discussion at York University did I became aware of the possibilities of working at the institution finally chosen.

The trip to York was curious indeed. The first reaction I received from my potential supervisor was that he had asked me for interview to suggest that I went elsewhere. He responded to the confused expression I offered in reply by adding that he knew I would have ignored his advice if he had not told me in person. He knew individuals were starting a research project on UK transport policy from a historical perspective elsewhere and thought my work would tie in extremely effectively with this work. So he sent me off with a new point of contact and a number of useful articles, urging me to apply to a university only five miles from my home town.

From selecting a supervisor to realizing the dream

It was after my first meeting with my potential supervisor that I realized the importance of supervision in the facilitation of the dream of doing a PhD. Before I arrived I had updated my proposal in the light of the articles I had received at York and with the help of a sociology lecturer who was a family friend. I had obviously done enough to convince my prospective supervisor that I was a student with whom she wished to work. From the outset, I was given the impression that my project was worthwhile, that she wished to be associated with it, and that it deserved funding. It is in this stage, from the interview with the supervisor until your day of enrolment, that some of the most important developments occur with the student–supervisor relationship. The curious paradox is that it is at this stage that the student is powerless to affect the development of the relationship. As a student of lobbying, my supervisor took it upon herself to mount a lobbying crusade to ensure I was nominated as the top-rank candidate in the department for a university award. Politics had been granted few awards before, and, although she never admitted as much, I am sure this fact drove my supervisor even harder to ensure my forms were completed again, and again, until they were right. Considering the tight schedule we were operating under – I only met her for the first time in March – it was a titanic effort to get all the paperwork in on time.

This is a crucial time for students, when they most need to be able to assert control over their own destiny, but are unable to do so. After submitting the proposal, the student can only hope that their potential supervisor will act with such commitment to their corner. With hindsight, and comparing my case to other students, it may be that if your potential supervisor is not willing to pull out a number of stops for you, then you may wish to reconsider your choice. Having an individual who can broker for you to secure money for field trips and conferences can be as important an element of the student–supervisor relationship as having a supervisor interested in, and motivated by, your work.

The second key role which my supervisor played at this time was to ensure that I remained motivated and committed to the PhD process. The period from filling in the ESRC forms in April to discovering you have been rejected in September can feel unbearably long. At times desperation struck and I sent off for forms for jobs undertaking a fixed research task. My supervisor ensured I never filled them in. She kept on telling me, while waiting for my ESRC rejection, that my project was worthy of funding and that if nothing materialized this year I could work part-time for a year and make some progress. At times her advice seemed galling and inappropriate. After all, it is all very well and good for a professor with money to advise someone with nothing not to apply for a job.

Perseverance paid off, and I spluttered and perspired my way through a half-hour long grilling from a fifteen-strong interdisciplinary panel of individuals who redefined the notion of 'constituency interest'. Everyone, it seemed, had a protégé and wished to bolster their faculty and would do everything in their power to ensure they were rewarded with a grant. However, I must have had friends of my own since I left the room with a full scholarship, fees, and a travel allowance for my fieldwork.

Getting down to business – the PhD from day to day

The first and most curious observation I remember from my first few days as a PhD student was the feeling of utter confusion. At times I wandered around the campus, totally familiar with its landscape, but utterly unfamiliar with its operation. Frequent trips to the swimming pool, students' union and tennis and squash courts in the summers of my youth had orientated me perfectly, but the feeling of being a student in such familiar surroundings felt alien and disconcerting.

My first proper supervisory meeting was similarly surreal. I had only heard that I had received my funding a week before the start of term, so when I arrived I had scarcely had the time to gee myself up for the onset of freshers' week. My initial feelings were that I was not worthy to be embarking on the process which would result in my membership of a most exclusive class, real doctors! PhD students were a weird bunch with goatee beards, weren't they? I entered the meeting a day or so after I arrived with a simple task. I wanted to settle in and, as far as possible, recover my sense of orientation. My first request to my supervisor was to let me spend a week or so gaining my bearings, finding somewhere to live and making some friends. To her credit she was extremely glad of this. She espoused adages such as 'happy minds are productive minds', and we left it at that. The key point to emerge from this is that I gained a considerable sense of confidence at a personal level from the way in which my supervisor approached her job. She seemed to have a keen sense of the psychological readjustment which is necessary as a PhD student and her ability to set me at ease, in tandem with her work behind the scenes in helping me to secure a grant, left me with a very positive personal relationship which throughout our working relationship was never lost.

Day-to-day working is not about first meetings, of course, and it is when we got into the true workings of the thesis that some familiar problems emerged. My first task was to write a piece examining literature on the theories of the state. I wished to take a broad sweep of the literature and then to undertake a progressive narrowing of the field by picking up threads from previous work. My supervisor was fully supportive of this approach and was of the opinion that the first year ought to be about a structured exploration of the literary landscape. There were no problems with style, content or comprehension. The real problems came in the conclusions which I reached. It was clear, having read some of her work, that my supervisor's methodology and theoretical framework favoured a pluralist perspective and that I had a number of sympathies with elements of Marxist analysis, especially their critique of pluralist methodology. The interesting thing about this realization, which occurred early in the first term, is the inaction which resulted from it. It was almost an unwritten code that was not mentioned in our meetings, and even though I felt periods of personal angst I always consoled myself with a theme which had emerged from the graduate seminar training programme. We talked at length about this issue, and the general feeling was that a PhD student's work can sometimes benefit from enhanced intellectual rigour if your supervisor has a different theoretical perspective to yourself. I still remain unsure about this advice; on the surface it does make sense to have a healthy clash of ideological perspectives, but having said that, clashes of ideology are almost as explosive as clashes of religion. When you consider that over centuries no international mediation has managed to overcome such cleavages, it makes you think that maybe intellectual ghettoization is not such an unhealthy option!

In practical terms the impact of this ideological conflict manifested itself in a number of ways, some of them predictable, some of them not. Predictably, the key problem at the outset was that when my supervisor suggested further material for reading it was often either inappropriate or out of step with the direction of my research. I always read it, but its key contribution often turned out to be a footnote which opened the door to other material. My concern was that there may have been times when I missed a key source or had not recognized the potential scope of the material I read. There is no doubt that this aspect of the student–supervisor relationship is important, but I feel on balance that it is not the most important aspect of the relationship. The key element, in the early part of the process, is the quality of feedback received on written work, and it is to this that I will now turn.

My supervisor gave detailed and extensive feedback on my work. Although my work often came back late, to the extent that I was midway into the next task when we discussed it, the comment was always focused and informative. She demanded precision with language and clarity of expression which ensured that my work was not open to criticism of ambiguity. She was very good on issues of structure and form, and I noticed a qualitative improvement in the standard of my work over the period in which I worked with her. The real strength of her feedback came through the interpretation and conflict over the theoretical and methodological issues I raised in my analysis. It was at this point that the clash of ideological perspectives served to considerably enhance the work which I produced. Often, I took a number of assertions for granted, or I simply ignored issues. She insisted that I was able to attend to 'my enemy' and that my analysis would not be open to accusations of simple flaws in reasoning.

The oral feedback which I received was more variable. My supervisor suffered from a problem which afflicts a number of people (I include myself among them), which is that they become passionate about their own work and often lose sight of what they are in the room to discuss. Frequently, she would draw an illustrative example from something she had worked on and then get side-tracked in discussing it in considerable detail. The result was that until I became used to her style I often left the room a little bewildered, with more questions than before. By the second or third meeting the balance of power had shifted a little and I became adept at strategically interrupting and hauling the conversation back on to the topic in hand. I found that simple things like half an hour of preparation before I went to see her and shopping lists of topics of conversation helped enormously in ensuring that the issues with which I was concerned were discussed in the meetings.

The key point is that the meetings which we had were informative, if a little difficult to manage, and invariably resulted in a real feeling of progress. She was willing to tell me that my work was good, when she felt it was, which is a positive habit a number of supervisors seem unwilling to adopt. As such, she was able to ensure that, as a student, I could experiment without fear of ridicule and progress towards development as a 'serious' academic. Overall, the real strength of her day-to-day style was her accessibility and willingness to engage in political argument, and while the central problem was of an ideological nature, and we largely failed to convert one another in this respect, she can't be held accountable for that! The other key point to make about the operation of her supervisory style (which was later to cause some problems) was her focus on what I would classify as an ideas-centred approach to thesis design. The impact of this was both positive and problematic. From a positive perspective, it resulted in a considerable sense of student-centred learning. Themes were picked up from reading, pursued for a while and rejected, amended or expanded as the case demanded. The result was a thesis which was constantly evolving, and although its central direction was never lost its form frequently changed. As a result the thesis lost its comparative element and I concentrated a considerable proportion of my time in the second year on completing a wide-ranging literature review and qualitative investigation of the role of Royal Commissions in the policy process, exploring the hypothesis that the 18th report of the Royal Commission on Environmental Pollution (Transport and the Environment) had a profound impact on the transport agenda.

This rapidly evolved into two substantive chapters of the thesis which, when I came later to change supervisors, were largely dropped. For a time I was bitter about this development, but with hindsight my reflection is more considered and rational. This development was a natural result of a difference of emphasis between my two supervisors. The first, as I have said, was an 'ideas person'. The thesis outline as such was a malleable document, which was to be frequently revised in light of the developments from the research process. In terms of the evolution of the research, a 'bottom up' focus was taken. The key theoretical model had to be in place, but the method of 'proving' or evaluating it was much more open to flexible reorientation.

In contrast, my second supervisor used a 'top down' method of supervision. She insisted on seeing a variety of thesis outlines, and a final document was collaboratively 'rubber stamped' as endorsed. In consequence, changes were much more difficult to countenance and interesting side angles were, as a result, left for pursuit at another time.

This experience of different methodological approaches has led me to conclude that both processes are completely compatible with the completion of a PhD. A structured bottom-up approach can, as in my case, be a useful tool to allow the student a sense of independence. From my own personal perspective, removing the Netherlands from the case study was a positive development which removed a considerable element of anxiety from my mind. The top-down approach is clearly important when researching a predefined research project or working towards the completion of the thesis. In this sense I would regard the process of completion to be roughly from Easter of the second year. A realistic discussion of what is possible under the constraints of time and word count can save considerable anguish and time if it is conducted early in the process. A top-down approach need not restrict a student unnecessarily, but can liberate them to investigate an issue in more depth. It is in the pursuit of this element of adding depth that I feel that some of my most productive work has been necessarily jettisoned as I attempted to incorporate my work within the theoretical structure which I set myself from the outset.

Finally, my experience is based on having had two supervisors at different stages of the PhD process. For the second, who came in from the summer of the second year, the urgency of ensuring the completion of the thesis 'on time', in tandem with a lack of knowledge about the work I had completed, led to some searching questions about my focus and the contribution made by my thesis. Coming into the process when she did has necessarily forced her to be extremely top-down in her working practice. As such it is difficult to compare supervisors, and I must restrict my analysis to some of the benefits and problems of these contrasting approaches. The fact that both individuals in question have a considerable record in supervising PhD students leads me to conclude that they both know how to get the job done and what a PhD looks like. There are many ways to skin a cat, as the saying goes, it's just that some of them have less of a psychological impact.

Problems and the academic transfer market

If it had not been for the existence of a growing academic transfer market, my first supervisor may never have left half-way into my PhD. The timing was unfortunate in that I was rapidly approaching the period in which the step from flexibility to discipline was becoming essential. The fact of the matter is that losing a supervisor (and it is invariably a considerable loss) can never happen at a good time for any student, but in my case the timing was particularly unfortunate. Her change of location was somewhat mitigated by the news that she would be happy to supervise those of us who wished to remain in her charge. She was rather too popular for her own good, I fear, and, happy as we were, we all wished to stay with her. Despite the theoretical reservations which I harboured in the first year, familiarity breeds a certain security. I was acutely aware of the importance of this period of the research process and did not wish to upset the metaphorical apple cart. With hindsight, it may be that at this point I should have made a switch when she left for her new institution. My experiences of supervision in absentia are not overly positive, although this was due to uncontrollable events rather than a failure of working relationship. She always seemed to be away when I called and was never very responsive when I got through.

This raises a general point which I feel all institutions must consider to ensure not only that the personal problems which afflict supervisors do not damage the individual student unreasonably, but that any career movement by the supervisor is covered by the department. From the student's point of view supervisors are individuals typically under high levels of stress. As such, they are peculiarly liable to prolonged periods of illness which can cause considerable difficulties for students who inevitably develop a culture of dependency when closely related to a single individual. Aside from concerns with illness, high-flying supervisors, who at the beginning of the process are in high demand, are particularly vulnerable to the growing phenomenon of the academic transfer market. The vagaries of this market are becoming considerably acute for students who are far from certain whether their supervisor will still be at their institution by the end of their research.

The problem in general terms, which I have experienced acutely, is that students remain the victim of a system which, from the research student's point of view, has few winners. For this reason I feel it is sensible that all students be supervised by a panel of individuals to ensure a sense of continuity. If they all leave, they will hopefully do it over a period of time and the disruption can be minimized! To illustrate my point, when I first completed my provisional search I had a shortlist of four departments and four individuals. All have now moved to other jobs. I cannot fault my supervisor on her willingness to help in this problem, or the standard of supervision I have now gained, but the lesson is there, and responsible departments ought to take note.

Conclusion: changing supervisors

The process of changing supervisors was protracted and problematic. My first supervisor's decision to relinquish her role in supervising her cohort was finally communicated to us deep in the third year. It was sudden but not altogether unexpected. The department, however, seemed to be completely unprepared for such an eventuality. The key problem which I presented to any potential supervisor was that I was over half-way into the PhD process. As such, I was neither close enough to the beginning for extensive, proactive involvement nor near enough to the end for early, and comparatively stress free, submission. The result of this was that I quickly developed the feeling of being 'damaged goods'. I explored a series of possibilities, some more seriously than others, before arriving at the door of my new supervisor. I was unfamiliar with my new supervisor's style of supervision and had only acquired a gut reaction to her methods, style and approach, via attendance at various meetings as the staff–student liaison representative for PhD students.

In the first meeting we had, I remember being struck by her understandable sense of the inevitable burden which I seemed to present to her. This feeling was dispelled after our first substantive meeting. The key point which emerged from this change of supervision was that as a supervisor she ought not to be judged by the criteria I had used to judge her predecessor. Supervisor number one was gregarious and outspoken. Her successor was quiet and methodical. From the comments which I received, each was highly effective, but in different ways. At the outset, however, I remember that it was very difficult for me to use any other criteria than those I was used to. It was only after our early meetings that this changed.

The first meeting we had was a strategic overview meeting with the aim of dissecting my thesis outline. The first thing which struck me was the efficiency of her reaction to the submission of my work. I handed the paper in and received it back that afternoon! The comments were extensive but expressed a certain sense of concern. In analysing the state of my PhD, her top-down approach came directly into conflict with the previous process which had been predominantly bottom-up. Much chopping and changing occurred, in which a period of intellectual self-doubt dominated the transitional period. The process of having work subjected to a critical eye at its time of most vulnerability is enlightening and exasperating. The new supervisor is unable to read between the lines or to offer you the benefit of the doubt. There is no place for excuses that you will do it next week. An evaluation of your progress and your proposed objective is offered with only limited grounds for appeal.

A key problem emerged in my case with the change of supervisor and the analysis of my thesis outline. Through the adoption of the ideas-centred research strategy I had undertaken a wide-ranging survey of the role of the Royal

Commission on Environmental Pollution (RCEP) in the policy process. The intention of this research was to compile two chapters from the findings: the first on the theoretical inadequacies of the existing literature on the role of the Royal Commission in the policy process, and the second on the role of the 18th report of the RCEP. With the change in supervision a large element of this work was dropped. My new supervisor argued that imposing my own criteria on the RCEP (i.e., attributing it as an agent of change) might blinker my analysis to broader developments. The problem was that I had to agree! Methodologically, there seemed to be a difficulty with such a case study if the aim of the research was to test the original hypothesis.

As a consequence, much of the work that I had compiled was deemed largely irrelevant and too detailed for the scope of the research. At the time this acknowledgement increased my sense of exasperation as I now feared I was six months behind schedule. The reality was, of course, much less traumatic. I had lost a month, maybe two, as a large amount of the research I had compiled was of a more general nature and therefore still usable.

The aim of this illustration is to underline a key point: a change of supervisor involves more than a change of working relationships in a personal sense. A change of supervisor can result in a transformation in the expectations of working practices. The result can be that the direction of research can be subjected to considerable pressure. Elements can be thrown out and chapters discarded. In some senses, it could be argued that your work is your own and should be defended as such. I would counter this by arguing that often you only know your work when you are forced to present it to those unfamiliar with it – a further argument for a panel-based system of supervision at best, or a system of periodic review at least.

Note

1. This conflict of interest resurfaced later in my experiences as a doctoral student. In this case, the supervisor can make contradictory demands on the student. In my case, pressures to complete on time, on the one hand, were contrasted with requests to slot in 'just one more hour of teaching' on the other.

8

On Being a Teaching Assistant

JOHN WILLIAMS

I was appointed to a teaching assistantship in September 1992, the first year of the scheme at my institution. Overall, my experience was a positive one, with some difficulties being the inevitable result of teething problems. American horror stories of 20 contact hours a week of teaching and nine years to complete the thesis were not repeated. I taught five one-hour seminars a week, gave occasional lectures and submitted my thesis almost exactly three years after I was appointed, although it later had to be significantly revised. Teaching assistantships have the potential to be a valuable means of providing extra funded research places. However, they also have the potential to become sources of cheap junior lecturers struggling to research a PhD in snatched moments while burdened with administration and demanding levels of teaching.

Reflecting on the status of a teaching assistant, I pondered whether any great political thinker has anything useful to say. The analogy of being a citizen in a Platonic Republic seems inappropriate, as does the notion of a Machiavellian Prince scheming to take and maintain power. Teaching assistants as an exploited, alienated proletariat struggling to throw off their chains had occasional appeal but does injustice to my general experience. Also too harsh, but still of use, is Hobbes' famous description of life in the state of nature. Can being a teaching assistant be characterized as 'Poor, solitary, nasty, brutish and short'?

Poor

Teaching assistants are employed by their university, being paid a salary and having tuition fees paid in exchange for a set number of hours spent teaching and writing a PhD. The justifications I was given for the salary level varied: initially being described as roughly equivalent to a Research Council grant plus about £10 an hour for up to 150 hours teaching; later as being based on a percentage of a lecturer's salary. A casual survey of advertisements for these posts suggests a general salary of approximately £6000 (in 1996).

Teaching assistants therefore do not escape the problem of student hardship, especially if they are carrying a heavy debt burden from undergraduate and Master's courses. Financial concerns can have a significant effect on your ability to do the job properly, both in terms of the general worry that accompanies scraping by and in terms of funding research. Unlike Research Council grants, it seems teaching assistantships need not automatically carry with them a certain amount of money for conference expenses or research trips to visit archives or conduct interviews. I was fortunate in that my PhD was mainly library based and also in being able to apply to central departmental funds for conferences I attended. However, especially in a time of tightening restrictions on funding, this seems a significant area for clarification. Conference fees and travelling expenses for research can quickly accumulate, especially when buying a book noticeably affects your standard of living for a week or two.

Moreover, since a teaching assistant's income is a salary, it is taxable and subject to National Insurance, unlike a Research Council grant or a university scholarship. Assuming the analogy of a Research Council grant plus an hourly rate for teaching, I was actually *receiving* less than £5 an hour for seminar teaching, and taking into account preparation and marking this figure fell to under £3 an hour. Hence the fears of the abuse of teaching assistantships as a cheap way to free up established members of staff to meet the increased research demands placed on them. Maintaining personal morale can be difficult enough while writing a thesis, feeling 'used' can make matters worse. My experience was generally good, working in a department that tried hard to avoid such things, but I know others are treated less 'generously'.

In short, there are significant financial issues raised by teaching assistantships, both in terms of access to research funds, obviously important to the success and pleasure of the research process, but also in more general terms of financial hardship and the possibility of exploitation. The deal can be a reasonably fair one, but there is considerable room for abuse if safeguards are not in place and departments decide to renege on their pledges. One hundred and fifty contact hours can easily double, or more, if you are preparing for two or three different courses, are involved in double-marking assessed essays and exam scripts, and find yourself carrying a good deal of course administration.

Solitary

Writing a PhD can feel a lonely business. The sense of struggling to find a way through a seemingly endless maze of material towards a target that probably changes several times as the thesis progresses seems to be a fairly universal experience. The ups and, in particular, downs of the research process raise questions about the support mechanisms in place for postgraduates. As a teaching assistant, my experience of 'isolation' was, in general, less intense than the experiences of more 'traditional' PhD students.

I worked in an office for a year before becoming a teaching assistant and found the rhythm of working office hours very helpful in writing a thesis. Treating it as a job and not letting it spill over into evenings and weekends more than was unavoidable helped me to maintain a sense of perspective. As a teaching assistant I had a half-share of an office, enabling me to keep more easily to office hours. Being able to go home to a place where I didn't work made relaxing a lot easier. As, technically, a member of staff, I also had the use of a phone and access to secretarial and other office support, all of which were very helpful.

Perhaps because of the novelty of teaching assistantships in the UK, my institution was keen to install a system of departmental 'mentors' to offer advice and guidance, particularly on teaching issues but available also for more general matters. The application of this scheme seemed pretty patchy, with some people finding supposed mentors unwilling or unable to provide much in the way of help. The support of senior members of the university's hierarchy is also essential to ensure teaching assistants have a heavyweight figure to whom they can appeal if departments attempt to make unreasonable demands.

I benefited from both safeguards in my first year and found that once everything had been made clear the scheme settled down to work reasonably well. One danger is being regarded as a research assistant, photocopying clerk or filing clerk for the person leading the course on which you teach. This happened to me in my early days, although an appeal up the chain of command saw the matter resolved and quickly forgotten.

The issue of status can also have other effects, some of which are not confined to teaching assistants but are familiar to other postgraduates who teach. The question of any disciplinary procedures that may need to be taken against undergraduates raises fears about the rug being pulled from under you by a department perhaps unwilling to back up individuals not regarded as 'proper' members of staff. Access to information can also be difficult. Although a member of staff, I was never invited to a staff meeting, and it took two years before I received departmental memos and circulars, even covering such mundane information as exam arrangements, changes to course options and other procedures.

Nasty

Researching and writing a PhD can be a 'nasty' process. I spent some fairly grim days ploughing through journal indexes looking for potentially useful sources and some fairly grim weeks perusing microfilms of newspapers, tracking the development of the Yugoslav crisis and the response of the European Community, taking notes because photocopying the relevant sections was prohibitively expensive. Even with the advantages of CD-ROM and on-line databases there seems to be no avoiding some lengthy bouts of boring, old-fashioned slog while writing a thesis, even one not involving searching primary archives or organizing, conducting and transcribing interviews.

This is without the writing process itself. Some people enjoy an ability to sit down and write, seemingly at will. I remember asking a professor at the start of a term's sabbatical what he was doing. He said he was writing a new edition of a book and had done the first couple of chapters so far. I was pretty impressed and commented that at that rate the first draft would be ready by the end of his term away. He replied that it would be done by the end of the following week. Few of us are that lucky. Others seem to have the happy knack of writing more slowly but getting it broadly right first time and being able to write every day, always producing something, even if it is just a couple of hundred words.

I wrote my thesis in fits and starts, writing nothing for periods of up to two months and then writing constantly, occasionally for as long again. This caused practical difficulties, as the only computers I had access to for my first two years were open-access terminals in communal rooms or, in my office, an ancient Amstrad with an 8086 processor, no hard drive and so little RAM that eight or ten sides filled it completely, forcing me to quit and start again. Trying to put together the result of two months of research in a noisy work room while balancing piles of notes and books in two square feet of desk space is not the easiest way to work!

Writing a library-based thesis meant fairly basic research techniques centred on organizing large amounts of paper. Research methods courses turned out to be one of those things, like first-year political theory courses, which I did not necessarily enjoy much, or even see the relevance of, at the time, but which turned out with hindsight to have been extremely useful. It reinforced a determination by my supervisors to generate as clearly defined a project as possible in a short space of time. I spent the first term writing nothing other than thesis outlines, until I had what looked like a reasonable way to approach the subject. Although the final version bore only a passing resemblance to my first term's expectations, largely through cutting down the amount of material to be included, this process was invaluable in finding my feet and being able to get started on what seemed like meaningful and positive work for the thesis. This process was repeated as each chapter came to be written. I would propose a fairly detailed structure and refine it with my supervisors, and then it was up to me to go away and do it. I would estimate when it would be done by, but I decided when I was happy with the results and presented it to my supervisors in a form which could, hopefully, stand as a working draft of each chapter, awaiting later revisions when it came to putting together a complete first draft of the thesis.

In terms of research design, I therefore had a fairly free hand. This was refreshing after a year spent working and having my commas moved and sentence order rearranged numerous times by various people. It could, however, mean some fairly lengthy gaps between supervisory meetings, sometimes of months while lengthy chapters were researched and written. Unless I was in real trouble, it was up to me to get to the end of a chapter before handing things over to supervisors. They wanted to see a whole chapter so they could get a proper feel for the purpose it was supposed to serve in the thesis as a whole. When one chapter, which became three in the final version, reached nearly 30,000 words I had the results of over six months of work which had been seen by no one other than myself. Fortunately it turned out to be all right but, with hindsight, this was letting things go a bit far. I did enjoy the expression on my supervisor's face, though, when I handed it in!

On reflection, it seems I received formal supervision rather less often than most other PhD students I know. However, the quality of the supervision was, I felt, high. When a problem arose with one of my supervisors being away, an outside 'expert' was found. My work was read properly and comments thought out, both in terms of the quality of the draft chapter and in terms of how it fitted into the thesis as a whole. The focus was firmly on putting together a working draft as quickly as possible, but without this becoming coercive in the sense of being told what to write and how to write it. Throughout I felt the thesis was mine and contained what I wanted to be in it. I never felt myself pressured to pander to a supervisor's agenda or to take directions they would have preferred to follow.

Therefore, my Hobbesian analogy rather breaks down. The researching and writing of a thesis was not a 'nasty' experience, but, in general, a rewarding and even enjoyable one, at least until it was submitted. It continues to amaze me that the end game of a PhD can be so unlike the rest of the experience.

After a hard, demanding and fair viva – in which the examiners concentrated on serious weaknesses in the way I had constructed a model of legitimacy – I had no quibble with the decision to refer the thesis, meaning that some fairly significant rewriting would be necessary. Two and a half hours of intensive questioning had left me disappointed, naturally, but able to see the value of the main argument put to me and how its incorporation into a revised thesis would strengthen the theoretical model considerably and produce a better thesis.

My optimism was badly damaged by an examiners' report which bore only a limited resemblance to the main line of questioning in the viva. What had provided the central element of the questioning was reduced to a secondary issue, and instead I was faced with making changes to areas I had been given limited or no opportunity to explain or defend. The amazing thing about PhD examinations is that, after three years of independent research, the report is binding and simple compliance is not only expected but required. Like a schoolchild who has their sums wrong, you have to come back with the 'right' answers. I found this extremely difficult to accept as the report required me to strip the thesis of many of the things I felt were central to its value and interest. The opportunity to produce a better thesis which the viva had seemed to offer was, to my mind, being thrown away. Making clear the strength of my feelings was not exactly welcomed.

The examination process for PhDs has a reputation of being a somewhat black art, shrouded in mystery, with formal guidelines being hazy. Phrases such as, 'A significant/original contribution to knowledge', and 'Worthy, in principle, of publication by a learned society', which represent the criteria on which examiners are asked to judge, are open to wide interpretation. Echoes of a bygone age of a rather cosy club of academics being able to feel in their bones what is and what is not good enough to be a PhD seem to hang over the process. Other, less official, hoops through which a thesis is expected to jump add to the lack of clarity. I fell foul of making insufficient reference to existing literature in the area of legitimacy in international relations, despite the fact that there is virtually no literature in that area. A formal literature review, on reflection, is an indispensable part of a thesis.

From the point of view of candidates, submitting a thesis can therefore be a bit of a lottery. Both my supervisors backed submission and expressed some surprise at the result. Without necessarily supporting the American idea of taught PhDs, there does seem to be a case for more specific and detailed guidelines on criteria for the examination of a thesis. At a time when so much attention is being paid to improving the teaching of research methods at the beginning of a PhD, to make it a more professional, effective and faster process, attention is overdue, at the other end, to the present examination system. Part of the process of how to produce a thesis more effectively lies in knowing the boundaries of the target.

Brutish

The question of brutishness in the life of a teaching assistant raises the issue of teaching. This is perhaps the most important way in which being a teaching assistant is different to being a 'normal' PhD student. Teaching is inevitable and unavoidable: you are contracted to do a certain number of hours, and therefore they have to be done. The option, available to Research Council or scholarship students, of deciding whether to accept some teaching is not available.

The task, increasingly familiar to postgraduates, of juggling research and teaching is therefore an inevitable part of being a teaching assistant. While I attended courses on research methods and an introductory course designed to give guidance on how to cope with teaching, no advice was forthcoming on how to combine the two roles. This meant rather a lot of trial and error. Fortunately, my life was made relatively easy by being assigned to one course for the whole of my three years. Therefore, preparation time for teaching was minimized. Being expected to teach on two or three different courses, which change each year, greatly increases the amount of time teaching takes up. I knew one teaching assistant who was even expected to devise her own course for the second year. Also, when I gave additional lectures or marked exams I was paid extra, while other teaching assistants in other institutions were expected to agree to such demands as a matter of course. As it was, I did little during my first term other than worry about and try and prepare for seminars. It was pretty daunting. I arrived at my new university, a new town, with new people, the week before the start of term and took my first seminar seven days later, the day *before* the first meeting on the course designed to offer us advice on teaching.

The training we received was mixed. Being the first year of the scheme, it was obviously designed to be comprehensive and was spread across Wednesday afternoons for about fifteen weeks. Some sessions were remarkably useful, others almost breathtakingly inept. I shall remember for a long time a session on visual aids which boiled down to a two-hour demonstration on the use of an overhead projector! The course was subsequently shortened to two days before the start of term and concentrated more on practical issues of how to run a seminar, mark essays, and so on. Refinements were continually being made, and follow-up sessions added, with a great deal of effort made to use the experience of those already in the teaching assistant scheme. I filled out questionnaires, was interviewed and read drafts of a handbook designed to provide a resource for those new to teaching. It is, of course, impossible to train anyone to be a good teacher in two days, but it is possible to offer ideas and instil some confidence, reducing the chances of 'brutish' being a fair description.

The use of teaching assistants seems most likely on core courses with large numbers of undergraduates, rather than on smaller, specialist, second- and third-year options. This raises the issue of the advisability of entrusting the teaching of basic aspects of a discipline to people of limited experience. Laying the right foundations properly is not only important to helping undergraduates get the best out of more specialist courses, it also maintains and develops their enthusiasm for the subject. Core courses usually have that status for a good reason, and if their teaching outside the lecture theatre is to be entrusted to teaching assistants and other postgraduates, the need for strong quality control and assessment mechanisms is increased. Whether or not these are always in place is questionable.

The impact of regular seminar teaching on the research process was both positive and negative. The negatives are fairly obvious and focus on the amount of time teaching can take up. There is always more preparation that can be done, and teaching seemed to have a habit of expanding to fill as much time as possible. Setting restrictions and keeping to them was therefore essential, especially in the second and third years as researching and writing become more intensive.

In the last year I packed all my teaching into one day, concentrating the effort and also ensuring I knew no research or writing could be done that day and therefore focusing my thinking on teaching. The costs of such a decision are, unfortunately, significant. Five seminars in a day is pretty exhausting, and when all five are on the same topic the dangers of not giving the last group the attention given to the first are heightened. Rushing through what you know has to be covered in thirty minutes when the first time it took fifty has to be guarded against.

Marking adds to the problem of time. I eventually got the time spent on a 2000-word essay down to about half an hour; except for the very good and the very bad, which take the longest. This included around half a side of comments, the minimum space in which I found it possible to say something useful about how to build on strengths and correct weaknesses rather than just identify them. Ninety essays a year meant about fifty hours of marking, or over a week of working time. Add exam scripts and longer assessed essays, and over two weeks disappears, along with the 'contact' time. As well as such 'formal' aspects of teaching, a certain amount of pastoral care is inevitable, without being formally made a personal tutor or equivalent to a group of students. Dealing with persistent absences, late essays and other academic problems is unavoidable. With most teaching assistants likely to be in their mid and late 20s, undergraduates sometimes feel happier talking about personal problems to someone closer to their age and with fresher memories of their experience. You inevitably do more than give them the number of the university's counselling service and tell them to talk to their official personal tutor. Some level of training, or at least written guidelines, on such issues for postgraduates would have helped me enormously.

The positive benefits of teaching alongside researching are considerable. I found having something else to think about and concentrate on a welcome diversion, especially during those inevitable periods when thinking about the thesis seemed impossible or unproductive and hours were spent looking at a blank screen or continually writing and deleting the opening couple of pages or so of a new chapter or section. I found this dispiriting, but trying to see it as providing an opportunity to take more time to lead better seminars provided comfort and a sense of purpose to what would otherwise be seen as 'wasted' time.

As well as providing a second focus, teaching can also be very enjoyable in its own right. The pleasure of leading a good seminar and watching students develop over the course of a year is considerable. This is not to say I didn't make some fairly horrible mistakes or lead some rotten seminars. But treating teaching as a valuable activity and a source of pleasure and reward, rather than a chore and a distraction from the 'real' business of research, made life as a teaching assistant a lot easier. I also hoped it would be useful in finding a permanent job after I submitted the thesis. This had certainly been held out as a positive benefit of accepting a teaching assistantship. Difficult choices have to be made. Early idealism and optimism about being able to help all my students gave way to a realization that some do not want to be helped and are happy to coast along doing the minimum necessary and no amount of encouragement or cajoling will change their minds. Watching people make the same mistakes as I did was difficult and sometimes frustrating, especially after advice on how to avoid them. Typing essay comments, after I had insisted on students submitting typed essays, took a prohibitively long time. Innovations such as asking students to comment on each others' papers in the hope of improving presentations was resisted. So too was asking students to read one another's essays and suggest a mark, having found I learned more about how to write a good essay by marking one than I did by writing ten. Indeed, the conservatism of undergraduates surprised me. Trying something too different can lead to howls of protest. I also found a certain amount of distance is inevitable, and trying to get by as being 'one of them' and 'just another student really' is very difficult and on reflection is to be avoided. Just because you drink with them does not mean you do not have to fail their essays if they are rotten. When it comes to more personal relationships, and the question of professional ethics, the situation seemed especially hazy, with no guidelines or rules.

I generally enjoyed my teaching, although at times it did seem like something to be got through or that was in the way of other (more important) things I had to do. My experience of teaching was enhanced, in part, because of support from the course director, who took my opinions about strengths and weaknesses in the course seriously. I felt like a member of a team trying to run a successful course and interested in improving it. This was not universal, with other teaching assistants being told what to teach and how to teach it by course directors uninterested in them except as a way to off-load teaching and administration.

Short

The pressures to complete a PhD in three years are growing. Teaching assistants are not immune to these pressures. I was asked fairly regularly from the end of my first year onwards whether or not I expected to finish in three years, with the implication that there was a right and wrong answer to the question. This was despite the expectation among those running the scheme that four years would be normal, with a certain amount of continuation into a fifth year not unusual. Therefore, the life of a teaching assistant is likely to be short. I was told six months before the end of my third year that my contract would not be renewed for a fourth year, unless I would need almost all of it to complete the thesis. This is understandable, as departments are not going to want people submitting and leaving after three or four months of the academic year, and may also reflect a genuine desire to offer the position to another person to maximize the number of people benefiting from the scheme. Completion rates, of course, can also affect funding. In short, the normal time pressures apply to teaching assistants as to any other PhD student. Balancing research with teaching is therefore vital. A third element of the equation is getting published. A publishing record is becoming crucial to the chances of gaining a good academic job after completing a PhD, and with the time pressures already great, teaching assistants face another burden as their short life comes towards its end.

I found the time to prepare one chapter of my thesis for publication in a book and to give a paper at a small conference. I was consistently advised by various senior academics that I should concentrate on completing the thesis as quickly as possible, rather than taking time to try and write journal articles and give several conference papers if they would limit my chances of finishing in three years. While the advice was given honestly, it did not take into account that I would submit my thesis six months before the deadline for the 1996 Research Assessment Exercise (RAE). This meant that as I started to look for jobs the requirements had shifted dramatically to a publications record long enough to qualify me for the RAE. Every application form stressed the need, in various words, for four publications. A submitted thesis and teaching experience seemed to count for little. This is a serious issue which faces all PhD students, and one which appears to have received little or no consideration among academics as a whole, let alone the team who established and implemented the RAE system. If the RAE continues to run in its present form, job prospects are apparently blighted every three years. Everybody I have spoken to agrees that the RAE is a significant factor, although it was the first time the vast majority of them had given it any thought.

Teaching assistants therefore find themselves significantly affected by the long-running debates over the relative value of research and teaching as aspects of being an academic. Under the same time pressures to complete a PhD in three years, constrained by significant teaching loads, they nevertheless face having to compete in a job market where research output becomes a dominant factor in appointments every three years and an important one all the time. Either the teaching load needs to be eased, rather defeating the object of teaching assistantships, or the time pressures need to be relaxed if teaching assistants are to be able to produce the research output increasingly important in the job market. Life as a teaching assistant may be just a bit too short.

Conclusion

The Hobbesian analogy turns out to be useful as a pointer to issues raised by the introduction of teaching assistantships to the UK, but rather inappropriate as a description of my experience. The worst epithets of nasty and brutish do not fairly describe my experience. Poor, short and occasionally solitary tend to go with the territory of being a PhD student. I do, however, think I was reasonably lucky in terms of the people I worked for and with, both in doing a PhD and in teaching, and things could have been both nastier and more brutish.

Teaching assistantship schemes seem likely to expand in the future. They offer potentially considerable benefits to departments and to research students. My experience is that being a teaching assistant is a pretty good way to get to do a PhD and to gain teaching experience that will, I hope, serve me well in an academic career. There are, however, several areas of concern. There is a serious risk of intensive exploitation through maximizing teaching and administration loads within what can be a remarkably flexible limit of 150 hours a year of teaching. Access to research funds is another issue where serious problems might arise. Both are exacerbated by the fairly intense time pressures placed on teaching assistants, especially in an era of Research Assessment Exercises when publications are crucial to job opportunities.

More generally, as a PhD student, I have concerns about the examination process with its hazy guidelines, especially for candidates, and the coercive nature of examiners' reports which can stipulate in considerable detail what stays in and what has to be thrown out of a referred thesis. The 're-submission fee' (usually around £150) for a referred thesis, not mentioned in the regulations, was also a 'nasty' surprise. This does not detract from what I found to be a generally rewarding and enjoyable experience. I submitted a thesis I was still interested in, I learned a lot about myself as well as about my subject, and I got more pleasure than pain out of teaching.

9

Juggling a Full-time Academic Post and a PhD

NISHA MALHAN

In the depths of despair in the final year of a PhD, the first academic appointment may appear to be a light at the end of the tunnel. Naturally, full-time employment is an appealing option that brings certain distinct advantages with it and spells an end to three years of scrimping and saving, living on a shoestring budget. A full-time lectureship, whether temporary or otherwise, is the next step on the road of academia, and legitimizes one's entrance into the profession. The euphoria I felt at having moved on to the next stage of my academic career by gaining a full-time lecturing post in the third year of my PhD soon gave way to coping with the practical demands of my first academic position, a difficult task in its own right. Despite the benefit of teaching experience as a postgraduate in two diverse institutions, and the familiarity of my home department, nothing could have prepared me for the tasks ahead. Indeed, the transition from being 'just another postgraduate' to being a member of staff was more difficult than I first envisaged. The transition on to the 'other side' was not complete, and at least in my own eyes could not be complete, until I had acquired the basic tool of the trade, the PhD. At an advanced stage in my PhD, but by no means home and dry, I still had a great deal of work to do. Without the PhD I felt in a state of limbo, neither a postgraduate student nor a lecturer. I quickly had to master the art of juggling the PhD and the job. Added to this pressure was the requirement to produce publications in time for a Research Assessment Exercise.

Why do it?

It seems an obvious question, why would a sane individual put themselves through the stress, depression and exhaustion of what is in effect two full-time jobs put together? Apart from the obvious reason of progressing on to a permanent full-time post at the end of a PhD, reasons for combining a PhD with a full-time lectureship vary immensely. In an era of increased cuts in postgraduate funding and stiffer competition for the meagre funds that are available for postgraduate research, a full-time lectureship represents an alternative source of funding the PhD. So postgraduates who would normally prefer to study full-time are prematurely forced into a job to complete. Institutions, particularly the new universities, are keen to raise their research profile, and as a consequence, in some cases, are prepared to make a contribution towards part-time fees. Of course, the financial rewards of a full-time job are enticing at any stage in the PhD when compared to the average £5000 on a student maintenance grant. There is increasingly a fear among PhD students that the opportunities for full-time employment at the end of a PhD are diminishing. In the last five years university graduate schools have increased their intake of postgraduates, and this expansion, as far as I can see, has not been matched by similar growth in the number of jobs. The result has been a plethora of PhD students competing for a smaller number of jobs. Hence, when one is in the fortunate position to be offered a job, regardless of the stage of the PhD, one invariably opts for employment. Of course, a job also means access to resources that a PhD student could not even dream of: be it a budget for conference attendance, access to experts in their field, information technology and library resources. The situation in the 1990s is that postgraduates are taking up full-time employment at all stages of their postgraduate careers; the first, second, third and in some cases even before they have started their PhDs.

Experiences in combining a full-time PhD and full-time career tend to vary according to the nature of the individual, the stage of the PhD and the attitude and conditions of the department and university. Although experiences vary, this chapter endeavours to outline some of the common problems in attempting to marry the two.

The PhD: an overview

Visions of the momentous events that swept across Germany in 1989, facilitating unification, sparked my initial interest in what became my PhD topic. What began as an MA dissertation about German unification ultimately became a finished PhD entitled 'The Implications of Unification for Germany's Role in the European Union'. The thesis analysed the nature of Germany's role in the EU after unification, focusing on two specific policy areas, migration and agriculture. As the purpose of this chapter is not to engage in a detailed discussion about the hypothesis of my PhD, I will accordingly refrain from dwelling on the content of my thesis, and rather set it in the context of the problems I came across in attempting to complete it within the stipulated ESRC four-year submission period.

Academia: a changing profession

Academic posts should come with a health warning: 'Lecturing can be injurious to your health.' The 1990s academic is confronted with a whole host of pressures and conflicting priorities. The nature of the profession has changed greatly in the era of Research Assessment Exercises and Teaching Quality Assessment. One resembles a juggler, being required to balance the balls of research, teaching and administration all at the same time. In the age of three-year rolling and temporary contracts, one cannot afford to ignore any of these three core elements.

Teaching

Teaching is supposed to constitute one-third of the duties of a lecturer. However, in reality one just has to ask a new lecturer to discover that this is not the case. Teaching loads vary from department to department and university to university. One can be in a fortunate position, like me, and have one's teaching hours protected while on probation. For others, the picture is not so rosy. One hears horror stories of new lecturers being loaded with teaching of anything up to twelve hours a week. Of course, the twelve contact hours do not include the time spent on preparation. Given short-term and temporary contracts, new lecturers are often loaded with an excessive amount of teaching on a variety of courses. On top of that, new lecturers are often required to design and develop new courses. The task of organizing and preparing new courses is arduous and time-consuming, leaving very little time for anything else. I can remember reorganizing courses and painstakingly putting together reading lists for the first time. It transpires that my experience was rather better compared to others'. I was in the fortunate position to be able to run my courses.

Unlike other professions, academics suffer from a lack of training. Postgraduates in the 1990s come to a full-time job with at least some teaching experience. However, most things are learned by 'muddling through' or 'by trial and error'. I recall constantly knocking on the door of sympathetic colleagues every time I had a silly question. The repertoire of an average PhD student rarely extends beyond having taken seminars. It is assumed that you know how to write a lecture, set an exam paper, mark a dissertation. The first year of any academic post is difficult and exhausting by all accounts. The truth is that during term time one rarely has an opportunity to do anything else but to prepare and take lectures and seminars. Keeping on top of the teaching, writing on average two lectures a week and preparing and conducting seminars, was enough without loading the PhD on top. It was like a constant cycle: no sooner would I finish one set of lectures than I had to start the whole process again. Someone once told me that as far as the teaching is concerned 'the first year is the worst year'. I would agree wholeheartedly with that statement. It does, however, get better; the motto is: survive the first year!

Research: publish or perish! The RAE, publications and the conference circuit

The profession is research-driven in the 1990s, with the number of articles one has published dictating whether one is employed or not. Although the situation is changing, most postgraduates tend to enter the job market with few or no publications at all. Therefore, once employed, there is an implicit expectation that one should publish in order to raise the research profile of the department, regardless of whether one is based in a 'research' or a 'teaching' university. Research activity, however, does not seem to include work on the PhD. The pressure to publish becomes the overriding concern. Coupled with the demands of teaching new courses for the first time, there is even less time for the PhD.

I was one of those postgraduate students who did not learn the rules of the game until the very end. I started my job at a crucial time in my PhD, in some senses the wrong time, eighteen months away from the Research Assessment Exercise (RAE) without any publications to my name. To say that I was under pressure to publish is an understatement. Unfortunately for me, the publication trail detracted from my thesis. Any opportunity to write that would have been useful for the thesis was taken up by writing a conference paper or an article. The conference circuit entailed a whole host of problems apart from just writing the paper. Organizing the funding was problematic. Getting the expenses back proved to be a real problem. At one point I was over £1000 in debt, with the bank refusing to give me any more money. The conference circuit proved beneficial; it gave me an outlet to test some of my ideas in public as well as provide me with the material for an article and the other three entries on my RAE form. At least I fulfilled one set of statistics, despite having messed up the league tables for my department as far as PhD submissions were concerned.

Administration

Most academics loathe administration, they do not see it as an essential part of their job. Unfortunately, whether it is personal tutoring, being an exam secretary, an admissions tutor or co-ordinating a course, administration takes up an inordinate amount of time. Fortunately, I had a negligible administration load and while I was finishing my PhD, in the second year of the job, most of it was taken away from me. Some concessions were made, the only thing that the university did not grant me was adequate time to finish my PhD without getting injured.

Marrying the two: problems and pressures

A juggler is an accurate description for an individual attempting to combine a full-time job and a PhD. The truth is that it is extremely difficult to juggle the two. Postgraduates often feel that the simpler solution would be to finish the PhD first and then start a job. However, it doesn't always work out like that, but if you *can* avoid combining the two, do so!

The basic problem is a conflict of priorities. Most academics, new or old, are grappling with the fundamental conflict between the two facets of an academics' job, teaching and research. Many an argument has broken out between colleagues about where the focus should lie. Most would like to get a balance between the two. One wants to give students a good deal. However, the pressure to publish overrides concerns about being a good teacher and being adequately prepared for classes. Younger academics face an additional challenge of having to complete their PhDs while fulfilling the other demands of the job.

What are the problems?

The first characteristic that comes to mind when I think back to my experience is isolation. The PhD is an isolating experience in itself; however, combining two roles was even worse. Despite the reality being that many young academics embark on this dual journey, I couldn't help feeling this sense of isolation that nobody else was in the same boat as me. Nobody seemed to understand the pressure I was under and the sacrifices I made to achieve my goal. Of course, towards the end of the thesis I realized that another member of staff was engaged in exactly the same process.

The PhD invariably gets put on hold in order to deal with more immediate demands. During term time it is practically impossible to do anything else apart from teach. The time one has left is dedicated to publications. Experiences do indeed vary; however, as a newly appointed lecturer with very few publications to my name, I felt covertly pressurized to fulfil these criteria. Hence, consciously or subconsciously, the PhD took a back seat that year and did not re-emerge until threatening letters from the Central University Administration informed me that I had exactly three months to submit my thesis. As an ESRC award holder I was bound to submit my thesis within the four-year stipulated period, lest the department should go down in the league tables. It is quite genuinely a toss up between the two: either you progress with the PhD and as a result have no publications, or vice versa. Ultimately you end up the loser from this vicious cycle, as both are necessary to get a job.

A real problem is actually having enough time for the PhD. A full-time job can be extremely disruptive for the PhD, particularly for continuity of work. Finding a continuous stretch of time to work on the thesis can be extremely difficult. The flow of work is constantly interrupted by the need to write lectures and prepare seminars. Gone are the days when one could devote a 100 per cent of one's time to research. When one starts work, *time* is a precious and much desired commodity.

My PhD suffered greatly due to my other commitments. I was at that stage in my PhD when I required an intensive period of time on the thesis to finish writing up. However, with the other aspects of the job this was not possible. Switching hats from teacher to PhD student, or more precisely from 'teaching mode' to 'PhD mode', proved to be difficult. By the time one had got into 'PhD mode' it was time to write another lecture. One felt like a schizophrenic, constantly changing moods. I adopted the teacher's hat all term, but this inevitably spilled over into the vacation. The first week of the vacation was taken up clearing up excesses from term-time, and the week before term was spent preparing again. My experience in the first year was of literally grabbing time for the PhD even during vacations, which didn't leave any time for a real vacation. It could have been worth it, but I really got the feeling that I was doing neither adequately.

There were also the practical problems of conducting research. Academics have to conduct research against a backdrop of diminishing resources for research. Grants for research trips are hard enough to get as an academic, but the problem is multiplied when you are a PhD student. It is difficult to conduct interviews, do archival research or simply visit other libraries if you happen to be located at the wrong end of the country and cannot afford the train fare. The problem is intensified if you have to conduct research abroad. Physical constraints such as geographical location and limited resources can seriously hinder progress on the PhD. Some departments may be generous enough or have funds available to finance research, others do not provide any help at all. A tip is to always dress up applications to funding councils. One does not necessarily have to mention the word PhD in the application. You never know, you might get lucky!

I have already discussed the problems associated with getting enough quality time to spend writing up the thesis. The same problems exist with regard to conducting research. Academics find it difficult to find a clear stretch of time to conduct research. Some departments are flexible in their approach to young academics, offering help with time for research and limited administration. However, many departments do not pay any heed to the research needs of younger members of staff in allocating the work load. Of course, the expectation is there that the PhD should be submitted within the period stated at the interview. Unfortunately, younger members of staff cannot qualify for sabbatical or study leave until they have been working for a few years.

My department was very generous with regard to funding. Funds were available for me to return to Germany to conduct residual research, even if it was only the airfare over there. Contacts made in Germany while conducting research proved very helpful. Friends were more than willing to provide me with a bed for the night. The only problem for me was fitting in the research trips with the conferences I was attending. I can recall getting on and off a plane at least six times in one month.

In these circumstances the student–supervisor relationship can suffer a great deal. At any stage in the PhD your supervisor tends to be, or is supposed to be, the main motivating force; the one from which you seek advice and feedback. It is sometimes difficult enough to get feedback from supervisors if you are in the same department, but if you happen to be at the other end of the country it can be near impossible. Lack of contact and advice and, what is more important, isolation from peers and the research environment can be very detrimental for the PhD, leaving you floundering in the wilderness and completely unmotivated. The department in which you are employed is not necessarily interested in *how* you finish the PhD, only that you do. Feedback may be difficult to come by from colleagues who do not necessarily share your research interests. Conversely, if there is no real pressure to finish from within your department of employment, and if your supervisor is not there constantly to remind you of your deadline, the thesis may never be finished. It is quite easy to lose motivation and to put the PhD off for yet another day. It is really a case of out of sight out of mind. Actually mustering up the motivation to sit there day after day and write when nobody is physically pressuring you can be difficult. Before you know it, the deadline is upon you and then you try to do the impossible.

From my perspective, I was in the rather unusual position of having secured a job in the department in which I was a postgraduate student. It certainly had its advantages. The whole set-up was familiar. I did not have to endure the physical disruption of having to get to know a different department and campus. Most of all, my supervisor was at the same institution and consequently advice and feedback were readily available. Of course the flip side of the coin was that the place was too familiar. The transition from postgraduate student to member of staff was particularly strange. I don't think that I quite made over to the 'other side'.

Like any other person in the first year of an academic job, I spent the first year concentrating on teaching and publications. Unfortunately for me, this was to the detriment of my PhD. The central university authorities were not concerned about my other obligations; for them, I was a PhD student who had to submit within four years. Hence, by the time the exam boards were over in June, I still had a PhD to finish, which required some work and an impossible deadline to submit by September. Eager to finish my PhD within the stipulated period, and with very little opportunity for an extension, I spent the summer glued to my computer, typing away on average twelve to fourteen hours a day. Unfortunately, typing at that pace, I injured both my wrists and suffered pains up to my neck that even the strongest painkiller would not shift. I still had this deadline hanging over me, with the university threatening to terminate my registration if I did not submit, so I carried on typing, against the advice of my doctor. I wish I had listened to him. Within two months of typing like that I was wearing a wooden brace on my right hand and was unable to do even the simplest of tasks, let alone type. Eventually I was given an extension on medical grounds, but I also had a brace on my hand for five months and a permanent injury. The problem is, once you have typing-related injuries they tend to stay with you.

I have continually referred to the problems associated with combining a job and a PhD. It all sounds like doom and gloom, but some of these problems can be surmounted. It is possible to survive this ordeal! A job at a well-respected institution is a difficult option to turn down. So what is the key to combining the two and coming out sane at the end of it?

Conclusion: how to complete a PhD with a full-time job

The best piece of advice I could give would be to be sensible and finish the PhD – or at least have it in an advanced stage – before starting employment. The only possible way to do that is to eat, sleep and breathe your PhD in your third year. If you happen to be one of the increasing number of people who are starting their job quite early on in the PhD, be realistic about what you can achieve and sensible about when you're likely to submit. If you are no longer working on the thesis full-time, then register part-time. Not only does this buy you time with submission, but the fees are also halved.

Be methodical and almost mechanical in your approach to the PhD. One needs to be focused on the goal of finishing the PhD, perhaps obsessively so. In the closing stages of a PhD one has to remain single-minded, there is no room for distraction. In essence one has to forget the articles, conference papers, administration and all the other requirements of the job. It is easier to adopt this attitude in the second year of a job. One has ready a set of lectures and seminars, and is certainly more confident and comfortable with students on a full-time basis.

This scenario does sound far-fetched, but it isn't. I was completely immersed in and obsessed with my PhD. My strategy was to lock myself away from the world from the July until the April that I submitted. The only way to complete the thesis was to ignore every other aspect of my job. Apart from the days I taught, I spent all my time working on the thesis. I shed all my other duties. The department was quite helpful in the second academic year, even the light administrative duties were removed. All my time was spent locked up in my office. Friends did not bother contacting me at home, I was never there. Soon my office number became my contact number. I did everything but sleep there.

I took each day at a time, chipping away slowly, knowing that each word I typed counted towards the final version. I set myself a timetable with small realistic goals, attempting to finish certain sections or chapters within a given period. I certainly did not attempt to climb the mountain in one day.

A tip is to become highly organized, making time for research. In the first year my working week was divided up into preparation days, teaching days and days that I did not want to see a student. I did the bulk of my teaching on two days, with a further day for preparation, and the rest of the week was left for my PhD. This scenario did not always work out, but at least I attempted to organize my week to be able to have some clear days for my research.

I was more mechanical in my approach towards work patterns in the second year. My day was divided up into shifts. I would often work till the early hours of the morning to reappear the next day at 11.00 a.m. My system was not used to a nine to five regime, so I just went with my body clock. It didn't matter what day of the week it was, I'd be there.

The all-important factor is to have a place where you can work; having a place to work outside the department could be useful, so as not to be disturbed constantly. Unfortunately this was not possible for me, as I lived in a hall of residence full of students, so I haunted my office after hours. There was complete peace and quiet, nobody to disturb me except the occasional security guard doing his rounds at 11.00 at night.

Some of the advice in this section may sound basic, but it is often the basic information we forget when under pressure. Apart from sheer perseverance and hard work, some of the above advice helped me finally to finish my PhD, even if I had transgressed ESRC boundaries. I breathed a sigh of relief the day that I submitted – the nightmare was finally over. In retrospect, it was just about worth it – apart from the injured hand, of course.

10

A Very British PhD – A View from Overseas

LAURA TEDESCO

In 1990 I was working in a research centre in Buenos Aires researching Anglo-Argentine relations after the 1982 conflict. One of the seminars that we organized was a joint venture with a British university. I was, then, a research assistant looking at Anglo-Argentine co-operation in the exploitation of the fisheries around Malvinas/Falklands. I was also in charge of the organization of the seminar, and so met the British academics attending the event. One of the professors from the British institution asked me if I had ever thought of doing a PhD abroad. Until that moment I had never thought about it.

The purpose of this chapter is to describe the problems encountered in the PhD research process, emphasizing in particular the problems experienced by a foreign student. When someone from the other side of the world – like Argentina – opts to study for a PhD she must start to prepare herself one year in advance. The first choice to make is between North America or Europe. This was quite easy for me; since I was working with British colleagues on the Malvinas/Falklands issue, I thought it would be easier to go to Britain (in other words it would be easier for me to get a scholarship to study in Britain!). Once you have fixed a location, attention is then drawn to the process of obtaining funds, and the need to perfect your knowledge of English. Eventually you will be accepted in one university, hopefully with a scholarship, and you will pass the English exam; and, then, you are prepared to go. But, are you?

My intention here is to tell the reader, through my personal experience, the problems that a foreign student might face while doing a PhD in Britain. I start by describing the topic of the thesis. Following that, the article is divided into three parts. The first discusses how to overcome the most difficult problem facing a foreign student, that is the English language. The second part analyses a problem that most PhD students face: developing the central ideas of the thesis. The third part describes the problems of the writing process. Finally, I offer a conclusion which recalls the main themes of the chapter and gives some advice on how to survive – and enjoy! – a PhD abroad.

The focus of the thesis

After many deliberations, the final title of my thesis was 'The Crisis of the Argentinian State: Democratisation and Economic Restructuring, 1976–1989'. The thesis examines the crisis of the Argentinian state during the 1983–9 democratic government. It suggests that the 1976 military dictatorship attempted to resolve the crisis of the Argentinian state by implementing economic structural reform and state terrorism. The consequences of these policies constrained the margin of manoeuvre of the 1983 democratic government. The main economic constraints were the huge external debt and the impoverishment of the working class. The main political constraint was the need to bring the military to trial while avoiding a direct confrontation with the armed forces.

The structure of the thesis

In its final version the thesis is divided into seven chapters. As it analyses the crisis of the Argentinian state, the first chapter reviews relevant aspects of contemporary state theory. This chapter does not attempt to offer a comprehensive review of all approaches to the state, rather it is an analysis of some of the main approaches to understanding the development of the capitalist state, its relation to economic policy and the notion of crisis. It draws in particular on Marxist approaches to the development of the capitalist state in the context of the globalization of capital to highlight the influence of global capital in the making of domestic economic strategy. The second chapter is a historical account of the economic and political situation of the 1950s, 1960s and early 1970s in Argentina. It highlights the development of the crisis of the Argentinian state which ultimately led to the 1976 military dictatorship. The third chapter analyses the economic structural reform applied by the 1976 military dictatorship. The main objective of this reform was to discipline society. The chapter highlights the main legacies of this reform for the incoming democratic government. It also studies the causes of the collapse of the military dictatorship and the transition process to discover how the collapse and the transition would influence the democratic government. The fourth chapter analyses the first two years of Alfonsín's government. It studies the first policies applied by the government to confront the main legacies of the dictatorship, namely the policies towards the unions, the armed forces, and the external debt. The fifth chapter studies the development of the crisis from the launching of the 1985 economic reform to the 1987 electoral defeat. Chapter 6 analyses the last two years (1987–9) of the democratic government, when the crisis was at its peak. It examines the increasing economic crisis and the role of the unions and the armed forces as the historical barriers to the restructuring of the state. The chapter also charts the main economic and political consequences of Alfonsín's government. The final chapter concludes by looking at the development of the crisis of the Argentinian state under the democratization process and examines the reasons why the crisis could not be resolved by the 1983–9 government. It also highlights the implications of the thesis for state theory, commenting on the relevance of its main approaches to the analysis of the development of the capitalist state, its social relations and its relations to global capital. There are three appendices in the thesis. The first offers basic statistics about the Argentinian political economy. The second presents a list of Cabinet members in Alfonsín's government and, finally, I included a brief account of how I tackled the research process.

Arriving in Britain: surviving the first months

The first problem for a foreign student is not the PhD but the language. Even if your English is very fluent – which in my case it was not – you have to quickly get used to expressing yourself in a foreign language, to read all the bibliography in English, to talk with your supervisor in English, to live speaking a foreign language. Although a pressing concern, the problem of the language cannot be quickly resolved, it is a matter of time.

In the first term of my PhD I took a course in academic writing which was not very useful. In my view, you learn how to write by reading and looking at how others write. However, I believe it is impossible to get it completely correct. I always write in English with Spanish style; the most difficult task is to adopt English grammar and style. This is something which is almost impossible to achieve. Thus, the main problem that a foreign student faces is that the writing process is much more difficult simply because of the language. In addition, we face this problem completely alone. However, this is a risk that foreign students take when deciding to do a PhD abroad. But it is hard to imagine, especially when one is still at home, how difficult the writing process will be.

This problem of the language gives rise to a further difficulty, that you cannot enjoy your writing. I use to enjoy my writing (even when I researched squid around the Malvinas/Falklands), but when my supervisor asked me (in the first term!) to write my first book review, I could not believe how difficult it was. I had to read in English, try to understand, and then explain by summarizing the main ideas and by giving my own opinion. I was terrified. However, the book reviews were a very useful exercise. They forced me to understand what I was reading and to think about it. However, the most useful point was that I got used to writing in English from the very beginning of the PhD. This is not just useful for a foreign student but is also important for native speakers. To start writing from the very beginning – although many of the things you write will not be of direct use later – develops useful skills that become essential if you are to complete on time.

The book reviews were discussed every Friday with my supervisor. As indicated, I found this process invaluable. During the first year of my PhD, I had weekly meetings with my supervisor. I was working on state theory and also trying to define the topic of my thesis. I am sure that it would have been very easy to get lost if I did not have his strict advice. I am convinced that the role of a supervisor is crucial, especially at the very beginning of the PhD. If you do not have the proper help, it is very easy to get lost in the maze of books to read and topics from which to chose.

After I became used to reading in English and to writing two or three pages per week, I was asked to write an extended essay on state theory. This was also a useful but frightening experience. However, I discovered that, after six months of reading and discussing with my supervisor all the book reviews I had written, it was quite easy to produce a chapter. At this point, I realized that the first six months of my PhD had been highly productive.

The first months were also full of very different experiences. During the first week, I had to learn how to use the library. This might be very straightforward for an English person or a European, but it is not quite the same for an Argentinian. In Argentina, there are no such libraries, so I had to struggle to learn how to take advantage of it. If I asked for help, I usually did not understand the answer and I was ashamed to ask again. Therefore, this is not the way. It is better to sit in front of the computer or the CD-ROM and start using the old method of 'trial and error'; after a few weeks, one undertands how it works. However, it takes longer to take full advantage of all the services provided for you by the library.

As a foreign student, I learned early on that one must take advantage of a British university by monitoring different courses. In my first year, I attended three different courses (on international political economy, international law and European integration). One realizes that it is impossible to combine a specific focus on research and coursework, and that the PhD must take precedence. I was unable to read most of the bibliography for the seminars, so I lost a lot of the discussion. However, it was good for me to take these courses. Not only have I learned about the issues taught by the courses, but I have also realized the main differences between this educational system and the Argentinian one. For good or ill, I am now a product of the strengths and weaknesses of both systems!

Monitoring courses is also a way of escaping from the isolation of PhD research and its almost obsessive specialization. I thought it unproductive to concentrate all my years in England studying about Argentina. Therefore, in my second year, I took a course on the international state, and I regret that I was unable to take any course in my last year since I spent most of the academic year in Argentina. For a foreign student, I believe it is essential to try to combine the research of the PhD with taught MA courses.

Choosing the topic of the thesis is one of the hardest tasks of the first year of the PhD. When I was leaving Argentina some of my colleagues who had also gone abroad to do a PhD told me that a day would come – especially in winter time! – when I would ask myself: 'What am I doing here?' They advised me not to try to find an answer because it would be almost impossible: throughout most of the first year the topic of the thesis is still not clear in your mind, you examine and read bibliography that you will probably not use in the end, and everything takes longer because of the language, and it is cold, dark and raining. When that day comes – and it can be a long 24 hours – temporarily put your research to one side, take a nice Latin American novel and calm down!

There is nothing you can do about the insecurities involved in studying for a PhD. At the beginning it seems like something you will never attain, that you will never finish. This feeling is always there, you know you have to do something original, and this is very intimidating. The topic of the thesis is a crucial point of the research, and it is the most difficult part: to define it in your mind is a very isolated task and puts you under considerable intellectual pressure. On balance, it is better to have the topic only loosely defined at the beginning and gradually let it take its definite form during the research process.

Developing the ideas of the thesis

Originally I proposed to study the impact of regional integration on national sovereignty, looking at Brazil and Argentina. However, I soon realized that the topic was too broad and that it would be quite difficult to develop a proper research project since the integration process in Latin America was just starting. By this time I was already working on my second chapter about the political economy of the military dictatorship. I realized then how the structural reform applied by the military government constrained the economic policy of the democratic government.

A journey to Argentina to look for material and carry out interviews with academics involved in the study of the economic policy of the military dictatorship helped me decide the definitive topic of the thesis. On the one hand, it was then clear that it would be impossible to find material (primary as well as secondary sources) about the integration process between Argentina and Brazil from the perspective that I wanted to emphasize. On the other hand, it was also clear that the first democratic government had not been studied in depth, despite many articles about its economic policy, its human rights policies and its relations with trade unions. There was no extensive study of the years of the first democratic government. Moreover, after having studied the economic policy of the military dictatorship, it seemed clear to me that the democratic government was constrained by the structural economic reform applied by the dictatorship.

The topic of the thesis started to become more clear: the constraints on the Argentinian state's economic policy during the democratization process. For this topic, primary and secondary sources would be available. However, at this point it is useful to recount the problems I encountered in the use of primary sources.

If the problem of primary sources is not a feature of all 'Third World' countries, it is undoubtedly a feature of Argentina. A country which had alternated for the last 50 years between a military dictatorship and democratic government did not of course have a tradition of keeping official documents. Democratic governments are aware of the next military government, and military dictatorships intentionally destroy official documents. Therefore my primary sources were mainly interviews, newspapers, some official documents (such as the speeches of the president and his cabinet members) and statistics from the Argentinian Central Bank, the International Monetary Fund, and the World Bank.

The most useful sources for my research were interviews. They were undertaken in a second journey to Argentina during the last part of my second year and the first part of my third year. Before going to Argentina, I had a draft of all the chapters of the thesis, excluding the introduction and the conclusion. This was essential, since I went to Argentina knowing what kind of information I needed and what kind of interviews I had to arrange. I organized all the interviews from England, sending letters to those I wanted to interview. Some of them refused my request; however, most of the senior members of the democratic government accepted. Throughout the interviews I learned a lot. The interviews gave me a deeper understanding of the central problems facing the democratic government. In the meantime, I was also searching for other primary and secondary sources. In addition, before leaving England my supervisor had read and corrected the drafts of all the chapters. Therefore I was also rereading the thesis and considering his corrections.

By the end of the second term of my third year I was back in England. I gave my supervisor all the corrected drafts and I started to work on the theoretical part of the thesis, going back to the essay on state theory which I had written in my first year. By this time I felt that the thesis was finished. I soon realized how wrong I was. The main task was now to conceptualize the main argument of the thesis and relate it to my essay on state theory. Thus, the main argument of the thesis began to take shape. The empirical information and the state theory essay suggested that the 'constraints on the Argentinian state's economic policy during the democratization process' could be conceptualized as a 'crisis of the Argentinian state'. Therefore, as I said, the main argument of the thesis took its definitive form during the final phase of the research process. The thesis was defined as a study of the crisis of the Argentinian state during the democratization process. Having organized my thoughts, I was able to rewrite the introduction and the conclusion, which are the central components of the project.

The final editing of the thesis consumes a considerable amount of time and is as important as the research process itself. It is essential to read all the drafts, to check that the main idea of the thesis is clear and that the work as a whole is coherent. It is also important to correct all the repetitions that one makes, and most notably it is time to correct the writing style.

The writing process

Each individual has her own way of writing. For me, it was very difficult to learn through reading books on how to write. However, it was very useful to read some bibliography (most notably, Becker, 1986; Burgess, 1982; Lichtman and French, 1978), especially since I was writing in a foreign language.

As a research worker in Argentina, I was used to writing after having read a couple of articles or books. I did the same in England, especially at the beginning of the PhD through the weekly book reviews. However, when I started to write about Argentina, I changed this practice and I preferred to read more before starting to write. My experience was that I read for three or four weeks and afterwards began to write a first version of the chapter. However, the writing took me less time than the reading. This is due to my method of writing in English.

As a foreign student, one cannot pay much attention to the style, the mistakes, the vocabulary or the grammar. The easiest thing is to write the ideas you have in your mind and, after a careful reading, to correct them. Here there is another problem – you might not even realize your own mistakes! And this is when a foreign student can be very isolated. As noted earlier, it is a matter of time, and patience. One easy mistake to find and deal with is constant repetition. I believe this occurs because you are not sure if the reader will understand what you want to say. In Spanish, I say it once and clearly, and I know that is enough; in English, I always have doubts.

Another difficult task is to decide the limits of the topic. While writing, it is very tempting to include all you have read. However, this carries the danger that the argument gets lost amidst too many facts. The thesis must have a limited objective. Most PhD students think of the thesis as *the* work of their life. It is hard to realize that the thesis is *just* the beginning. I also found it very useful to set deadlines and not to allow myself to take extensions. This made my research more organized and gave a general overview of the possibility of reaching my final deadline. It is also helpful to limit the reading, since there are so many things you could read. Indeed, I used to read a lot more, simply to avoid having to start writing.

Another problem I found when the drafts were being written was that my thesis began to seem very obvious. I believe that after three years with Alfonsín's government in my mind I thought that everything was very obvious. I think this was related to the fact that I was living in Argentina during Alfonsín's government, so I could remember what I was reading and writing about and I also had my own recollections and points of view about those days. Moreover, I think that this occurs because after three years the material is so familiar, although there is still scope for some original observations. While I believe that originality is one of the main objectives of a PhD thesis, I think that it is much more important to contribute to the knowledge of the reader. In this sense, I hope my thesis explains why the amazing experience of living under democracy after seven years of military dictatorship ended in hyperinflation, looting and disappointment.

Conclusion

There are many things to consider before doing a PhD. As I said, the thesis is only the beginning; thereafter its topic will become your specialization either in politics or in international studies. I understand I made a mistake. Before going to England, my specialization was in international studies. However, my thesis ended up as a work in politics. After completing it, I had a job in the Ministry of Foreign Affairs back in Argentina, and now I have a lectureship in politics!

Students are often advised that when you choose your topic you have to think about your future job. What do you want to do next? I never thought like this. I chose the topic because I liked it, and I very much enjoyed doing the thesis. However, I would like to do something with the final product. It was not possible to get it published in England straight away because studies on Argentinian politics represent a small market. Therefore, when you chose your topic, it is wise to think also about your future career.

As a foreign student, I experienced a paradox: either you study about your country – which is easier to do and useful in getting a job at home – or you study something different, which might give you the opportunity to get a job abroad. I do not have an answer to this. However, I believe that you have to be very interested in the topic, it must make you think, it must motivate you. At some point you have to love it! If not, it is impossible to continue to work on it. Therefore, you have to be very careful when choosing your topic, and very careful when discussing it with your supervisor. Although this was not my case, it is very common that he or she has a special area of study and wants you to produce a work on it. In this, you have to be very strong, because if you did not like the topic, the PhD would be a great sacrifice.

The relationship with your supervisor is a central issue. Coming from abroad, you might not know him/her. Therefore, in the first months you have to decide if you want to work with him/her or change supervisors. If you think that he/she is interested in your work and finds the time to discuss it with you, it is fine. But if this is not the case, it might be good to change your supervisor. I had a very good supervisor, he was interested in my topic, read all the drafts, made very good comments, always had time to discuss it with me, and even corrected my English mistakes. After every meeting he suggested further reading, or an idea to consider. He read the whole thesis at least three times. When he said that I was ready to submit, I was very confident because I knew he was doing his job very well. The result was that I finished my thesis in three years and I passed the viva without any problem, and the thesis did not need correction. Without his advice, it might have been different.

Another problem you might face is how to obtain funds to do your PhD. In my case, I had a scholarship from the British Council for my first year, and from an Argentinian institution (*Consejo Nacional de Investigaciones Científicas y Técnicas*) for the last two years. The Argentinian institution did not pay the fees, so I had to obtain other funds to pay them. Again, your supervisor should be a great help. Although not a financial supervisor, he or she might advise that you apply to different bodies. You might also ask advice in your department and the university. Most universities have an International Office whose director can be very helpful. Finally, we found a way to pay the fees. You often have to be prepared to push hard in respect of the financial and practical arrangements for your studies.

You should also be prepared for independent study. Although I was used to research in my previous work, the PhD is something completely different. In Argentina I had deadlines to fulfil; if I did not meet them, I could be sacked. With the PhD you have to organize your time, you are the director, even if your supervisor is very strict with deadlines, you have the last word. Everything depends on you. And the sooner you finish the PhD, the better!

The PhD is very isolating, therefore when you are leaving home you should understand that for the next three years you will be struggling with the language, and living with another culture. However, a PhD abroad is not just a degree, it is a whole experience of life. Suddenly I was mixing with people from Sri Lanka, Greece, Spain, Portugal, Taiwan, and, of course, England. Because you have chosen politics and international studies you are going to be very interested in how people think and live in so many different cultures.

In other words, if you have the opportunity to leave your country for some years to do a PhD, you should not concentrate all your energies on work in the library. When I left Argentina, my country was undergoing hyperinflation, military rebellions, and trying to survive the crisis of the external debt. So anything in England, even travelling from Heathrow to Coventry train station, was completely new for me. University life was unknown, I had never seen a university campus. Therefore I tried to take advantage of this opportunity, not only for getting a degree but also to learn how people live, think and act on the other side of the world – and especially how the 'First World' thinks about the 'Third'. In most cases you will get the PhD, return home and, believe it or not, you will miss your years abroad.

Part 2

Methods and Procedures in Qualitative Research

11

The Practice of Political Theory

———

CHRIS WOODARD

New PhD students may know a good deal about political theory without knowing how it's done. There is a temptation to think of the practice of doing political theory as just a matter of constructing arguments and writing them down. Perhaps it is just this in one sense, but it also involves tricky decisions about which advice to take, when to start writing and when to stop rewriting, what to do when things seem to fall to pieces, and so on. This chapter, like the others in this book, is about these hidden dramas of the PhD student. I shall not say much about the content of my research, nor about *methodology* in any narrow sense, having to do with philosophies of social science, formal research techniques, and so on. Instead I'll try to emphasize the untidiness of research in my experience, its non-linearity, and the benefits of a certain kind of psychological attitude given these features of the research process. First, however, I should say at least something about what it is that I claim has merited three years of study and thousands of words of dry prose.

Explanation of my research area

My PhD is about the importance of discriminating between political possibilities which are worth entertaining and those which are not, and about the basis on which we should make such discriminations. The 'political possibilities' in question may be events, actions, states of affairs, or institutional arrangements. An event, for example, may be possible in some sense without being worth taking seriously – perhaps because it is too unlikely. Why is it important to judge whether possibilities are or are not worth entertaining when we are trying to decide what to do? The answer is that which possibilities we entertain will help determine which course of action looks best, perhaps reversing the recommendation of some line of reasoning about what to do. Hence, if deliberation is to be a rational process, we must be able to give reasons for thinking that one possibility is worth entertaining, while another is not.

To the extent that this topic has been treated before, it has been assumed that discriminating between relevant and irrelevant possibilities is a matter only of making the best use of our various predictions and predictive theories. On this view, a possibility is worth entertaining if our predictions tell us that it will occur, or is likely to occur, or, at the very minimum, if they do not tell us that it won't occur. I think that being predicted is very important to making a possibility relevant (and so worth entertaining), but this is not the whole story. In some circumstances we should entertain possibilities which, we predict, will not be realized. Moreover, sometimes we should act on this basis, choosing a course of action which, we expect, will have the best consequences only if others behave as we predict they won't. This seems paradoxical, but I believe that it makes sense in some situations in which joint actions are available to more than one actor. Hence, defending my view takes me into discussions of the rationality of joint action – discussions which I never planned to get into, and the relevance of which, in fact, I did not realize until well into my third year.

All this is pertinent only in so far as it gives an idea of the kind of territory I've been trying to research. My concerns are, I think, pretty abstract by most standards. While the research falls within the boundaries of political theory or political philosophy, the problems which it deals with do not keep many political theorists awake at night. Indeed, while much has been written on what may be called second-order issues about prescriptive political argument, most of it has been concerned with problems about value conflict, or the cognitive or other status of evaluative claims, or the differences between deontological and consequentialist reasoning, and so on; not many people seem to have found the issues I discuss to be both interesting and problematic – sometimes the first but not the second.

As I'll explain later, I had some trouble in the early stages of research in identifying a relevant body of literature. But whether or not there is an obvious place to look for relevant literature, new PhD students working on theoretical issues face a problem. The problem is that making substantive progress with the research, and getting clear about the claims to be made, are tasks so intimately bound together that it is very difficult to break them into stages: first getting clear, then finding relevant literature, then making some progress of one's own. It would be nice, perhaps, if research progressed in a linear fashion – with, as the textbooks would have it, an initial stage of problem definition, then a stage of breaking the whole problem into smaller parts, then a neat series of solutions to the sub-problems. In my experience, however, this picture could not be much more misleading. It *may* have some relevance to empirical studies, which perhaps do admit of a *certain amount* of straightforward disaggregation (though even here I'm doubtful), but when the research is very abstract I think it is better to picture a spiral, circling round and round the topic, hopefully reaching a better understanding of the issues and a better articulation of the central claims each time.

Definition of the project and progress in articulating the central arguments go hand in hand. If someone had told me at the start that what I was really talking about was the grounds on which we should discriminate between relevant and irrelevant possibilities, I would not have believed them, and scarcely have understood what they were talking about. The project itself, and not just the claims one makes, may change dramatically as a result of the spiralling process. I'll try to illustrate what this feels like in the next few sections, by recounting the ways in which I redefined my topic over the first eighteen months, before turning to some more thematic issues at the end of this chapter.

The initial definition of the project

The first attempt to define a project suitable for three years' full-time research took place one Tuesday evening, after work. I had been out of academic study for some while, and I had heard of an opportunity to apply at the last moment for a teaching assistantship, so I had to develop a research proposal very quickly indeed, without the chance to do any preparatory reading. Fortunately, I already had what I thought was a killer idea, which I was hatching for proposal the following year; I'd simply have to follow it up sooner. At this stage, I formulated the conclusion for which I wanted to argue like this: an explanation is not commanding of our attention just because it is consistent with the available evidence about the relevant phenomena. (Note how different the final formulation of the topic – let alone the argument – was!) My idea was that there may be many explanations of a certain phenomenon which are equally consistent with the evidence, and yet not equally satisfactory with respect to some theoretical or practical purpose. I was thinking particularly of sociobiological explanations of human action: the better ones seem to be consistent with the evidence (more males are aggressive, etc.), but nevertheless they seemed to me to be unsatisfactory. So, I wanted to pursue the question of what the further criteria for good explanation are.

All this made perfect sense when travelling on the tube to and from work. However, it did not escape even the interview for the teaching assistantship unscathed: my lack of relevant reading was swiftly and decisively exposed; though fortunately this was not considered to be a conclusive reason to reject me. Still, having cleared that hurdle, my first task was to turn a bald conclusion into a viable piece of research. As yet, I had no idea of the area or areas of literature which would be relevant to my intended argument – having a conclusion but no area of research is, perhaps, the opposite predicament to that of most 'green' research students.

Man with conclusion seeks relevant body of literature

Rereading early PhD work can be a source of great amusement. In the very early stages of my work, I had a particular tendency to diagram revolutionary new theories (or so I thought) on a single side of A4 paper, the only tasks then being to while away the remaining two years and ten months, and to fill the remaining 399 pages. My problem was that of someone who is convinced by a conclusion, but doesn't know the argument for it; or worse, doesn't even know where *to look* for the argument. At this stage I had two supervisors, whom I used to meet separately. This certainly influenced the way in which I set about finding an argument for my conclusion. One supervisor was particularly interested in the philosophy of natural and social science; the other was more interested in the philosophy of mind. Both disciplines seemed to have some promise as resources for a set of claims about the criteria for good explanations (which is how I defined my topic then), and indeed my first work was in familiarizing myself with some of the major debates and writers in each area, and in trying to see their relevance to my (still highly inarticulate) position. After about three months or so of this twin-track approach, however, I came to think that the preoccupations of philosophers of science were incompatible with my interests in the status of apparently true explanatory claims. They typically want to describe actual scientific practice accurately – at the same time as developing a normative account of its proper method or logical structure. In contrast, I was wanting to talk about a *more general* class of claims which are supposed to be true, and so the requirement to describe scientific practice accurately made little sense in relation to my arguments.

For this reason, I soon concentrated on the approach via the philosophy of mind. The idea here was that the various debates about the relationship between mind and world might help me say something about what ought to follow from some explanatory claims apparently being true. Moreover, all this stuff was just intrinsically interesting. This factor shouldn't be overlooked: I was so taken with these arguments about mind and world, and with connected arguments about the nature of language, that I was (I can now see, in retrospect), more or less determined that I was going to find a way of arguing for my conclusion here. Indeed, the results of this determination were long-lasting – it took more than a year for me to see that such arguments had much less to offer in support of my conclusion than I had thought. The final dissertation has only the odd echo in a footnote here and there of this work which occupied me through much of the first year and into the second. Still, the trip was interesting.

Here, then, in the philosophy of mind and of language, I found what I took to be my core literature. Fairly rapidly, my earlier schemes for intellectual revolution, which had spread so luxuriantly over a whole side of paper, became a significantly more realistic 4000-word plan of an argument. And by the end of the first summer, I had written an admittedly very rough first draft of a chapter – this felt like progress at last. Then came an earthquake.

When research seems to go backwards

I had invested quite a lot of time and effort in trying to develop an argument using one particular philosophical treatment of language. Then as my second year began, the supervisor of mine whose particular interests included philosophy of mind and language took over full-time supervision of my work. As a result, my central argument came under closer scrutiny, and it began to seem that it could not work, for fairly abstruse but nevertheless good reasons. I had, of course, always realized that this sort of thing can happen, but it was in any case a shock. My first instinct was, rightly, to try to save the argument if I could; this took me up to Christmas of the second year, but it seemed then that I would have to make a fairly major structural change in the way I hoped to go about arguing for my conclusion.

I was lucky enough at this time to be accepted for an ERASMUS exchange visit to the European University Institute in Florence for four months. In addition to sunshine and good coffee, this visit offered me the chance to spend some time away from the usual routine (and teaching duties), and to reflect on the broad outlines of my thesis. I had been sent away with a specific problem to solve: up until now, I had formulated the conclusion for which I wanted to argue in terms of a claim about the concept of *truth*; the problem was to find a way of stating my claim which did not refer to this concept. Instead of saying something like: there must be more to a good explanation than its being true, and this extra thing is . . ., I was charged with the task of finding an alternative way of expressing the thought behind this claim.

The first two months or so of the stay in Florence was punctuated by a series of occasions when I thought I had cracked the problem, only to realize a few days later that the new approach could not work either. One of the good, exciting things about theoretical work is that it is possible to take very large steps in a very short space of time; however, it is also possible to concede ground very quickly. This is what seemed to be happening to me, and for some time I doubted whether anything at all could be rescued from my project. I was conscious also that the eighteen-month mark was rapidly approaching: I wanted to have at least an idea of a workable argument to form the backbone of the thesis by that stage.

I remember one Sunday afternoon in particular. Slightly the worse for wear and quite despondent, I asked myself whether it wasn't too late to scrap the existing project and do something else. One of the things which contributed to my gloom was that I knew I was taking a risk in trying to borrow arguments for use in political philosophy from an area of philosophy in which I'm no expert. It looked as if I was now being found out. So here I was, a pathetic figure sitting on a bench, contemplating my overdue comeuppance. Then no more than two days later I was in the library rereading a key article, and it triggered an idea about how to solve my problem. Not only that, it seemed to be a way of retaining much of the benefit from the work I'd done throughout the first year and the first term of the second year. Naturally I was very excited, though apprehensive of another disappointment. This time, however, the new idea survived subsequent reflection. Not only that, it was a vast improvement on the kind of argument I had been trying to work out before: I'd not only rescued my work, but improved it greatly. And the new idea set off a whole series of new connections, while also inviting an elegant structure for the thesis as a whole. So what seemed like disaster turned out really quite well.

The point of this story is that you should be prepared to change arguments and even the definition of the project quite radically, even well into the research. I think this is more likely to happen in very theoretical topics than it is in more empirical areas. The episode I've just described was not the last time that the ground seemed to fall away from under me, and nor was the apparent solution which I found then as good as I thought at the time. But since then I've been better prepared to deal with it. Often I've had to make quite radical changes both to the overall shape of my argument and to its details. In coping with these changes it is very important to have the correct frame of mind, as I'll now try to explain.

Faking nonchalance

A certain kind of psychological attitude is of great help in the research process: the best way I've found of describing it is to say that it is a kind of *faked nonchalance*. This attitude is useful just because it is a defence against despair, and there are a lot of opportunities for despair when writing a PhD. For me the central difficulty is a result of the point I made earlier, that it can be very difficult to organize research as a series of discrete sub-problems to be solved. The problem then is that it is near enough impossible, especially in the first year or two, to know whether the work that one is currently doing will ultimately turn out well: there is always scope for worrying that this or that piece of work, or even this or that general approach, will eventually fail; the only way of answering this worry decisively is to finish the PhD. Few other tasks can so defiantly resist being broken down into proximate goals as does a PhD – and the result is that there is a great deal of potential for anxiety, since one can never know that one is going in the right direction. This is why I think we need to try to cultivate faked nonchalance: it is a kind of nonchalance, because once you've realized the nature of the research student's predicament, it would be foolish to pursue all worries about each aspect of the process remorselessly; it is faked in a way, however, since there is of course a need to worry sufficiently to maintain momentum, and to seek out genuine problems with the work. At a practical level, faking nonchalance amounts to discriminating among worries: pursue those which offer some hope of resolution, or which are so central that they cannot properly be ignored, but as part of the same deal, do ignore, or at least file away, those worries which either cannot be resolved, or which are peripheral. And be self-conscious in this process. Think:

I could worry about this but I'm deliberately not going to, because (a) it's not absolutely central, and (b) there's not much I can do about it.

The advantage of faking nonchalance is that it brings some psychological stability to what could otherwise be a very traumatic time. After all, there's endless potential to worry about *those other books which I've not read yet and which certainly revolutionize my field* (they probably don't – this is the 'magic books' fallacy); there's always more to do, and more cognate disciplines to become acquainted with, and so on. What appeared to be a nicely defined topic, unsullied by previous attention, can rapidly turn out to be a messy collection of old chestnuts, which quite simply have been approached before from a different angle. In itself, this need not cause problems with regard to the requirement to be original, I think – since even well-examined topics can usually be examined again profitably in a new way. But it does mean that the better one articulates one's project, the more connections become apparent, and the more obvious it is that many things will have to be taken for granted in the dissertation itself.

So perhaps the main message of this section is: do take some things for granted; don't try to justify every assumption (reasoning gets into trouble when it goes in pursuit of 'the unconditioned', as Kant put it). Theoreticians in particular like to question as many assumptions as possible, but this tendency has to be restrained if progress is to be made. The trick, of course, is to know which assumptions to question, given that they cannot all be questioned at the same time, nor within the compass of a PhD. Sadly, there is no straightforward method for deciding which to question and which to accept. But so long as one is aware of the most major and controversial assumptions one is making, there needn't be a big problem about making them.

Where's the political theory?

One of the problems facing a PhD student pursuing very abstract research, which probably does not arise so acutely for other politics and international studies PhDs, has to do with the artificial academic boundaries between the study of politics and other closely related disciplines. I'm thinking here particularly of philosophy, though theoretical aspects of economics, sociology, law and psychology could also be relevant. The problem has two aspects: the first is the possibility of a charge of amateurism being laid at the door of the student who does make significant use of material from other disciplines, without having significant formal training in that discipline; the second concerns the requirement to retain enough traditionally recognized material from the study of politics for the final dissertation to count, plausibly, as indeed a PhD in politics and international studies – rather than a PhD in philosophy, or economics.

I mentioned earlier that I've worried about the first of these sub-problems. It is a serious problem and it should not be brushed off lightly. I would not wish to encourage theoretically inclined students to plunder arguments from other disciplines at will, since it is obvious that mistakes can easily be made in trying to do this. There must remain cases, however, in which the student and his or her supervisor are happy that the material has been used properly, and that it is relevant. In these cases – and I think it is important that the student takes advice from his or her supervisor about this – the second aspect of the problem may nevertheless remain. In my case, I have taken, used and developed a good deal of material from various branches of philosophy, and I hope that I have done so conscientiously. Supposing that I have been conscientious, however, there may still remain a problem about the proportion of arguments in the final thesis which look like the kind of arguments one regularly encounters in politics departments. What should be done then?

Unfortunately, I can see that where there is a strict word limit on the dissertation, one might have to compromise, by removing some highly relevant and important *alien* arguments, to replace them with more obviously political material. (This is just a special case of the more general point, that one has to think carefully about which arguments to leave off the page, when a limited number of pages are available.) There are a number of obvious steps one can take before reaching this unhappy pass, however. One is to make sure that the case for including the alien material is made quite clearly and emphatically, early on in the dissertation, so that the examiners at least know that it is coming. Another strategy is to make strenuous efforts to apply the alien material to more obviously political examples. For instance, some of the philosophical material which I'm interested in has to do with ethical reasoning; in introducing and using this, I make sure to point out why I think it can be transposed to a discussion of prescriptive political argument, and I try to develop political illustrations of the relevant points. A third method is of course to make sure that the alien arguments do play an important part in the argument which is developed in the PhD – that they cannot, for example, be replaced with points which have been made in the traditional political literature. Having convinced yourself of this, make the case plain as far as possible in the dissertation, perhaps in the conclusion. Finally, be careful in choosing your external examiner. Find out whether they are sympathetic to interdisciplinary work: some established academics are enthusiastic about such work, others are much more sceptical.

Changing work habits

New PhD students will already have a good idea of which kind of working routine suits them best. In this section I shall discuss briefly how my own working habits have changed, but the point of this, it should be emphasized, is *not* to recommend those habits to others! Instead, I think there is something to be said about the ways in which a person's habits can change as the project he or she is engaged with itself changes and (hopefully) progresses.

One of the first tasks that I was asked to do was to write a chapter plan for my dissertation. I thought at the time that this was a useful exercise, and I still do, despite the lack of resemblance between my thoughts about the likely contents of my dissertation at the beginning of the first year and the contents of the finished product. It was useful partly as a way of communicating to my supervisors what I thought I'd like to do, without getting bogged down in detailed, and at that stage probably highly unsatisfactory, claims. It was useful also, however, as a way of impressing upon me the importance of continually revising one's overall view of the project, while at the same time working on particular aspects of the whole. I really think that these two kinds of exercise should run in tandem as far as possible. I've spent a good deal of my time as a PhD student thinking and writing about the contents of chapters whose arguments I had no clear idea about. This apparently irrational labour was done with the aim of not just getting each individual argument straight, but of having at least a sketchy idea of where the various arguments were leading, and of what other arguments needed to follow. And even at the stage of writing fairly well-developed drafts of chapters, it's surprising how much one needs to keep an eye on the precise order of exposition – on the issue of exactly when to marshal which argumentative troops. Attending to these factors can have very significant effects on the contents of each chapter, and also on the quality of the thesis as a whole.

Before I started my PhD, I hadn't fully realized that arguments and issues do not form *themselves* into family units, each one of which corresponds neatly to a chapter heading. The writer has not only to formulate the arguments, and to make sure that they are valid, and so on, but also to decide the running order. It can make a great deal of difference exactly when a key distinction is introduced, for example. (These are the too-little discussed arts of rhetoric, in the good sense of the word.) This is another aspect of the non-linearity of the research process which I've been trying to emphasize throughout this chapter. There is a need to combine, in a more or less untidy and imperfect way, thought and work devoted to particular issues and arguments, with thought and work devoted to the as-yet admittedly ill-perceived whole. The guiding hope is that out of this shall emerge an articulate and coherent body of arguments. To the extent that it does, it will be as a result of a great deal of work on successive drafts. When not having fun designing plans for the thesis as a whole, I tended, early on, to write fairly short essays exploring topics which interested me, or on writers whose thoughts seemed to be important for my subject. These essays of about two to five thousand words provided the basis for discussion at supervisory meetings, when the next topic to be investigated would be jointly decided. I found this system to be highly satisfactory for the first year or so. For one thing, there was no pressure to conjure up a central argument for the whole thesis right from the start – the essays had at least as much to do with providing background knowledge and the opportunity to improve my writing as they did with the intended content of the thesis. Perhaps this is particularly useful for those, like me, who have not taken a Master's degree. In any case, this relatively relaxed method allowed me to make plenty of mistakes with a good deal of impunity. In total I wrote something like 40- or 50,000 words in the first twelve months, and not a single sentence of that work appears on the pages of the finished dissertation. But surely this is as it should be – it would be an indictment of the extent to which I had progressed in three years of full-time study if that work had survived to the final dissertation.

By about the summer of the first year, however, I began to want to write not only chapter plans, but also chapter drafts. I shan't recount again the story of the demise of these early attempts (it's too painful!). It will suffice to say that trying to write a chapter demands a different kind of schedule and working arrangement than does trying to write an exploratory essay on a topic which one knows little about. I used to allow two or three weeks for each essay, whereas now I allow two or three months for a draft chapter, if writing it involves substantial new work and new reading. At this stage in the process, it seems sensible to get as much of the hard work of reading dull but seminal books done as possible – in order to leave the final period of rewriting relatively free from such pressures.

It's worth emphasizing one more time how long the process of writing a draft of the whole thesis can take. The first draft of the thesis took until the start of the summer of the third year. I started this task half-way through my second year – and I had a complete draft only fourteen months later. Add to that at least six months for rewriting. In my case the rewrite took longer, since the revisions which I made were substantial, usually involving a literal rewrite rather than a cut, paste and fiddle. Remember also to allow sufficient time for supervisors to read and discuss the emerging draft chapters. Particularly if they have several other doctoral students, it can take up to two months from the date when the draft was handed in for the process of discussion to be completed. In these circumstances, there seems to be little choice other than to press ahead with the next chapter, in the hope that the previous one was not so drastically inadequate as to jeopardize the later ones.

Finally in this section, a word on writing style. Clarity of exposition is always at a premium, but in theoretical work it is especially important. There is, however, more to writing a readable dissertation than being clear. When I began to write draft chapters, I noticed how much more of an interest I began to pay to matters of style when reading others' work. In particular, I found myself picking up books which seemed to me to be well-written, specifically to see how their authors had gone about organizing each chapter, what sort of things they said in the introduction, and so on. This is another surprising element of trying to write a PhD: I realized that there was much to be learned about writing a long piece of work, as opposed to mere undergraduate essays, and that it was far from transparent. When I had previously read books, I had not been fully aware of the various conventions and tried and tested techniques for propelling the argument and the reader along. One thing worth mentioning is that readable books rarely take the form of a single continuous argument, beginning in chapter 1 and finishing with the conclusion. Perhaps I was naive, but I imagined that such a continuous argument was the thing to aim for. In fact, however, it is probably better to divide your material into chapters along the lines of *aspects of the topic*, rather than *stages of the argument*. This helps readability, and it also helps limit the damage caused by weak links in your argument, should there be any.

Conclusion

The message of this chapter can be spelled out quite simply. The first point is that, with a few exceptions, the new PhD student is unlikely to have a sufficiently well-defined project to be able to break the task of writing a dissertation into a series of sub-problems, each one of which can then be tackled and resolved in turn. I think this is true of all PhDs in politics and international studies, but it is perhaps especially the case when the project is very abstract. This is because very abstract research does not admit of much distinction between clarifying the problem and the claims to be made, on one hand, and sorting out the arguments for them on the other. There is no empirical fieldwork to be done; instead, the process is one of adjusting and attuning one's view of the local terrain, to perceive more clearly the connections between various claims and controversies. Think of a spiral around the topic, rather than a series of discrete sub-problems. (Certainly do not think of the dissertation as a series of thirty discrete essays!)

The second point has to do with the strategies available for coping with this predicament. The only sensible response, it seems to me, is to attempt to keep some distance from one's current worries during the work. There are bad days, bad weeks, even bad months. If one tries to get a feel of the significance of these bad periods, as elements in an unfolding story of disaster for the project, despair is inevitable. Instead, try to let them run off your back – up to a point (draw the line at bad years, perhaps!). As I've said, I think of this detachment as a kind of faked nonchalance. It's not real nonchalance, nor should it be if you are seriously interested in your project. It is, however, a blend of resilience, and a certain amount of faith. Have some, but not too much, faith in the system for training doctoral students at your university. Have more faith in your own abilities. After all, you've made it this far – and the PhD is nothing more than a kind of apprenticeship. Those dour inhabitants of the rooms up and down the politics corridor just want to make sure that (a) you're keen enough to stay the course, and (b) you're not utterly stupid. We all know that academic books and journals contain a good deal of hot air and bluster alongside the better material. If the PhD is a membership card to this club, it can't be *that* difficult to get one of your own.

12

Combining Disciplines:
How to Build a Good Enough Bridge

STEVEN SMITH

This chapter looks at some of the problems I encountered with interdisciplinary research. Indeed, many of my bridge-building 'solutions' have failed, but I am learning that this experience of failure is an essential part of the research process. However, persistence leads to *some* measure of success, and that, realistically, is all we should aim for, especially with a PhD. In short, I only need to build a bridge that is 'good enough', something that can carry traffic but without necessarily winning any design awards!

A 'sanitized' summary of my research

My research looks at some of the difficulties associated with moving from philosophical generalities to specific policies, by exploring how a bridge might be built between political philosophy and social policy analysis. It is in the light of these findings that I critically evaluate the relationship between the Centre-Left and the New Right.

I compare the preoccupations of political philosophers with the often very different preoccupations of social policy analysts and argue that these differences not only provide important clues as to why there is a divide between political philosophy and social policy analysis, but also offer reasons as to why a division is often said to exist between the Centre-Left and New Right. Most importantly, relatively small differences in philosophical value commitment can still lead to large differences in the way groups of people are treated by government when these commitments find expression in policy implementation.

More specifically, I start from non-positivist and non-utilitarian premises, and focus on the way the concepts of individual autonomy and equality are used by political philosophers and social policy-makers, looking at UK training, education, social security and community care policy. My central hypothesis is that, despite the possible differences in the outcomes of policy implementation referred to above, the Centre-Left and the New Right share a number of important value commitments which have profoundly affected the kinds of welfare policies which are promoted by each position.

Coping with mess and confusion

The above summary, although it is part of the 300-word blurb at the front of my thesis, disguises the haphazard way the project has come together. It is the process of researching through mess and confusion that I will now look at, focusing on some of the coping strategies I have devised as a result.

My ideas and arguments are often worked out in a very irregular and *ad hoc* way. Even during the final writing-up stages I found myself repeatedly clearing up the mess that other people and myself had helped to make. For example, just before submitting a third draft of my thesis to my supervisors I gave a seminar paper based on one of my chapters to a group of PhD students. This led to subtle but important changes in some of my ideas as well as to a reinforcement of existing arguments. However, I have tried not to panic about the confusion but instead to view it as an essential and creative aspect of the research process which can be worked with constructively. For example, I have frequently made lists of apparently unrelated questions arising from my research and then have identified any patterns or common themes emerging between them. Also, during the first year, when the confusion was at its peak, I generated a number of hypotheses (however daft some of them seemed). This activity made me think very laterally about the issues at stake and, although I needed at some point to prune these hypotheses down, I became positively engaged in the various materials I was having to deal with. I find that the trick is not to allow the confusion to demotivate me, but to initiate discrete tasks in response to it. Out of this process shapes emerge, however blurred at first, which then give me something from which to develop my ideas and arguments. In summary, often my research feels out of control, but I have learned that research is not about getting everything in the right order *before* you start.

When I had started to settle on one main hypothesis (for me this was not until the end of the first year), I asked myself whether I could 'own' it (i.e., whether I was personally committed to it). Does this fit in with *my* understanding of the world? Will this sustain *my* interest when trying to construct detailed arguments in relation to it? Once I was able to answer these questions in the affirmative, then I was less prone to feeling as if my supervisors were overly controlling my research. They might send me off in directions I am not particularly interested in or I think are a distraction, but if I know roughly where I am coming back to, and more importantly that the place is 'mine', then I am reassured that it is me who is steering the project. Moreover, having 'my place' gives me a position to argue from when I really do disagree with particular advice or suggestions about what to do. In any case, many of the various directions in which I have been sent, although at the time they might have felt irrelevant, turned out to be very useful excursions.

From the start of my research I was encouraged by my supervisors and in methodology seminars to get into the habit of writing. This was excellent advice. It is important that I see my arguments on paper or the computer screen, as their weaknesses reveal themselves more clearly than if they stay in my head. These initial efforts at writing, however half-baked, are not wasted, especially as they can be easily edited/cut and pasted with a word-processor. In addition, writing prevents me from becoming too precious about my ideas, as I get very used to seeing them develop. Apart from being a healthy lesson in academic humility, on the other side of the coin, this process also accustoms me to changing my views in a way that still accommodates central hypotheses and arguments.

One area in which my research practice was deficient was in regard to note-taking and cataloguing. For example, in my hurry to get things read, I quite often failed to make page number references throughout my notes, particularly in the early stages. I have been paying the price later on when I have had to double-check my references. However, after the first few months I did get a reasonable filing system up and running. I divided my notes under about a dozen subject headings which roughly corresponded to the issues I explored in my essay-writing to date, with contents pages for each section. This enabled me to manage efficiently the accumulation of material, especially as I began to make links across fairly disparate material. Also, after about nine or ten months I spent ten days to two weeks thoroughly reading over my notes (i.e., not skim-reading but slowly identifying central themes and research questions). In the process of rereading, I page numbered the notes and devised a fairly detailed alphabetical index of about twenty subject areas, developed from the original twelve-part division in my filing system. I have found this index an invaluable tool. After the first year, it enabled me to get thoroughly on top of the issues (it's surprising how much information and how many ideas and arguments I forgot along the way), and, when it came to writing up the thesis proper, I could find the appropriate references in my notes relatively quickly. Most importantly, it was through thoroughly rereading my notes that I hit on my central hypothesis regarding the Centre-Left and the New Right.

PhD students often panic, fearing that they have missed *the* article/book which will expose all their ideas and arguments as fraudulent. A nasty voice tells them that if they don't read *all* of the literature then they will fail their PhD – either because they will say something that someone else has already said, or that they will base their thesis on a fallacy that everyone knew about years ago. Consequently, particularly in the first months (but I'm still prone to this now), I ended up trying to consume too much too quickly. In retrospect, part of my confusion, especially in the first year, was symptomatic of skipping from one commentator to another in the hope that I would become some kind of expert on all of them. Although there is sometimes good reason for skim-reading a lot of material to get the gist of the arguments/issues, it is a strategy that, in my experience, should be used sparingly as it is likely to result in serious misunderstandings. I find that it's much more useful to understand one book or even one chapter thoroughly than to half-understand ten books or ten chapters. More specifically, it was when I started to focus on one or two commentators (forgetting the rest – or at least putting them on hold) that I started to get under the skin of the arguments. Guided by my supervisors, it was important that I focused on respected commentators. However, by piggy-backing on their vantage points, I could then better spot their strengths and weaknesses, and was able to identify where I might come in.

It is easy to become tied up in knots about the detail of which bit of the thesis will go where and why, when at the end of the day there are probably a number of ways in which it can be organized. Particularly towards the end of writing up the first draft, at night I would often be exhausted but unable to sleep for thinking about it all. However, there are a couple of strategies that can be employed to alleviate this problem. First, it would have helped if I had read a few PhDs to see how other students had put them together. I read one thesis early on in my studies but found it rather intimidating and so was put off reading any more until the final writing-up stages. It was at this latter point when I more fully realized, not only that the standard of a PhD is lower than I first thought, but that there are a number of organizational options available even if you are working within a fairly formalized PhD-type structure. Second, in any case, I also find that once my arguments are out of my head and in the computer then I generally stop worrying about their organization. Apart from this being another reason for getting into the habit of writing up arguments, I have become very aware of how important it is to find ways of switching off from the thesis. For example, I devise a weekly timetable of thesis work (in my head or on paper) which, although demanding, is something I know I can stick to. However, I build into this timetable 'switch-off' periods. This might be other work (e.g., teaching and marking, as well as child-care responsibilities), but it also includes more relaxing activities (e.g., longish walks, playing the trumpet, and watching TV).

Finally, I have found that I either need to be very self-disciplined when seeking to complete a PhD on time, or have a discipline imposed upon me in some way. I am fortunate that a lot of my motivation is derived from the latter, due to personal circumstances which are essentially beyond my control, reinforced by the approach of my supervisors emphasizing the submission of written work. In regard to the former, because I have been teaching part-time throughout my studies, and have family commitments which include helping to look after young children, I have to be very organized about my studies or I would not get anything done. Moreover, for the previous ten years (after my first degree) I have spent most of my time in paid work and so have got used to getting up early and working until at least the early evening. This routine has not been broken with my PhD and is reinforced by the relative urgency of having to get back to full-time paid work in order to pay bills. I have concluded, therefore, that it is not necessarily a disadvantage to do a PhD part-time as, depending upon experience and the nature of other commitments, it is possible to finish just as quickly as full-time students because you have to be more focused about completion.

Good enough bridge-building

There are a number of reasons why a PhD thesis ends up the way it does. Some of these reasons are very rational (whether premeditated or *post hoc* rationalizations), others are not. In this section I examine both types of reasons, looking specifically at the business of combining disparate disciplines, exploring the process behind the development of my central ideas and arguments.

Why I chose my subject area

First, I will look at some of my personal reasons for wanting to combine political philosophy and social policy, highlighting the ways in which my views about the two subject areas have changed over the years. My conclusions provide a broader context for understanding how I am combining political philosophy and social policy in my PhD.

My first love is political philosophy/theory. Throughout my BA in politics I opted for courses that had a theoretical focus and tried to avoid those subjects which were rooted in empirical analysis. In short, I considered subjects relating to empirical research very dull, including social policy analysis, or social/public administration, as it was called. However, I now believe that this judgement led to a distorted view of the relationship between social policy and political philosophy. Even when I did become more interested in the former, I had the academically snobbish view often acquired by political philosophers that political philosophy/normative debate is a superior type of analysis to empirical research.[1] This attitude is very counter-productive when considering how one discipline might combine with another. A more balanced attitude recognizes that there are bound to be strengths and weaknesses in any discipline, and that areas of weakness in one discipline are often compensated for by strengths in another. When I started my PhD I had more or less reached this conclusion, but it took me about ten years to get there.

It was in my time as a welfare practitioner (mainly in social work) and in social policy research that, to my surprise, I began to enjoy grappling with the detail of social policy and became much more sympathetic towards academics and others who analysed it. This sympathy has been reinforced by my spending the last four years teaching as a part-time tutor for the Open University (OU). The OU course material helped me appreciate the importance of interdisciplinary study. More specifically, it has become clear (and has been further clarified throughout my PhD), why many social policy-makers and analysts understandably avoid using analysis developed by political philosophers. Most social policy-makers/analysts conclude that political philosophy cannot assist them, as at best it obscures issues, and at worst is completely irrelevant when justifying specific policies. This problem motivated me to find ways of bridging the gaps between political philosophy and social policy.

However, during the first discussion with my two supervisors I was told that any contemporary 'bridge-building' between political philosophy and social policy analysis has so far been minimal. I subsequently found that this lack of communication between disciplines has advantages and disadvantages for the PhD student. I can explore new ideas relatively easily, but I am vulnerable to committing errors which could probably be avoided had more work been done in the area. Having two supervisors (one covering political philosophy and the other social policy) is a considerable help, in so far as there is expertise on either side of the division. Moreover, joint supervision allows for a better exchange of ideas as it provides an antidote to the academic prejudices referred to above. I can see that two supervisors might cause difficulties if there are major differences between them, or between the supervisors and the student. However, in my experience the differences which have occurred are not substantial enough to cause problems. This was no doubt helped by the fact that they had both jointly supervised a successful PhD student who, like myself, was concerned with the relationship between political philosophy and social policy.

Changing focus – practicalities, compromise and new possibilities

I will now look in more detail at the way the focus of the thesis changed. Anticipating that there would be difficulties combining two disciplines, I sought to incorporate, as much as possible, the knowledge I had already gained in social policy and political philosophy. Consequently, my first research proposal was based on how the concept of 'welfare rights' related to the 'work ethic', looking specifically at the development of post-1945 UK social security legislation. However, after the first meeting with my supervisors, it was decided to drop the term 'work ethic' as it was thought to be too vague and instead to focus on 'deservedness'. Initially, I was reluctant to do this as the former notion, while very broad, highlighted what I believe to be important issues relating to how paid employment relates to social policy. Nevertheless, despite these concerns, I thought that the debate regarding the 'deserving' and 'undeserving' poor often explored by contemporary social policy analysts would probably raise this issue just as well. Moreover, given that the idea of 'desert' is extensively debated in political philosophy, particularly in relation to conceptions of 'justice', I concluded that it made better sense to go where my supervisors were leading rather than stick with my original plan.

However, in the final thesis, although I have often referred to the concept of 'deservedness', as a way of illustrating some of the similarities between the Centre-Left and the New Right, I have not made it a focal point. This second change of focus was mainly a result of the first six to nine months of my research. Because I have ended up exploring a number of policy areas and normative concepts rather than just one of each, my interest in the concept of 'deservedness' has diminished. It was only after the first year, when I had identified my main hypothesis, that it re-emerged, but only as one of a number of arguments to back up my principal position regarding the Centre-Left and the New Right.

Initially, my supervisors also thought that encompassing post-1945 legislation was probably too ambitious a task. One of the reasons given for this reservation was that numerous policy changes would have occurred in this period, making any in-depth analysis difficult. Consequently, I was persuaded by the idea that the post-1973 period would probably be adequate for my research needs. Nevertheless, in the event, although my main focus has probably been on this narrower time period, I have not kept to it rigidly. The issue of what time period I use has become less important the more my thesis has developed. In the first stages of research I explored aspects of a variety of policy areas, rather than trying to cover in detail one area such as social security. Moreover, I compared and contrasted different normative justifications for these policies, in the hope that this would give me some clue as to how political philosophy relates to social policy. In the later stages of my research my ideas and arguments have focused more specifically on those policies that are readily associated with either the Centre-Left or the New Right. Again, this has not involved keeping rigidly to one time period or exploring in detail one policy area or one type of value.

In summary, then, choosing a subject area is necessarily a matter of negotiation and compromise. Indeed, the notion of choice is misleading as there are so many factors bearing on your decision which are essentially outside of your control, particularly in the first year or so. However, I have found that what feels like a compromise at one point can end up a springboard into other more interesting and fruitful areas. For example, I discovered, contrary to my expectations, that when two disciplines are being combined it is still possible to cover a wide range of issues within the disciplines. In my case this was made possible by four factors. First, two supervisors (each covering one discipline) provides a kind of safety net for exploring a range of subject areas. Secondly, I have tended to focus on areas within the two disciplines I already know something about. This cut down extra reading and gave me a certain degree of confidence in my own knowledge-base. Thirdly, the rather *ad hoc*/experimental way I explored the relationship between the two disciplines, especially in the first year, inevitably led me to look at a number of different areas, rather than just one or two as originally intended. Fourthly, it was out of this experimental process that a more specific methodology developed which has allowed for a broader exploration of areas.

Steven Smith

Which came first – methodology or hypothesis?

One of the first questions I explored was to what extent could political philosophy lead to specific policy recommendations? This question was prompted by my supervisors, who are very aware of the difficulties of 'converting' political philosophy into social policy. Initially, I found addressing this question quite disconcerting as it challenged my main research premiss – that a bridge ought to be built between the disciplines. However, I think it is important to face up to this type of question at an early stage as it has reoccurred in one form or another throughout my studies. In any event, tackling this issue taught me a lot in the first year. It was during these early explorations that I started to examine political philosophers who had already made attempts at bridging the gap between political philosophy and social policy (Goodin, 1982; Plant *et al.*, 1980; Weale, 1978). The main lesson I learned was to avoid abstract and obscure illustrations when making a philosophical point, and instead to use real-life examples from the world of social policy. This need to provide an antidote to philosophical abstraction also prompted me to look at material outside of academia, such as 'think-tank' documents, government statements/papers, and publications from pressure groups. This allowed me to explore the detail of social policy-making and at the same time to establish explicit links with the political philosophy literature. For example, when I started to examine some of the highly abstract philosophical arguments relating to the concept of equality, I was able to connect these with policy issues raised by the disability rights movement. This movement frequently uses the language of equality, rights and justice to articulate its political demands and so provides considerable bridge-building material.

It was also during this period that I found that the contemporary social-policy political philosophers referred to above provided bridge-building solutions which were increasingly unsatisfactory for my purposes. They often stopped short of applying their philosophical analysis to specific social policy implementation, preferring instead to focus, as one commentator put it, on more general policy 'intentions' (Goodin, 1988, p. 14). Throughout my thesis I have been able to exploit what I consider to be this arbitrary decision, by arguing that it is precisely at the point of policy implementation and recommendation that subtle differences in philosophical emphasis can have an important impact. Also, identifying this weakness in contemporary 'bridge-building' allowed me to develop a relatively systematic methodology in response to it. The methodology has been library-based, partly by default, as I simply had not thought about the possibilities of, say, doing interviews with policy-makers. However, I also have easy access to the Bodleian Library in Oxford. Although it is not a lending library, I found I could work there very efficiently, being able to refer to such an enormous range of material and sources. Consequently, I started to characterize particular theoretical debates (inside and outside of political philosophy) which then could be 'mapped-out' or compared against policy-makers' justifications of specific social policy. Reinforced by the expectations from my supervisors that I produce written material for supervision, I quickly developed a note-taking system (in standard linear form) where I extracted discrete sections from the non-academic material referred to above, and then wrote essays speculating on the nature of the response from various theoretical literature. It was through this process that I began to notice interesting facets of the relationship between social policy analysis and political philosophy. For example, I highlighted a number of similarities and differences between the preoccupations of social policy-makers, social policy analysts (particularly from sociology),[2] and political philosophers. I was able to identify the way all of these sources discussed at some length the same concepts but had produced very different 'spins' on the debate. For example, social policy-makers (whether from the Centre-Left or the New Right) often refer to the concept of individual autonomy in terms of a person's accessibility to the labour market, whereas political philosophers explore what are competing ideas of 'self-mastery'. Sociologists, on the other hand, seek to 'problematize' the concept of individual autonomy (i.e., question its universal validity) by referring to issues relating to, say, the cultural specificity of liberal values (which includes the value of individual autonomy) and the problems of 'modernity'. It was these different preoccupations within debate that then allowed me to identify some of the strengths and weaknesses of each approach, and explore the possibility that answers to problems in one area might be found in another.

Admittedly, in the first nine months or so I was often frustrated with the 'mapping-out' approach, as my supervisors and I were not quite sure where it was all leading. I had continuously to ask myself what the thesis was *not* trying to explore, in order sufficiently to narrow the bodies of literature that I had to refer to. My first answers to this problem were often vague and unsure, causing lots of headaches. It was not until the end of the first year, when I had identified my central hypothesis, that my use of the 'mapping-out' methodology became much clearer. The more I use this system, the greater light it seems to be shedding on the relationship between political philosophy and social policy. Most importantly, it led to what became a principal subtext to the main hypothesis – that issues often 'change weight' as they cross the divide between political philosophy and social policy. For example, I argue that relatively small differences in philosophical emphasis may nevertheless still have a large impact on people's lives when 'translated' into social policy. Moreover, this 'changing weight' notion not only gives more substance to my exploration of the relationship between political philosophy and social policy analysis, but has also provided a way of exploring what I believe are important caveats to the claim that the Centre-Left and the New Right share considerable value commitments.

Finally, there arises the interesting 'chicken and egg' question; did the methodology or the hypothesis come first? I believe that in my case it was mostly the former that led to the latter, which is an odd way of doing things – at least according to the more orthodox textbooks on research methodology. Moreover, as I have already highlighted, the methodology was first developed in a fairly *ad hoc* and unsystematic way. Nevertheless, I believe that even though this might be described as a 'non-rational' developmental process, it is still, I believe, an unavoidable and very positive aspect of research. The methodology has allowed me to become interested in explaining the relationship *between* positions, rather than defending particular political and philosophical concepts and values. This has suited the development of my own ideas – because my principal research interest has led to my becoming increasingly interdisciplinary and eclectic when constructing explanations. This in turn has given me the analytical space I need to compare and contrast two broad ideologies such as the Centre-Left and the New Right.

Conclusion

Although there is no 'master plan' for completing a PhD, my experience leads me to three general conclusions.

First, students should be prepared for a lot of confusion, particularly in their first year. This is a very common experience for all PhD students, but especially perhaps for those trying to combine disparate disciplines. In the initial stages, there will be a preoccupation with identifying what the thesis is *not* trying to do in order to determine exactly where the 'bridge' between disciplines will be located. This can be very frustrating as it can delay the business of building the bridge proper, and make a student feel that he or she is seriously floundering. However, it is important not to panic when your research seems to be developing in a very *ad hoc* and even irrational way – this is an inevitable *and* creative aspect of the research process.

Second, combining two disciplines does not necessarily confine a student to a small range of issues within either of the subject areas. However, when considering the range of issues to be examined, a number of factors and questions have to be taken into account and addressed: (i) The type and quality of supervision available: Does the student need more than one supervisor? Does the supervisor(s) have experience in combining the two disciplines? (ii) The existing knowledge of the student: How can his/her previous knowledge or experience be used most effectively to combine the two disciplines? Does he or she have a special interest in *both* subject areas? How likely is it that one subject area will overly dominate the other? (iii) The type of methodology chosen: Does it commit the student to a particular argument or explanation which might get them bogged down in one discipline rather than the other? What kinds of hypotheses are available?

Finally, when combining two disciplines there needs to be a genuine commitment to interdisciplinary research. The basic premiss should be that a combination of two disciplines can produce better explanations than those generated from a single academic area. When developing arguments derived from one of the disciplines, it is essential that students continually ask what the commentators from the other are likely to say in response. It is through this two-way reflection process that academic prejudices are continually challenged and bridge-building is made possible.

Notes

1. I must confess that in my weaker moments I still adhere to this view. It is important to point out that this kind of attitude is exhibited not only by political philosophers. Empirical researchers often dismiss or downgrade in importance normative/philosophical debate, on what I consider to be equally academically prejudiced grounds that political philosophy is 'subjective', 'unscientific' and generally irrelevant to the 'real world of politics'.
2. This was helped by the fact that I was teaching an OU social policy course which used sociological theory extensively.

13

Border Crossings: Opportunities and Challenges in Comparative Research

MICHAEL O'NEILL

The best piece of advice I received from my supervisor was to continue with comparative research. I was considering turning my research into a single-case study for financial and logistical considerations. It might not have been apparent at the time, but in the intervening years I have come to see the wisdom in my supervisor's advice.

As political scientists, we have been schooled in the comparative method virtually from our first lectures in university. For example, country-specific courses (American politics, politics in the UK, etc.) or overview courses (introduction to politics, introduction to international relations, etc.) which refer to historical and political developments across polities and time lead us to see the world in terms of the similarities and differences among states. Our national experience is regularly, whether consciously or unconsciously, projected on to other polities. Asking ourselves, for example, how Bill Clinton came to be president or whether the French National Assembly can block a European single currency casts these political events in terms of their similarity or difference with those of our own experience. Why not, then, use this natural way of seeing the world in our research?

Although in the following pages I will primarily discuss cross-national research, comparative research need not imply work that is an offshoot of the larger area of international relations. Moreover, whether you are comparing cities or countries, the methods of comparative research remain largely the same, only the subjects (the cases) vary. There are as many valuable lessons for politics in comparing Birmingham and Coventry as there are in comparing Canada and the UK. Even in cross-national research the unit of analysis need not be the state. Any number of institutions, sub-national entities and actors can be considered in cross-national comparative research. To return to my earlier example, you can compare the municipal policies of Moose Jaw and Coventry just as readily as you can compare those of Coventry and Birmingham. The only limitation on such work is the ability to develop variables and concepts that 'travel' (Dogan and Pelassy, 1980, p. 11; also Dogan and Pelassy, 1984; Bahry, 1981). I will return to this issue below.

Why do comparative research?

Comparative research presents a number of advantages to the researcher in political science – although there are also a number of disadvantages to this approach. A comparative or cross-national focus enables us to escape the confines of a single culture or case, what Rose calls 'ethnocentric blinkers' (Rose, 1988, p. 219). Moreover, as new arrivals in the world of academia, comparative research enables us to cut across the masses of single-state, single-case studies that are currently piling up on the desks of journal editors and make up the vast majority of the output of researchers around the world. This is especially the case if you choose to focus on infrequently compared units – for example a Western state and an Asian one. Comparative research is also a useful way of broadening one's knowledge. In a competitive academic environment where we are likely to be expected to teach and research in several areas, having a greater number of specialities could be a significant advantage.

Another advantage of comparative research concerns the boredom factor. Don't let anybody tell you otherwise – no matter how original your subject is, and how great an idea you thought it was when you dreamed up your funding application, there will come a time when you'll tire of your subject. This is generally just a phase, but one which most graduate researchers experience. While the boredom factor will affect any subject – even in comparative research – the ability to drop one case and switch to the other offers a useful way of 'changing' what you are working on without the downtime. This, I found, was particularly true during the writing process, when long hours at the word-processor coupled with reading and researching one subject exclusively took a psychological and physical toll. The temporary diversion offered by picking up articles on something related (in my case reading on the UK when I got tired of the Canada section I was writing) proved most valuable.

There are, of course, disadvantages to comparative – particularly cross-national – research. It can prove costly. Rather than basing your work entirely on the contents of the library, good cross-national research will necessitate travel to the country or countries you are comparing. Reference material resources will often prove more difficult to find. Even work concerning relatively large and wealthy countries will face the difficulty of accessing relevant documents and other sources in one home country. In my case, even very general material on Canada was hard to come by in British libraries. I can only imagine the difficulties had I chosen to compare Canada with a country other than Britain, where I was based. Finally, language is always a problem. Many of us mistakenly believe that the rest of the world speaks and writes in English. While a surprising number of people and sources are available in English, this is not always the case. If you want the true story, particularly if your work requires interviews and/or access to non-public documents, a more than passable ability in the language of the country you are studying is a minimal requirement. This is especially the case in areas where there is a lot of research being published or on-going, such as industrial policy. If you can't speak the language, your work will be competing with – and be evaluated against – that of others (usually termed 'specialists') who do. Many of these issues will be dealt with below.

However, as noted above, the best piece of advice I received in starting my dissertation was to stick to a comparative framework. In the following pages I will walk you through my research project, identify some of the problems I encountered and discuss how I dealt with them. I will also provide an overview of the comparative method and how I adapted it for my work. I do not pretend to be able to answer all the questions in this area of research, which is why I hope the references will prove useful. I will try throughout to highlight areas where comparative work has saved me time and where it has added to my workload.

No research framework is a panacea – mine certainly isn't – but that which I describe below is closest, I feel, to what comes naturally to us as researchers in politics. As Dogan and Pelassy write (1980, p. 3), 'the comparative method is to the social sciences what the experimental is to the natural sciences'.

The New Right in power in Canada and Great Britain: notes on my research project

Too little attention seems to be spent working out the process leading from the inspiration phase of the research to its conceptualization. Yet this has proved critical to my work, especially in the closing months. A little like a Euro-rail tourist, the inspiration to embark on a project generally determines where you're going and how you're going to get there. In my case, the research I turned into my current dissertation topic, the New Right in government, was my second choice. Most of us begin with a topic or issue which interests us, in my case health care, and only later do we attempt to turn it into concepts that can be studied. The earlier you can conceptualize your topic, however, the more focused your research will be. The time savings alone militate in favour of taking a good hard look at what it is you want to do and how you plan to do it.

The inspiration for my research topic came to me during a concert by Art Blakey's Double Quartet at the 1992 Montreal Jazz Festival. Although I had been accepted for a PhD, I found I was unhappy with my original research proposal. Put another way, I couldn't imagine sustaining my interest on my original topic for very long – let alone three years. By the intermission I had the germ of the idea more or less worked out, and by the end of the concert I had pretty much resolved to give it a go. However, much still needed to be done. Over the next few weeks and months I visited university libraries and met with one lecturer who worked in a related field. I received encouraging words from the latter, and found little in the way of similar work in the former. Yet, now that I look back upon it, I really didn't have my research topic worked out. While I had a relatively interesting set of ideas, I didn't have any concepts to go out and measure. This fairly simple endeavour proved a major lacuna in my work and caused much delay later as I hunted around for a 'what' to study within the larger topic of health policy. Some might argue that such a search is the whole purpose of the first year of your PhD, but, with increasing pressures on funding and from funding bodies to finish in three years, a better use of the first year might be to spend more time breaking the subject matter down to a workable series of concepts rather than trying to read all there is on the general topic which interests you. Conceptualization will also help you find the theoretical framework that will anchor your research throughout. You need more than an interesting subject to write a good PhD, you also need well-defined concepts and variables, a method to measure these, and a framework that will hold it all together.

My dissertation, in this sense, is a good example of what not to do. My original idea, to work on health policy in Canada and the United Kingdom, became an examination of the New Right in government with health care policy as my case study – my independent variable being the ideology of the New Right in power and my dependent variable, health care system policy. Although confident that little similar work had been done, and encouraged by the comments of the academics I consulted along the way, I still faced the problem of what I was measuring and how. This is where the lack of concepts affected my research. In the first instance, I drifted towards performing a strict policy analysis/programme evaluation piece. Later I looked at policy networks and communities and other variants of the interest group school. In short, the research project lost its bearings. I still had a topic, but something as vast as health care could be studied in any number of ways. I was frequently developing new frameworks to address my subject, none of which lasted very long. This confusion also affected the ability of my supervisor to chart a course for my work. If I didn't know what I was doing, how would my supervisor?

Eventually, these issues sorted themselves out near the start of the final year, so that I can now describe my topic (as excerpted from my CV) as: 'Policy change under Conservative government: health policy under Thatcher and Mulroney'. In its present form the research aims to explore the link between New Right ideology and the making of public policy. Taking the Thatcher and Mulroney governments as examples of the New Right in government, this research considers the areas of policy convergence and divergence between them using health as a case study. This study concludes that the 1990s variants of Conservativism differed in rhetoric and in their overall impact. The Thatcher government was found to be a more effective agent of change than the Mulroney government, with institutional differences between Canada and Great Britain as the main explanatory variable.

The ability to pass the cocktail test, that is to describe the subject of your dissertation in five sentences or less without once referring to your case study (e.g., health) is proof that you've made it past simply having a subject to study. The research strategy (or methodology) used in my work is a relatively straightforward and conventional one. Although much cross-national research relies on survey data to determine the degree of difference and similarity between countries, my own study used conventional bibliographic resources supplemented by elite interviews and government documents. On this point Dunleavy and Rhodes have noted (1990, p. 5), 'Cross referencing published documentation, mass media coverage and participant interviews may not give fully authoritative accounts but they produce more insights than the prevailing reliance on memoirs, diaries and platitudinous observations by ex-ministers.' However, it proved inevitable that some use had to be made of the 'platitudinous' memoirs of ex-prime ministers in my research.

As my goal was to measure the influence of the New Right on public policy, and in particular the welfare state, much of these sources were utilized to confirm or 'falsify' my basic hypothesis, that is, that the New Right has had a remarkable effect on public policy, and particularly social policy. I believed this to be more the case in the United Kingdom under Thatcher than in Canada under Mulroney. This hypothesis did not survive my research, but it led me to investigate other possible explanations such as the prevalence of institutional considerations in determining the ability of governments to act in certain areas of public policy. The fact that my early hypothesis was 'falsified' did not invalidate my research – in fact it gave it a more interesting focus as I had to explain why a conclusion that had almost entered the conventional wisdom of political science was not sustained by my research. Once again, the importance of deciding early on what it is you are trying to measure across countries is critical.

My research project was not concerned with theory-building or challenging a major body of literature. Moreover, as I was working with a comparative set that had been neglected in the past I did not have to worry too much about the existing literature. In the course of my research I was using the work of other researchers rather than seeking to undermine it. This in itself simplified my task to a large degree, as I could take most material as written. On the other hand, this also complicated my work as I found myself hunting for secondary source material on the Canadian half of my research. This is probably the most common problem faced by those doing cross-national research. If one polity in your comparative pair is the country in which you are working and/or residing, this is a significant although manageable concern. In my case, I was able to find much material on Britain in the university's library. However, and this came as a great surprise to me, material on Canada was hard to come by and often several years out of date. Relatively basic sources of information such as the *Canadian Journal of Political Science* were not commonly held by British university libraries. If your comparative pair includes two countries removed from your place of residence or study, this problem is further compounded, especially if you select relatively small, underdeveloped or geographically removed cases. Language is also a consideration. Unless your university has a specialism in certain non-English speaking nations, the chances are that books and journals will be difficult to find. For example, although it is a major industrial power only a select few universities will stock Japanese journals. Why? Few people read Japanese and, secondly, Japan is not geopolitically located where traditional British economic and political interests lie. Finding German-language journals, on the other hand, is becoming comparatively easier. Nor should you think that because a country is influential in world affairs source material will be easy to find. While teaching an American politics course I was amazed at how little current material there was on the library shelves. The situation with journals was only marginally better.

While secondary sources can be difficult to come by, official documents such as reports or the debates of legislatures are sometimes impossible to find. Joining specialized associations or contacting other academics can be useful in this event. In my case a combination of both led me to find the largest stocks of Canadian official documents. While inter-library loans and the use of information technology have gone a long way to make previously difficult to obtain materials available, the chances are that in-depth research will require fieldwork in the country or countries which you are studying. The political culture of these countries will often determine how successful you will be in acquiring the material which you require. In my case, surprisingly, accessing British official documents proved to be a problem. The Canadian tradition of 'open government', epitomized in the federal access to information legislation, meant that documents were both freely available and provided at no charge. Access to government department libraries was unrestricted and photocopying on site was also free of charge. This permitted me to gather a large quantity of both secondary and tertiary material. Letter inquiries to provincial governments yielded more documentary material – most of which could not find a place within this thesis. This generosity also extended to representatives of many of the interest groups interviewed. Unfortunately for future research, the neo-liberal proclivities of Canada's governments may signal the end, in the name of balancing the budget, of this generosity and access.

Access to British documentation was more difficult. Beyond Command papers, parliamentary debates and legislation, which are available in HMSO shops and libraries, no official documents were made available to me by the departments I consulted. Thus, while letters to Canadian government departments were sufficient to procure documents without charge, acquiring British official documents was more costly and in some instances simply impossible because of Britain's Official Secrets Act. Before embarking on a research project, and certainly before considering fieldwork, it is important to take into account possible legislative or cultural matters which may inhibit successful completion of one's research.

Political culture was also responsible, I believe, for the striking difference in my success rate in securing interviews. More familiar with speaking to the media and knowledgeable reading legislation which in most cases guarantees the accessibility of information, Canadian government officials were quite willing to meet with a university-based researcher. This availability also extended to the non-governmental sector. In Britain, however, where Whitehall is more cautious in its approach to the outside world, access was at once more difficult to achieve and the interviews themselves rarely strayed outside of the confines of the Civil Service's veil of impartiality.

Conclusion: the comparative method

Having outlined my experience of cross-national research, it is important to set comparative research within its academic context. A good first step in putting together a comparative or cross-national research project is to look at how other researchers have gone about it. A number of books have been written about the comparative method and several more cross-national comparative studies have been published. These will prove useful in composing your project and determining the concepts you wish to study and how to proceed. The works I discuss and list below are but a small piece of a very large iceberg but should prove useful at one time or another.

As I noted above, the method of comparative politics research has a long history in political inquiry. Dogan and Pelassy trace this tradition through the works of Aristotle, Rousseau, de Tocqueville, Marx, Weber, Pareto and others (1980, p. 3). In its most traditional form, cross-national or comparative research focused primarily on the character of political systems and was largely descriptive and static. Researchers in the traditional form of comparative politics were more interested in documents such as constitutions or in comparing the activities of legislatures rather than explaining why countries differed or were similar. These studies were particularly prevalent in the United States in the late 1960s and were conducted under the auspices of the Committee on Comparative Politics which was headed by leading researchers of the period such as Lucien Pye and Sydney Verba (Dogan and Pelassy, 1980, p. 10). The underlying assumption of their work was that looking at other polities' political structures and institutions made possible a better understanding of our own. This notion has continued to animate much comparative research to this day, although the questions asked now are often much more dynamic. Years later the work sponsored by the Committee continues to inspire much comparative research.

The first task of comparative research is to determine the differences or similarities among polities, institutions or agents – once again emphasizing the fact that comparative research need not be cross-national research. Determining these differences or similarities requires conceptualization. A concept must be clearly defined and strong enough to survive its use across nations and cultures. In other words, it is essential to develop questions which travel. This can be done by using variables that measure the same concept across space, time and cultures, or by using concepts that are specific to each case and then comparing these among units in the comparative set (Rose, 1988, p. 220; Bahry, 1981, p. 231; see also Sartori, 1970).

In the case of my research, measuring the influence of the New Right on government policy required a mix of both common and country-specific concepts. The preponderance of neo-liberal ideas in the 1980s across the West made the comparison of the discourses of the British and Canadian governments possible, but part of the analysis had to be rooted in the different traditions of conservatism in both countries. Thus, my approach was to combine cross-national and single-case variables. In selecting which cases to study one must also keep in mind whether one is looking for differences or similarities. Comparative research involves generally two strategies, either a most-similar or most-different systems design (Bahry, 1981, p. 231). In short, if one chooses to compare systems considered similar, then any finding of difference invalidates the similarities between systems as the explanatory variable. My study used a most-different systems approach, where I expected the differences between Canada's federal system and Britain's unitary system to be a significant explanatory variable. Although this was not entirely confirmed by my findings, differences in political system did prove to have an impact on the outcome of New Right policies. Again, it may be useful to consider how others have undertaken comparative research – if only to gain appreciation for the techniques which may or may not work with the project you have in mind.

I should like to make a closing comment on quantitative research. Because of the problems inherent in developing variables and concepts that travel, many involved in comparative or cross-national research have turned to quantitative methods to address their subjects. Beyond reliance on international survey data, much comparative research will utilize statistics from national governments. It may prove valuable to consider if and how such material can be utilized in your research. Although much of this data is sometimes incompatible, it may be possible to develop a trend which is comparable across institutions, nations or agents. In my research, government data concerning the amount of money spent on health services was a useful addition to my argument, although my proof, so to speak, is found mostly in other sources such as legislative debates. While the Canadian and British governments calculate health spending in different ways, the identification of a comparable national trend was made relatively easily. Data from international bodies such as the United Nations or the OECD may prove similarly useful. In constructing a comparative research project, quantitative sources should be investigated and, where possible, the research questions should consider these sources.

Comparative research is one of the most natural ways of conducting political inquiry, for it offers opportunities to gain a better understanding not only of another polity but also of our own. However, while cross-national research transcends culture and nation-bound research, the conceptual difficulties inherent in the method add significantly to the problems with this approach. Perhaps this explains why much cross-national research is quantitative rather than qualitative. In the end, it is my belief that in an academic environment where postgraduates are increasingly called upon to develop broad areas of expertise, as well as develop publishable research, comparative research – although at times more complex than single-case studies – better equips us than single-case analysis.

14

On the Record: An Introduction to Interviewing

GAIL STEDWARD

'Interviewing is not easy' (Denzin, 1970, p. 186), but it is challenging, informative, the preferred empirical tool of political scientists, and it can actually be fun. I have used interviews extensively in several research projects spanning a broad range of topics. In my PhD project interviews have been a valuable method of gathering data. In particular, the interview is a great vehicle for bringing a research topic to life. It is also an excellent method of obtaining data about contemporary subjects which have not been extensively studied and for which there is little literature. My PhD research examines the influence of anti-racism on British national public policy in the areas of racist violence and harassment, asylum and immigration. In the course of my research I have conducted interviews with anti-racist activists, office-bearers and officers of relevant interest groups, civil servants in London and Brussels, Members of Parliament and Members of the European Parliament.

Interviewing is a vast topic, so at the outset I should clarify the intention of this chapter. The primary focus is pragmatic – that is, on doing depth and semi-structured interviews, identifying good practice and problems which you may encounter and I have experienced. Each of the component parts of the interview process is discussed: identifying interviewees and securing interviews; determining interview content; conducting the interview; and recording and writing up the data generated. Aside from a brief discussion on why one might choose interviewing as a method, and contrasting theoretical accounts of interviewing with practical applications, the chapter does not dwell on the theory of interviewing. Finally, it should be noted that the discussion of interviewing in this chapter is based on one-to-one rather than group interviews.

Why choose the interview as a method?

Political scientists appear to have a rather limited repertoire of research methods, compared, for example, to the range of methods employed in sociological research or in social research more generally. Without doubt the favoured method in political science is the interview. Custom and practice are not good reasons for adopting a method. Rather you should consider the following points.

First, is an interview the 'best' or only method available to gather the information required? Interviews can be very time-consuming and expensive. Aside from the time actually spent interviewing and travelling to the interview, you need to account for preparation, obtaining and setting up interviews, writing up, and content analysis. Remember too that interviews should wherever possible be used in conjunction with other methods, for example the examination of primary archive material or participant observation.

Second, given the nature of this research method, you should also give some consideration as to whether it is right for you. Techniques can be learned and skills developed, but it is an unalterable fact that some people will never make good interviewers because they are uncomfortable with the process. Whether this is the result of shyness or a dislike of asking questions of complete strangers is immaterial. Just as I know that I lack the qualities necessary to become a fighter pilot, some may have misgivings about interviewing. Read on and then decide!

Having considered these preliminary questions, it's worth reviewing, in a theoretical sense, what an interview involves. 'Elite' interviews, as they are often called in political science, generally take the form of an unstructured or semi-structured conversation between interviewer and interviewee. The 'elite' interview is, as the name suggests, often (but not exclusively) conducted with a person of some status or influence within an organization. The interviewee responds to the interviewer's inquiries, and unlike a tightly structured interview of the sort used in consumer research, the interviewee is encouraged to introduce her/his own ideas, not just in response to questions but in suggesting areas of enquiry to the researcher. It would be simplistic to categorize interviews into merely structured or unstructured typologies. Rather, there is a continuum from which researchers select lines of enquiry, seeking open or closed responses to a greater or lesser degree. At one end of the continuum lies the free interview, where the interviewer allows the respondent to lead the discussion (within parameters set by the researcher in the sense that s/he is interested in a particular topic area). At the other end is the tightly structured interview, dominated by the questionnaire, from which the interviewer must not deviate. Where the elite interview lies on this continuum depends on a number of factors, such as the time available for the interview, or the level of rapport between interviewer and interviewee; it is not static. As ever, practice will deviate from the theoretical accounts of textbooks.

Identifying interviewees and securing interviews

Having decided that interviews will yield valuable data for your research, the next question is: 'With whom?' There are a number of ways to identify potential interviewees. Inevitably sources are dependent on your subject area. For example, I have used reference sources such as the *Civil Service Yearbook*, the *European Union*

Institutions Yearbook, Dods Parliamentary Companion, Annual Reports and other publications from groups with an interest in the field, and the press. The point is to gather as much information as possible to enable you to target appropriate individuals to interview. Looking at an organization's Annual Report, for instance, will ensure that you don't approach the General Secretary when the European Policy Officer will be more helpful. Another example will illustrate the importance of cross-referencing sources: having identified the MPs who sat on the House of Commons Home Affairs Committee's investigation of racist attacks in 1993/4 (Committee members are listed in the report), I checked the names against general reference sources to identify long-serving and new members as well as group literature, supporters lists and press to determine individuals with a long-standing or special interest in the subject. Not only does this process help to identify key interviewees, it also helps to shape the interview questions. Once you get started, you can take advantage of existing networks in your field and 'snowball' – that is, pick up further contacts from those you have already made. You should also use your supervisor and any other personal contacts you may have in the area. An obvious, but alarmingly under-utilized resource, is to be found in the persons of subject and reference librarians, who often know exactly where you should look to find a particular piece of information.

Having targeted your interviewees, the next step is to gain access. The importance of your first contact with a potential interviewee cannot be over-emphasized. You do not want to lose an interview because of a shoddy or ill-thought-out letter or mumbled telephone call. A good letter at this stage can not only secure an interview, but can save valuable time when you meet by keeping introductions to a minimum. I do not recommend identifying yourself as a student at this stage. This is not to say that you should lie about your status, but rather that you will have more success if you describe yourself as a researcher, although not everyone would agree (see Dexter, 1970). At the actual interview you should be perfectly frank. The letter that you send to a potential interviewee should not be too long but should always contain certain information (see Appendix A). Correspond on departmental headed-notepaper so the recipient of your request knows you have an institutional affiliation. It's a good idea to draw attention to how you can be contacted; for example, if you work from home your home telephone number is a more useful contact point than the department (but see discussion of security, pp.157–8 below). Briefly outline the nature of your research and, importantly, emphasize that element of your project which fits with the interview you are seeking; for example, in my letter to members of the Home Affairs Committee: 'I am undertaking a case study of the Home Affairs Committee Inquiry of racial attacks as part of an ESRC- funded research project . . .' rather than the more general: 'My research examines anti-racist policy influence . . .' I always tell interviewees how long the interview will take (usually 45–60 minutes) and the main areas of discussion. I also think that it's worth pointing out to interviewees some benefit of their participation (if you can't think of one, then ask yourself why anyone would agree to be interviewed by you!). It is telling that this part of the process is called *negotiating* access. I follow up such a letter with a phone call seeking an appointment.

The way you handle the phone call is as important as the letter. The best advice I can give is based on my own experience, and it is very simple; be prepared, polite and persistent. Clarity of purpose and expression are important. You may be asked to give more details about the research. You may well encounter a Personal Assistant whose primary purpose appears to be to deflect people like you. Gatekeeping is one of the roles of a PA, and you have to seek admission. This is just part of the interview process. Bear in mind that the person you want to interview might actually answer the telephone herself or that you might be put straight through. If you are telephoning overseas, in my case to European Union institutions, and you do not speak the language, do take the trouble to learn a few appropriate phrases and responses. Occasionally it may be appropriate to telephone a potential interviewee rather than send an introductory letter ('cold calling'). I have done this successfully when I have obtained a personal recommendation from a colleague or friend of the interviewee, which can then be used as an opening gambit, or when I have already met the person I wish to interview.

Determining interview content

By the time you secure an interview, you will, of course, have decided on the general if not the specific content of the interview. Considerations prior to the interview and during it will determine how structured it will be. Time, costs and personality, of the interviewer and interviewee, are important determinants. Economic considerations figure in the determination of methods not just in commercial research, but in the design of any piece of research, and thought must be given to the relative costs of approaches (see Why choose the interview as a method?, above). The cost of analysing large quantities of qualitative data, for example, can be prohibitive. More likely, practical or economic factors will intervene from the point of view of the interviewee, who may be willing to give an hour of her time for a semi-structured interview but will be unwilling to donate an afternoon for a free interview.

Compromises may have to be made, between an ideal of an information-gathering exercise and the reality of what can practically be achieved. My solution has been to draw up an interview schedule which covers the areas I know I want to have information on, but which also gives interviewees opportunities to contribute their perspective (see the example of an interview schedule in Appendix B). By this I mean they do not simply respond to my prompting, but are given the opportunity to introduce their own concerns. I have done this by placing 'open' or non-directive questions throughout the schedule as well as ending the interview with the traditional 'Is there anything I have missed which you think is important?' type of question. By scattering such questions throughout the interview I have greatly increased my chances of obtaining a higher yield of original information than by the usual 'bombshell at the end' approach. Rather, signals are sent to the interviewee throughout the interview that I know that she has superior knowledge and that I'm open to suggestion. It's almost an inversion of the traditional power dynamic between interviewer and interviewee. More practically, it also ensures that the interviewee is not too tired and that you do not run out of time before you elicit her views without prompting from your agenda.

Even if you have never interviewed before, you have almost certainly been interviewed yourself, whether for a job or in a consumer survey – draw on that experience. The golden rule is to make the most of the time you have allotted. Think carefully about the type of questions you include. The easiest way to do this is to ask yourself the following:

What sort of information will this question provide?
The individual question or the entire interview may be exploratory, in which case you may have no idea what will be thrown up. Generally, though, from background reading you will have some idea of what you're aiming at. Does the question you've constructed help or hinder you? Is it clear or ambiguous?

Can I get this information elsewhere?
If yes, then why include it in the interview? (Perhaps to co-ordinate the information you have found elsewhere.)

Do I really need this information?
If no, then take the questions eliciting it out.

The points raised above are illustrative of the sort of economy you have to apply simply because you have to prioritize the collection of data within a limited time frame.

In addition to reflecting on these questions, the benefits of piloting (i.e., testing) an interview schedule are manifold and cannot be exaggerated. When piloting, you're looking out for ambiguities in your questions (signalled not just by requests for clarification or rephrasing by your interviewee, but also by an off-beat response), a logical flow between the questions you ask (aim for a smooth path which does not disorientate your interviewee) and checking the timing of your interview schedule. You can pilot a schedule on friends or colleagues and again in the field. At its best, this means a proper pilot and review process. In practice, you'll probably fine tune in response to your experience. A short cut to introductions, which can eat into your valuable interview time, is to send a confirmation letter to your interviewee, in which you can include a short summary of your project. Obviously it depends on individuals, but in my experience interviewees are rarely fascinated by the finer points of the research to the extent that they want to receive much in the way of background information prior to the meeting. They are usually interested in where you're from, who's funding you and the very briefest of details about the project. As noted above, I always cover this in the first instance and take a copy along to the interview. When I actually meet interviewees, and particularly if there is a good rapport, I have been asked for more details at that stage. You do have to strike a balance between dealing with the interviewee's queries and getting a good interview completed. You can often cut out the need for background questions by reading in advance relevant primary and secondary sources such as annual reports or *Who's Who*. In interviewing, I do find that there is a tension between meeting my research objectives and completing an interview in a relatively short time frame, and adhering to the conventions of 'normal' social interaction. I shall expand on this point below.

Doing interviews – practice, problems and solutions

A point closely allied with timing is the timetabling of your interviews. It's worth remembering that an interview secured with one person in an organization can open doors to other contacts. Make the most of your opportunities; don't timetable your interviews so tightly that you haven't got time to be introduced to someone who could turn out to be a valuable contact. When interviewing European Union officials in Brussels, for instance, I found myself being propelled along corridors to meet 'X who's working on a related topic' or 'Y who's interested in this area'. In this way I secured what turned out to be the most interesting and useful interview of my Brussels fieldwork. I've had this experience before, but for any readers who are thinking of interviewing European Union officials, my advice is that they are particularly likely to help you in this way. You can also initiate this kind of contact yourself, particularly if you feel an interview has gone well. 'I'd very much like to speak to Z, do you think that would be possible?' can often lead you to a personal introduction. Similarly, I've been given the opportunity to use organization and personal archives, when interviewees have volunteered these resources to me. Of course you can't always take up these offers on the spot, and it is possible to schedule another appointment, but the moment can pass and I do think that some opportunities present themselves rarely and should be grabbed. By way of illustration, in my asylum and immigration case study, one MP interviewee arranged for me to examine his files that afternoon in his constituency office. Another example, taken from my racist violence and harassment case study, illustrates what can happen if you don't strike while the iron is hot. The MP I interviewed offered to take me up to his office to get copies of relevant documents from his files. As I had another appointment to keep (NB: MPs are often running late), he agreed to post the papers to me. Needless to say he forgot and I spent the next three weeks chasing him up. Happily, this resulted in my gaining access to his entire file for a morning. This example has a happy ending – but you can see how easy it is to let chances slip by. It also says a lot about the necessity of persistence.

Timetabling is not just about efficient use of your time, it's also about being effective. Good interviewing is hard work. For this reason, as well as those above, I counsel against packing your interviews too tightly. While there are occasions when you have to do this, in my case, for example, in Brussels, I try to avoid doing too many in a block. As a rough guide, and obviously there are no hard-and-fast rules, as each interview is different, I'd recommend no more than four in a day. This also takes into consideration the writing-up process, which I discuss below. I have found that building in time for review of an interview, and reflection on the process, pays off in terms of increasing and enriching the yield of data from an interview and in developing skills. I also find it helpful to trade tips and experiences with other researchers. It's a sad fact that there is little published discussion of reflexivity in the research process (see Hoggett *et al.*, 1994), something which this volume seeks to redress. Likewise, I am unaware of published accounts of the important practicalities of coming face to face with your interviewee.

Security and personal safety

I've had some rather interesting experiences, when it actually came to meeting my interviewees, which are salutary. Two examples of mistaken identity give me the chance to talk about other issues in interviewing. The first took place in a tube station in South London, where I had arranged to meet an activist from an anti-racist organization. For reasons of security we had agreed to meet at the station and then retire to a local cafe to conduct the interview. Needless to say, I approached the wrong man in the tube station and by grace and good timing was saved from an accusation of soliciting, or marching off with a complete stranger, or, in a less paranoid vein, simply behaving inappropriately. Security was always an issue in my research because of the subject matter. The reason that I could not interview this individual at his organization's office is because it was at a secret location due to arson attacks and death threats from extreme right-wing/fascist groups. This example is extreme but illustrative. Security and personal safety are issues for any researcher doing interviews on her own, and it is not an exclusively gendered issue. However, a woman interviewing is more likely to encounter sexual harassment than a man. In many research projects, you may think about conducting interviews with strangers in their homes, for example, or you will frequently be in unfamiliar locations, sometimes at night. You should give consideration to issues of personal security, whether that means doing what many researchers now do and pairing up with another researcher (you reciprocate on their interviews), carrying a personal alarm and mobile phone or phoning back to someone at an agreed time. Rather less dramatically, but in its own way deeply disturbing, was an occasion when I had arranged an interview with a northern Labour MP in the House of Commons. At the House, the procedure is that you present yourself at the visitors' desk in the Members' Lobby. On every other occasion that I had visited, the system had been foolproof. Very many of those who are meeting have never clapped eyes on each other before, so the system is geared for this; the man at the desk nods at you and winks at your MP, and in this archaic and eccentric manner you are united. Except that on this occasion I was paired with someone who turned out to be a southern Conservative MP who thought that I was a reporter from the *Sun*. In this instance it very quickly became clear that neither of us was who the other thought, but it's an example of how important it is to check identities before heading off to Annie's Bar, or wherever.

Bars, of course, should generally be avoided, although in the case of the House of Commons business is often transacted therein. It's an obvious point, but no less important for that, to caution against interviews conducted under the influence of alcohol. Similarly, interviewees may suggest that you interview them over lunch. This sounds like a great idea until you are faced with the prospect of trying to take notes and eat crispy noodles at the same time, or, worse still, have to transcribe a tape recording of munching and crunching among those valuable sound bites. Such situations have distractions inbuilt which make your task more difficult. Food and drink are not the only culprits. Many interviewees repeatedly veer off the subject that you're there to ask them about. In a way a successful interview is like a sheep-dog trial. It's your task to keep the interviewee on course without worrying him too much or snapping at his heels. There are various ways in which you can draw an interview back if you feel the interviewee is straying. Phrases such as, 'I'm very interested in what you said about such and such . . . could you tell me a bit more about that?' or, 'You made a very interesting point about X . . . could we go back to that?' are very useful. The trick, of course, is to aim for a balance between covering the points you have in mind and, as noted above, taking advantage of the interviewee's knowledge on a subject to introduce avenues you hadn't thought of.

Building rapport

At the beginning of an interview it's a good idea to set out the path you intend to follow. Having already apprised the interviewee of my general intent and main areas of discussion (set out in the letter contact), I quickly remind her of these and add that I'll leave time at the end for unprompted contributions. This assures the interviewee that you're not just cutting up what they say into neat justifications of your preset ideas. In practice, as noted above, I tend to ask open and also unscheduled questions throughout the interview. While this more discursive approach is a feature of elite interviewing, it has to be said that it becomes easier with experience, I do not recommend too unstructured an approach when you're starting out (for discussion of the unstructured interview as a conversation, see Burgess, 1982). Taking a structured approach makes it easier for the interviewee to follow and for you to control. If this sounds authoritarian, I say it only to remind you that an interview is a special type of conversation with a precise objective. If, like me, you enjoy the process of meeting new people and conversing with them, it can be very easy to lose sight of your objective. There is a paradox inherent in becoming experienced in interviewing; the more skilled you become, the more it seems like a 'normal' conversation. It's important to remember that it never actually is.

I have found feminist critiques (Oakley, 1981; Finch, 1984) of the theory of interviewing presented in standard textbooks to be very accurate in practice. Oakley, in her discussion of women interviewing women, raises the fundamental issue of how unworkable much of the received wisdom on interviewing techniques is. Note my point above about an interview being a special kind of conversation, special, but a conversation nevertheless. This means that certain social norms have to be complied with or else the whole enterprise runs into the ground. As Oakley points out, in the standard accounts the interviewee is presented as the passive participant in the encounter whose role is limited to responding to questions from the interviewer. In practice this simply is not the case, interviewees do ask questions, and, as Oakley notes, you cannot ignore them. For instance, I've often been asked by politicians if I have any political ambitions. My opinions on particular strategies have been solicited by activists in campaigning organizations. I've also been asked for more general information about myself – how I came to be pursuing this project, what I did before, what I think about living in England (I'm Scottish) – that is a part of everyday social encounters. I have indeed found Oakley's observations to be particularly true when interviewing women, or when sharing some other characteristic with an interviewee. As noted by Finch (1984, p. 167), women interviewing other women can often effectively short cut the process of building 'rapport' with interviewees, a process deemed essential for effective interviewing. Class, nationality, ethnicity or other characteristics shared with an interviewee can perform the same function. In our field personal politics can be a variable. Finch and Oakley note that such a situation of empathy and trust can become exploitative if one does not guard against it. This is particularly the case when researching sensitive subjects, and indeed *interviewers* may have to consider protecting themselves as well as interviewees (Brannen, 1988). In my PhD research, for instance, I found descriptions of cases of racist violence and harassment very disturbing. My solution to this relates back to the point I made above on securing interviews. Essentially, I conceive of the interview process as an imperfect exchange process. Thus my attempt to think about what an interviewee can get out of the interview is not just a carrot to tempt her into giving me an interview, it is actually a genuine offer. Obviously I am aware that I will be seeking more than I can give, but I think that the intention of reciprocity is important. This issue is thrown into sharp relief when interviewing members of an underprivileged or discriminated against group, and it has been an issue which has been very important in my PhD research on anti-racism. My interviewing practice, in particular receptivity to interviewees, and has been informed by consideration of such matters. In practical terms, this has involved answering queries, engaging in discussion of broader issues with interviewees, and providing information and contacts for interviewees.

In some contrast to the implied power relation in interviewing discussed above, is my experience as a student researcher. Having worked as a researcher in central and local government before returning to university to do a PhD, the experience of researching as a student again was something of a culture shock. It was not the novelty so much as the feeling of *déjà vu* (I already had experience of postgraduate research, having completed an MPhil) and the knowledge of what I now lacked. I was accustomed, for example, to working in an equal-status research environment; now I was working alone at the bottom of a hierarchy. I was used to a decent salary and full organizational and economic support for my work; now I was living on a grant with limited expenses and little administrative back up. As noted above, these sorts of factors impinge on the type and quality of research that is produced.

In terms of the interview process, there is no doubt in my mind that the traditional view of the power dynamic in an interview, with the interviewer being the dominant actor, is called into question when a student conducts an 'elite' interview. This is a result of students typically being accorded low social status because of their perceived characteristics of youth and inexperience. Dexter acknowledges as much when he suggests that students capitalize on their non-threatening low status to obtain interviews (Dexter, 1970, p. 32). As noted above, I am more inclined to think that potential interviewees will be put off by the perception that it will not be a particularly useful exercise for them. In my experience reciprocity oils the wheels more than charming ignorance. I raise this issue in the spirit of the critiques above; to demonstrate the contrast between theoretical accounts of interviewing and real-life experience. Sexism, racism, homophobia, classism or general patronizing are spanners that can be chucked into the smooth running of your interview machinery at any time. The accounts of methodology presented in textbooks are 'sanitised versions of a much messier reality' (Hoggett *et al.*, 1994, p. 69); this is nowhere more true than in the theoretical descriptions of interviewing. If this sounds too depressing, I should say equally that very rarely do texts ever say how enjoyable interviewing can be!

Recording interview data

Interview data should be recorded during the interview, or if for some reason this is not possible, immediately after. In addition to recording the content of the interview, I find it useful to take a note of other contextual information, for example where the interview took place and my impressions of the interviewee. This is useful for jogging your memory when you come back to the written-up interview as a source document, particularly if you have carried out a large number of interviews. As for the full record of the interview, anyone who has put off writing up notes or transcription of tapes will tell you how important it is to do this as soon after the interview as possible. This is another factor which may influence the timetabling of interviews. Whether you've taped the interview or taken notes, there are usually some observations or expansions that you will want to jot down. Wherever possible after an interview, I like to retire to a quiet spot, preferably one that serves tea or coffee, to do this.

Whether you choose to tape or rely on note-taking is influenced by specific and general factors, such as personal preference (yours and that of the interviewee), location of the interview, and your assessment of the most appropriate method for a particular interview. Each has advantages and disadvantages, and both methods can of course be combined. Having had a particularly disastrous experience of using a tape recorder which mysteriously played back hiss and crackle (a mobile phone was implicated), and having no notes, I now do both. A tape recorder has the advantage of recording far more detail than you can ever hope to write down during an interview. While tone of voice and emphasis can be recorded in notes (you quickly develop your own shorthand) with a tape recording these nuances are integral. Perhaps the greatest asset in taping your interviews lies in your ability to use these real-life experiences of interviewing to review your performance and develop your skills. It is very instructive to read a standard textbook account of interviewing and then to listen to yourself in practice.

Two phrases occur frequently in interviews. From the interviewer, 'Can I quote you on this?'; and from the interviewee, 'This is off the record.' The first is relatively easy to deal with and usually elicits a straightforward response. Some interviewees actually fashion sound bites for you (you can tell I've been spending a lot of time with MPs). Sometimes they request to see any quotes in context if you intend to publish. Off-the-record comments are almost inevitably interesting, and it can be an irritating prospect that you haven't got such a free rein with this information. How you record 'off the record' depends very much on the nature of the information and the disposition of the interviewee. Your options are to switch off the tape recorder, put down your pen or draw attention to the fact that you're noting that this information is off the record and keep writing. Given what I've said about such information usually being of interest, it's worth following up what category of 'off the record' it falls into. The interviewee may be happy with a non-attributable quote, for example, or it may be strictly background information for you only. Don't despair if it's the latter, you've learned something you didn't know before, and you may find, as I have, that you pick up corroborative information from another source.

Conclusion

It's been my aim in this chapter to provide an introduction to interviewing based on my experience for those who are inexperienced in the process. As I said at the beginning, I don't think that good interviewing is easy, but I do think it's an immensely satisfying part of the qualitative research process – not least because it gets you away from books to talk to real people about something which interests you both.

As indicated above, I do think that too many of the textual representations of interviewing provide an inaccurate picture of what the process actually entails. This is a curious paradox, given that interview data is often used to lend greater 'authenticity' to a piece of research. Yet, if the dominant paradigms of interviewing were followed in practice, the real-life interview would yield very little, indeed the process would probably collapse. Thus in practice something else is happening – we are all breaking the rules and usually keeping quiet about it. Until we tell 'our truth' about interviewing, honestly talking to each other about what we really do, new researchers will continue to be confronted with the alarming disjunction between interviewing theory and practice. This is particularly the case for the isolated, under-resourced PhD student. Some researchers (e.g., Brannen, 1988; Finch, 1984; Hoggett *et al.*, 1994; Oakley, 1981) are willing to tell it like it is and open their actual experience of the method to question and discussion. This demystification of the process is to be applauded and is the corollary of the actions we are engaged in as social scientists; the attempt to investigate, explain, understand and change.

Appendix A

MP
House of Commons
London SW1A 0AA

21 March 1995

Dear

HOME AFFAIRS COMMITTEE: RACIAL ATTACKS AND HARASSMENT

I am undertaking a case study of the above inquiry as part of an ESRC-funded research project on the role of anti-racist groups in the policy process. I am writing to you to request a short interview based on your experience as a member of the Select Committee.

The interview will take approximately 45–60 minutes. The main areas of discussion will cover your assessment of the role of anti-racist groups in this issue; your impressions of this 'lobby', including your evaluation of the evidence put to the Committee; your support for the creation of a separate offence of racially motivated violence; and assistance with amendment drafting on the Criminal Justice and Public Order Bill. As the focus of group attention, your views on the content and nature of lobbying are extremely important. Aside from producing an academic study, this research will produce information of value to MPs and help groups to tailor their submissions more effectively.

I hope that you will wish to participate in this research. I will telephone you in the next few days to arrange a convenient time for interview. In the meantime, should you require any further information about the research, please do not hesitate to contact me.

Yours sincerely

Gail Stedward

Appendix B

Following from the letter contained in Appendix A, here is a section of an interview schedule I have used (details have been omitted to avoid identifying the interviewee):

Personal/background

1. I know that you have a stated interest in this area, from both the legal and 'race relations' viewpoint, and that you are a member of [relevant organization]. Do you have contact with any other interested groups?

Home Affairs Committee

1. Why did the Home Affairs Committee take up this issue?
    (check for)

    *   group pressure

    *   perception of problem (media, constituency)

    *   particular members of Committee pushing issue

2. The 1994 investigation has much wider scope than previous inquiries (e.g., witnesses called). Was this a deliberate policy to open up debate?

    *   an attempt to bring in groups which the Home Office might not consult?

    *   a view shared by whole Committee?

3. How did the Committee decide which groups to invite as witnesses?

    *   already on Home Affairs Committee circulation list

    *   nominated by Committee members

    *   suggested by Committee Clerk

    *   policy community

    [possibility of interviewing Clerk? Name and how to contact?]

4. Do you have a perception of an anti-racist lobby?

    *   disparate groups

    *   coalition

    *   aims and tactics

    *   effective

5. Which evidence did you find most useful/impressive/convincing?

   - why

   - and converse?

   - assessment of anti-racist contribution

6. I know that you supported the creation of a new offence of racially motivated violence. Was this a view you already held, or were you influenced by the evidence presented to the Committee?

   - to what extent was the Committee divide on the issue party political?

   - how damaging to the case for a new offence was the Committee's lack of consensus?

   - which groups assisted with amendment drafting to the Criminal Justice and Public Order Bill?

   - Home Affairs Committee attempt to amend a Government Bill, is this an unusual strategy?

15

Using Archives in Political Research

RHIANNON VICKERS

This chapter explores several themes connected to using archives in political research. In the first section I shall discuss how I came to choose my thesis topic, which was in itself for me part of the learning process, and the implications that this had for my research. In the second I shall look at some of the pitfalls, and benefits, of teaching while researching and writing a PhD, and of gaining a lectureship and moving to a new institution. Thirdly, I shall turn to the research process itself, looking at some of the archive centres that I visited, how I set about using archives, and addressing some of the methodological questions that this raises. Finally, I shall comment on one of the problems I found in the early stages of my thesis, namely presenting my work and attempting to engage other academics in a debate about my research.

Choice of thesis topic

The choice of my thesis topic arose in a roundabout way. I was unexpectedly given the opportunity of beginning a PhD when I obtained a job as a teaching assistant on a first-year research methods course. Consequently, I had a fortnight to prepare a detailed research proposal. I had always been interested in the Cold War and felt that the end of the Cold War might be an area where I could find a number of issues to research. In the course of discussions with staff the international trade union movement was mentioned and how various changes had taken place within it during the past few years. This fired my imagination, although I had little background knowledge of trade unions or the international union movement. I did some preliminary reading, and decided I would like to investigate the impact of the end of the Cold War on international trade unionism.

When it came to considering how I could sensibly write a PhD on such a large topic, I found that I would face serious problems of gaining access to up-to-date information, given the limited time and resources available to doctoral students. This was rather disheartening. However, my supervisor suggested that I look at the beginning of the Cold War and the international trade union movement, as the archives of the Trades Union Congress (TUC) were conveniently held at the Modern Records Centre at Warwick.

At first I was rather reluctant, but I started to read round the subject and again developed an interest. The topic seemed more manageable, as I could get access to relevant archives. While going back in time meant that my research would not have the immediacy that I would have liked, it also meant that events would not be changing as I studied them.

Thus I began investigating the origins of the Cold War and the international trade union movement, primarily the role of Britain in the setting up of the new trade union international, the World Federation of Trade Unions (WFTU), after the Second World War. The split of the WFTU into communist and anti-communist camps in 1947 seemed to be of particular interest. However, the more I researched the topic, the more it seemed that the focus of my topic should in fact be the Marshall Plan. It became impossible for me to understand the reasons for the split of the WFTU and the failure to create world trade union solidarity between East and West without understanding the impact that the Marshall Plan had on the politics of trade unions at this time. What seemed to be of special interest was the way the trade union leadership in Britain co-operated with the Labour government in a policy which they acknowledged could deepen divisions within trade unions in Britain and internationally between communists and non-communists. In this way my focus shifted from the creation and divisions of the trade union internationals at this time, to the effect that the Marshall Plan had on the politics of British trade unions, and the role that the unions played in the Marshall Plan apparatus. The title for my thesis became 'Manipulating Hegemony: British Trade Unions and the Marshall Plan'.

Implications of my choice of thesis topic

My choice of topic had two main implications. Firstly, it determined what sort of primary research I could do. As the topic was historical in nature, it meant that the main source of information that I would be using was documentary evidence. Using archives and studying historical documents was not something I had done before, my previous research experience having been based on studying aggregate and survey data. This was a little daunting, and I was not sure how I would respond to researching an area which to me at the time seemed vague and 'non-scientific'. However, my supervisor's confidence in this type of research convinced me that it could not be as awful as I was anticipating. The other research method I intended to use at the time was semi-structured interviews. Again, this was not something I had experience of, but the more I spoke to other academics about my work, and the more I took a risk in approaching people to interview, the easier it became. The people I interviewed included academics from various fields with expertise relevant to my topic, researchers who had worked for the international trade union movement, and trade unionists who were either active in the early postwar period or had considerable knowledge of it. Obviously the main problem I encountered with this research method was that most of the people who would be useful to interview were either deceased or very difficult to track down. Some had an autobiography or biography, which proved useful for gaining information on their personality or viewpoints. Some people I managed to contact after being put in touch with them by a third party. Often it was the case that I would unexpectedly meet someone at a conference or a meeting, or at an archive centre, who turned out to be interesting to speak to for my research, and so I had no time to prepare a formal interview. While this presented obvious problems, I found that such unstructured interviews were very helpful, not only for finding out about other people's experiences or opinions, but also for clarifying my own ideas.

The second implication of my choice of topic was that I found I no longer quite seemed to 'fit' into a politics department. I believe this to be partly due to the reaction I received from some other academics. A number of people felt my topic was not suitable for a politics student, being 'historical' and hence of no practical value, and moreover it was about trade unions. I was also told by several people that I would never get a job on the basis of my research.

On this first point, my research has convinced me that the study of politics should not be confined to the current decade. One of the interesting aspects of my research is the way that it has changed my understanding of current issues, and the way that parallels can be drawn with recent events. For instance, the extent to which the trade union movement in Britain should co-operate with a Labour government is a pertinent question today. Also, following the end of the Cold War, a Marshall Plan for Eastern Europe was widely discussed, which in turn opened up questions about the postwar period. Moreover, the fiftieth anniversary of the Marshall Plan in 1997 was quite timely in terms of generating interest in the topic more generally.

Certainly I have found that researchers who study similar topics to myself tend to be in economic history, contemporary history or industrial relations departments. Nevertheless, I feel I have benefited from having contact with people outside my own department, and in many ways this is a strength rather than a weakness. It does mean that it can be difficult to know where to be placed within the discipline of politics, but I have become comfortable with a transdisciplinary approach to my work, so that this is no longer a major cause for concern.

Teaching while researching a thesis

As indicated above, I funded my thesis by working as a teaching assistant on a research methods course. This meant that during the first term of my PhD I did not complete a great deal of research. I found the preparation for the teaching took up a great deal of my time: if I had not prepared properly for a seminar this resulted in immediate embarrassment in front of students, whereas if I had not done enough work on my thesis then all I had to do, apart from dealing with the guilt, was try and avoid seeing my supervisor. This tension, between getting on with my own research and doing the teaching, was something that I found continued throughout the PhD.

Another factor which slowed down my research was that because I was teaching research methods I was offered a number of opportunities to take part in courses myself. While this mainly consisted of one-day computing sessions, I did attend the Essex Summer School in Data Analysis at the end of my first year. This took four weeks out of my research time in the summer holidays, and while it was a valuable experience in many ways, it did mean that I lost a large chunk of clear research time.

I also lost time on my research at the end of my second year. This was because I gained a lectureship in research methods, and so found that just as I was getting used to teaching at one institution, I had to uproot. Phillips and Pugh, in *How to Get a PhD*, reflect the view held by many people I spoke to at the time, that:

> *Taking a new job before finishing is a way of not getting a PhD. At the very least it will put off completion for several years . . . until the intellectual learning curve of the new job allows it – or else you join the ranks of those the Americans call the 'ABDs': the 'all-but-dissertation' brigade.* (1994, p. 44)

While I can see their point, to have refused a lectureship would have been foolish. All in all, I would rather be working under pressure than worrying that I might finish the thesis only to end up unemployed.

Starting a new job

Gaining the lectureship had a big impact on my work. Moving to a new institution, setting up new courses and having more responsibility was stressful. I kept my original supervisor, which I found to be less of a problem than I'd anticipated. While it was of course easier than ever to avoid speaking to him, if I did need to contact him there was always e-mail. On the positive side, being a lecturer rather than a postgraduate meant that other academics did treat me more seriously; I had greater access to research funding; and I was given new opportunities such as being invited to join committees, and convene panels for conferences. This all helped to give me more self-confidence, and the motivation to build up links with academics in other departments and institutions.

The major problem I have found combining teaching and research was that to make any progress with the thesis I needed several clear days to immerse myself in it: spending a few hours on it here and there did not seem to be productive. I found this aspect incredibly frustrating, as each time I had been away from the thesis for a few days it took a couple of painful hours to get back into the right frame of mind for actually tackling it. While Leeds was understanding in not expecting a large list of publications from me, the feeling that I should be pushing myself to publish was an added pressure, as was my desire to give conference papers on my theme. These needs, to teach, to get on with the thesis, to publish and to give papers, meant that I was permanently performing a balancing act with my work.

Doing research

I spent the first two terms of my PhD research reading secondary sources. This was necessary to give me a 'feel' for my topic, as I had hardly any background knowledge about trade unions, the international trade union movement, the early postwar period or the Marshall Plan. Spending time in this way also helped to integrate me back into the academic world, as it had been over a year since I had seriously tried to understand and analyse other people's work.

In the course of the first year I wrote three descriptive pieces for my supervisor before I produced a serious attempt to delineate my precise focus. This was largely because of teaching commitments and because my topic had shifted so much in focus, but also partly because I lacked the confidence to commit myself to explaining what my thesis was about, and it took a while for me to have substantive ideas about how to interpret my research. By the summer of the first year I had produced a literature review that I was fairly happy with in which I set out my main theme and how this differed from other people's work. This literature review actually proved an invaluable means for reminding me of the detail of my topic every time I was away from the research in my second year.

Primary research

My primary research did not begin until about ten months into the PhD. This was because my focus had shifted so much that I did not feel prepared to work through archival holdings until I had a clear idea of what I was doing. Also, I felt somewhat daunted about the whole thing, and the idea of spending hours on end in an archive centre did not greatly appeal. I did not conduct many interviews until the third year of my research, as up until that point I did not feel terribly confident about them and was not persistent enough in establishing contacts. Once I started to interview properly, I did find the semi- and unstructured interviews to be a valuable source of information. In this next section I shall focus on archival work, as this was my main source of primary data.

Archival work

Most of the archival work I carried out was on the TUC archive at the Modern Records Centre at the University of Warwick. Initially, I was reluctant to use the Modern Records Centre, finding the whole idea of archival research a little off-putting. However, once I had grown used to the place and could find my way round their cataloguing system I found that I actually enjoyed it. During the summer of my first year of study I visited the Modern Records Centre intermittently to ferret around in the files. By the following spring I was spending as much time as possible there, and feeling that I was making solid progress in finding relevant information. A work pattern emerged such that I would spend all my time in the archives for about a fortnight, reach saturation point, and then have a week away. The amount of information I gathered from the archives varied. Sometimes I would use files that were a goldmine of information, and sometimes I would spend what seemed an eternity working through files that turned out to have nothing much of interest. This, I have since realized, is typical of archival analysis.

How I used the archives

Before ordering files, I would spend a considerable amount of time looking through indexes and guides to see which files might be of interest. Some of my references came from secondary accounts I had read, some from conversations with archivists, and some from my investigations into the archive guides. Once I had ordered a file I developed a process of having a quick look at the file as a whole, and then writing down all the required references for it along with a two-sentence description of what it contained. After that I would work through the file, sometimes fairly quickly, but often very meticulously, depending on how relevant I felt the file to be. This was a very time-consuming process, and is also quite tiring. Sometimes I would order a file which would turn out to be huge, and on other occasions a file would consist of no more than three pages. One problem I found was that often the files that I had assumed would be particularly relevant were not so, whereas others I just happened to look at on the off-chance were very valuable. This would suggest that there were other files I did not look at which may have contained useful information. It was not always possible to tell whether the information I sought had ever existed, had been shredded, or whether it was kept elsewhere. Also, it was not always obvious that a document was important until I had looked at other files, which meant that I would often have to return to files I had already looked at to reconsider their significance. In the case of TUC files in particular, it was often necessary to work on several files at once as they contained different types of documents relating to the same issue or event, and did not make sense in isolation from one another.

I found that the more archival work I did the easier the process became. While at first I found it difficult to know what to look for, or how to assess the importance of documents, this improved with experience.

Initially, I did not have access to an easily portable laptop computer and so had to make longhand notes from the documents I consulted, which was a rather laborious process. As archive centres have a pencil only rule, I felt a constant worry that my notes would fade or become illegible. To counter this I tended to write up afterwards on a computer a record of the files I had consulted with a summary of their contents. This was again very time-consuming and tedious, but these records proved invaluable. I consulted so many files which often related to each other that it was vital to have lists of the contents of each. Even so, I sometimes lost track of exactly where pieces of information I had found were held, and would have a frustrating time looking through my files for a particular letter that I had just remembered would fit in as evidence elsewhere.

The archive sources I used

The main archive repository I consulted was the TUC archive at the Modern Records Centre. This contained information on TUC activities relating to the Marshall Plan, on its relationship with unions in Britain, and its relationship with other national union centres and the organs of the international trade union movement. Two of the main topics of interest were the involvement of the TUC in the Anglo-American Council on Productivity, and the European Recovery Trade Union Advisory Committee. Other sources that I used at the Modern Records Centre included the files of the Federation of British Industries (the predecessor to the Confederation of British Industries), the files of individual trade unions, especially engineering, of local Trades Councils, and of individuals who had been prominent in the union movement. I also looked at items such as the Trades Union Annual Congress Reports to see what resolution had been put forward at Congress, and also at journals and papers relating to the union movement. The types of documents that I consulted included minutes of meetings, internal memos, letters, published and unpublished reports, conference resolutions, pamphlets, and newspaper and journal articles.

Other archival sources included the TUC library at the TUC headquarters in London. This did not contain much in the way of official records, but did have copies of relevant published pamphlets and, importantly, the Productivity Reports of the Anglo-American Council on Productivity. I consulted records of the Labour Party and the Communist Party held at the National Museum of Labour History in Manchester, official documents at the Public Record Office in Kew, and holdings of various individuals held at the British Library of Political and Economic Science (at the London School of Economics). I also received funding for a trip to consult archives at the International Institute of Social History in Amsterdam. While this turned out to be a wonderful place to work, overlooking the docks in Amsterdam, I found that the documents I consulted on the international trade union movement were duplicates of items already covered at the TUC archive at the Modern Records Centre. While this was disappointing, it was also reassuring, implying I had covered my sources thoroughly.

I found a number of differences between the various archive centres that I used. Most are very pleasant places to work, in particular the Modern Records Centre and the International Institute of Social History, but my experiences did vary. Some, especially the Public Record Office, have very strict rules and regulations about consulting and copying documents, whereas others have a more relaxed approach. One of the main problems I found concerned the photocopying of documents which were of particular interest to me: strict copyright rules have to be complied with, and it tends to be an expensive and time-consuming process at archive centres. Further problems arise in the way in which the files are indexed. Some archival centres have very easy to use guides, others are often rather vague, cataloguing large groups of files under one heading. The main set of archives that I needed to consult in Amsterdam were in the process of being catalogued; and at one archive centre I used, some groups of documents had no referencing system. This means that the process of working out which files are likely to be of interest and recording correct reference numbers for them can be extremely convoluted and frustrating, which emphasizes the necessity of writing in advance to archive centres to ascertain whether documents will be available.

Conclusion: methodological questions

At the beginning of my research I felt rather isolated in a politics department studying a historical topic. I could not consult new data sets that I could have gained through survey analysis (of which I had a little experience), and I could not use statistical analysis to impress myself and others. Instead, I was re-evaluating and reinterpreting existing information from the late 1940s and early 1950s. I was anxious to avoid using an *ad hoc* historical descriptive narrative, and to take a more rigorous approach in which I would explain the significance of events. I found that I was coming up with hypotheses that I was trying to test: I was looking at past events, but trying to do so with the analytical skills I had learned from my study of politics. This was actually very difficult, as I found it much easier and less intellectually demanding just to tell a story or describe events rather than to analyse and to lay out hypotheses that could be tested. Rather to my surprise, I found that this 'hypothesis framing' approach was being recommended when doing historical research in education:

A fact that many students fail to realize is that historical research usually requires the setting up of specific, testable hypotheses. Without such hypotheses, historical research often becomes little more than an aimless gathering of facts. In searching the materials that make up the source of historical research data, unless the student's attention is aimed at information relating to specific questions or concerned with specific hypotheses, [s]he has little chance of extracting a body of data from the available documents that can be synthesized to provide new knowledge or new understanding of the topic studied. (Borg, 1963, pp. 189–90)

Having completed a considerable amount of secondary reading and thinking before I launched myself into the archival work, I found that I was working with a set of hypotheses and ideas, whether I was always fully aware of them or not. I found it helpful to try to keep these in mind when looking through files, as it was very easy just to note down a lot of information without really thinking where it fitted into the wider picture of my research. When I approached files because I thought they might possibly be interesting but was not sure why, and did not stop to think about why the information might be relevant or useful, I often felt that I had been wasting time. I found the work most rewarding when I had a focus, made a conscious effort to analyse the information as I went along, and tried to relate it to the broader picture of my research as a whole.

One aspect of using documents that did concern me, especially at the beginning, was whether or not I was being 'objective' in my research. The only primary research I had carried out before I started the PhD was of a quantitative, not a qualitative, nature, and I was concerned that my findings would be too much based upon interpretation. Mapping out my ideas before consulting the files helped in this respect. I do not feel that this skewed my work, as I constantly reviewed my ideas and hypotheses in the light of information that I gained as I proceeded with my research. Furthermore, without delineating my own ideas and concerns before approaching the archives, it would have been very easy simply to assimilate the theories of the academic accounts I had been reading in my study of secondary work.

A final important issue that confronts all research students is that of presenting work to others. At first I found it difficult to talk about my thesis as it was so specialized and so personal. Translating hours of work into a few sensible sentences is difficult. I also found it difficult to know how to order my work when it came to presenting it as a coherent written whole. It seemed that I had a choice of presenting things chronologically, thematically, or by having a chapter on each important organization or group of people involved. I ended up having a combination of the three: information was presented to a certain extent in a chronological order, as this made sense, but was divided up on the whole according to different groups, which reflected different interests and themes in the thesis. Actually writing could be difficult, as I worried I was not doing justice to my research, and could find myself 'intimidated' by the task in front of me, suffering at times from what I have seen described as 'thesis paranoia' (Duncker, 1996). Allowing other people to read and comment on written work was also a worry in that they might think that my work was not good enough. As Pamela Richards puts it in *Writing for Social Scientists*: 'For me, sitting down to write is risky because it means that I have to open myself to scrutiny. To do that requires that I trust myself, and it also means that I have to trust my colleagues' (Richards in Becker, 1986, p. 113).

Trusting the archives is another matter. Archive documentation should be considered as raw data and therefore is subject to interpretation. The main limitation of such data is the tendency to produce 'top-down' studies (skewed by the thoughts of elites). As indicated by Keith Middlemas, between the study of 'high politics' and that of the social history of the working class, 'lies a gulf both in method and understanding' (1979, p. 12). In my experience, archival analysis alone cannot bridge that gulf and must therefore be supplemented wherever possible with oral histories and interview techniques.

16

Breaking Free Through the Use of Unusual Sources

STEPHEN DAY

[The Internet] is crucial for scholars who don't wish to be marginalised, who live in a country where their particular discipline is not strong or who don't live close to a major institution. It vastly increases the opportunities for people in this region [eastern Europe] to participate in their disciplines.[1]

With the explosion of information technology and conference opportunities in the last few years, it is appropriate that a book dealing with the experiences of PhD students in the 1990s should include a chapter that deals with unusual sources. There are a plethora of issues that one has to deal with when commencing a PhD – the student–supervisor relationship, how to begin, etc. – hence thoughts relating to information technology, conference attending and networking are often relegated to the back of one's mind. Are they really just another set of hazards or, on the contrary, a potential remedy for so many of the ills already mentioned in previous chapters? The opportunity to explore the information superhighway, to scan the airwaves with a short-wave receiver and to get away from one's institution networking, 'bouncing off' your ideas with other research students or established academics can make it seem as though there is light at the end of the tunnel. It must be stressed, however, that this is not a 'something for nothing' exercise where everything is laid before you. Although the element of luck is often an essential requirement, forward planning and perseverance are fundamental prerequisites for survival. The changing nature of academic departments to a more market-orientated world means that to survive we have to adopt a certain set of techniques. It is up to each individual to decide the exact balance. I was told by a politics professor that, as PhD students, 'our function was to act as extrapolators', that we should use those around us and establish strategic relationships. Alternatively, we can take a much more 'human' approach where the cultivation of relationships becomes a two-way process of interaction, where networking is a friendly pursuit and not a cold, calculating, instrumental pursuit of ends. This chapter will therefore begin with an overview of my project and the experiences that I have had in the course of my PhD studies. The substantive part of it will deal with my experiences in breaking free from my institution, which for the purposes of many aspects of my project remains a rather constraining factor.

Beginning research

I came to my institution after spending a summer worrying about where I would take my MA and pondering ending up on the 'dole'. I had a few interviews for teaching assistantships, but these always seemed destined to go to the internal candidates. I also waited in vain for one institution, who held out the possibility of a studentship. In terms of my PhD topic, which analyses the realignment and re-emergence of the post-communist left in Poland and Slovakia, it was much better suited than my final-choice institution in terms of resources, the ability to teach Slavic languages and international links with East and Central European academic institutions, but unfortunately the studentship came to nothing.

Towards the end of August, after scouring the pages of Tuesday's *Guardian*, I came across an advertisement for an editorial assistant for a new academic journal. I had been doing some editorial work at my previous institution, I had teaching experience, a good MA and what I considered an interesting PhD outline. The interview went well, and a day later I was told that I had the job. My project now had an institutional base. I suppose I was so glad at getting the funding that I did not really consider the appropriateness of the institution for my project; in fact, I knew next to nothing about the politics department or the university. I soon found out that the institution, in fact, offered very little in the way of substantive materials for my sort of work. Firstly, the library (as is the case in most institutions) had a patchy collection of contemporary, post-1989, literature, although it did possess a few of the essential journals relating to communist and post-communist studies,[2] as well as a number of the theoretical journals dealing with political parties and party-systems.[3] Secondly, for the first eighteen months there was no research room for non-teaching assistants in the department with on-line computer facilities (there were, of course, computers all over campus, but they were more often than not occupied). Finally there was nobody in the department who specialized in my area of East and Central European politics. This, again, is probably a common phenomenon, and one which in itself is not necessarily a problem. I believe that the most important factor is a supervisor who is both enthusiastic and prepared to embark upon the learning process with the student. Therefore, instead of choosing a supervisor, which for many research students is a primary consideration when deciding where to study, I had mine appointed without any 'real' idea as to who they were, or their appropriateness for my project.

Setting the scene and understanding the limits of my project

In a nutshell, my project analyses the dynamics of political change in East and Central Europe through an analysis of the legal successor parties to the communist parties in Poland and Slovakia, namely Social Democracy of the Republic of Poland (SDRP) and the Party of the Democratic Left (SDL). The inspiration for this project came from a number of sources over many years. Firstly, I was inspired by Mikhail Gorbachev, whose style not only took everyone by surprise, but also led me to visit the Soviet Union in the autumn of 1988. Secondly, at the 1985 Labour Party conference I came across Eric Heffer MP, who was part of a group connected with 'socialist dissidents' in the Eastern bloc. A few years later I organized my degree so that I could study, albeit superficially, communist systems. As the events of 1989 unfolded it was then that my focus really changed. I was bound up totally with the romanticism of the period, those Monday-night demonstrations in Leipzig, and the desire of many to create a 'real' democratic socialist alternative. I remember feeling very disappointed when *Neues Forum*[4] failed to make an impact on the East German electorate. Internationally the left (both communist and social democratic) was in retreat, but this was not to be the end of history à la Fukuyama (1989). The flip-side of orthodox communism (i.e., capitalism) would now be subject to a thorough examination. No longer could its defects remain cloaked behind the jibe, 'If you don't like it here, why not go over the Berlin Wall and live in Russia?'

I soon began to question the decision of the 'new democracies' to follow the remedies prescribed by the International Monetary Fund (IMF), and felt uneasy with the apparent hegemonic position achieved by the Anglo-American vision of capitalism and democracy. The costs of change were falling disproportionately on the backs of ordinary people. Wasn't there another alternative, I kept asking myself? It was from this point onwards that I knew I wanted to continue my studies further in the direction of East and Central Europe. I looked around for specific MA courses that might be of interest, but so many of them, at established centres, still seemed to treat the region as a peripheral component of Soviet and post-Soviet studies. I was persuaded to return to Exeter,[5] where I was able to focus specifically on the region that was of interest to me. The MA lacked a language component (other than Russian), which I now realize was a big drawback, but the experience of working on my own, especially the dissertation, has enabled me to cope with the loneliness of the PhD.

1989 was undoubtedly an *annus mirabilis*, but the likelihood that such a complex process of change could develop in a linear, sequential and unproblematic fashion was pure fiction. Conceptually, my project is an attempt to understand not only the theoretical nature of political change, in terms of democratization and consolidation, but also the practical effects of such change on political parties and party-systems in general and the successor parties in particular. By dealing with change in this way, my aim is to highlight, draw upon and modify ideas relating to democratization and its outcomes; to put forward an objective and analytical explanation for the realignment and re-emergence of the successor parties; and hopefully to show that the stronger the forces of the social democratic left, the greater the chances for democratic stability. Therefore, in terms of variables, the role of the successor parties remains the focus of the study (i.e., dependent), while political parties and their adaptability contribute to the focus (i.e., independent variable), and the process of democratization and consolidation act as the intermediate variables influencing the course of the independent variable.

Because of the complex nature of the whole transformation process, I am forced to use an eclectic array of methodological tools and approaches which includes the use of sources that might not immediately spring to mind, such as the Internet, short-wave radio and networking.

Flying blind

The biggest problem that I had to face during the course of my first year was that my main supervisor was on sabbatical and hence had no real input into the project. While I was able to cope with this situation because of the structures that I had established outside of my institution, I am sure that many students would have found it difficult to cope, especially in terms of laying the foundations for a PhD. Even so, it took some time before I was able to pull in the reins of the project (I had to remember that this was a PhD and not a lifetime's work), initiate an effective research strategy and develop a single theme around which the PhD would be based. It was not until Christmas of the second year that I decided to drop Hungary in favour of Slovakia. This did not pose any problems from a theoretical perspective, and I had not amassed a great deal of work on Hungary and the Hungarian Socialist Party (HSP). Much of the reasoning behind this decision lay with the problems of language (Hungarian, a Finno-Urgic language which is related to Finnish, must be the hardest European language to learn); the decline of sources, via friends, coming from Hungary; and the fact that the comparison between the HSP and the SLD had become quite popular since the electoral victory of both parties in 1993 (Poland) and 1994 (Hungary). While I had a wealth of material on Poland and Slovakia, I was unclear as to what to do with it, and hence tended to wander down many different avenues. It wasn't until the end of the second year that things began to come together. This coming together process was facilitated by what I felt to be a coming together of the student–supervisor relationship. All of us at last seemed to be on the same wavelength, and I started to value the advice and guidance that I was being given.

In contrast, the logistical support of the department was very good from the day I arrived. I was offered teaching, and it was indicated that money was available for conferences. Obviously I was eager to take up both opportunities. I taught for the first two years of the PhD on a first-year introduction to a politics course and a second- and third-year option on Soviet and post-Soviet politics. In terms of conferences, I attended one domestic and two international (Warsaw and Sophia), which were fully paid for, as well as a summer language school in Krakow, which was partially funded, in 1996. There was also use of the photocopier, fax machine and departmental office for international telephone calls. The department was always prepared to put money up-front for conferences, instead of the usual practice of the research student paying in advance, often via an overdraft. However, my relationship with the department was one of give and take; for example, with a friend we started a graduate seminar programme which the department would later highlight in ESRC visits, as an example of student involvement. I also spent most of one summer sorting out the 'donkey work' for a conference on the notion of civil society and its relationship to democracy, which was traded off for a conference in Warsaw, and photocopying essential articles for a new course, which was paid on the basis of an hourly rate.

It was only when into my third year that I began to feel focused. My status changed in the course of my studies as I was fortunate enough to get an ESRC scholarship for the last two years of the PhD, which was obviously a personal boost after the previous failure. This gave me, at long last, the ability to spend more than just two or three weeks in Poland and Slovakia at any one time, via additional funds to spend a year in the field. The year abroad was even more fruitful as I already had well-established links with professors (whom I met, by chance, at a conference) of the Institute of Sociology, Jagiellonian University, Krakow. They were of immense help in enabling me to gain the status of a visiting academic researcher, which enabled me to have a supervisor, language training, accommodation in the university and access to political elites in Poland. The year abroad also enabled me finally to lay to rest the ghost of language acquisition, which was always my biggest weakness.[6]

Attempting to build an independent structure

It is my 'own' attempt to build an independent structure outside of the confines of my home institution that has enabled me to have any chance of completing the thesis. This section consists of four subsections: lucky breaks; networking and conference attendance; new technology resources in the form of the Internet; and alternative media resources such as the radio.

Lucky breaks

In March 1994, quite unexpectedly, I received a letter from the Labour Party asking if I would undertake some exploratory work on their behalf in Romania under the auspices of the Westminster Foundation for Democracy.[7] Previously I had sent them a Curriculum Vitae and an outline of my interests *vis-à-vis* East and Central Europe. My task was to ascertain, via elite interviews (both structured and unstructured), presentations and general observation, which parties could benefit from contact with the Labour Party. It was my first experience of elite interviewing. I remember feeling quite intimidated on several occasions. This did not stem from any sense of deference, but was due to their reaction to probing questions. During one interview I suggested to a member of the ruling party that perhaps it had been a tactical mistake to form a coalition with parties considered by the West to be extremist. From that moment onwards he became quite agitated. I kept thinking, 'I want to leave, now!' All in all, however, it was an excellent apprenticeship for my PhD, especially as it enabled me to develop a specific approach and a tried and tested set of questions. I always begin by explaining my project, why I am doing it and what I hope to achieve. I go on to stress my quest for objectivity and the fact that, if necessary, anything they say will be treated with the utmost confidence. Finally I mention that during the questioning there will be times when I will play the devil's advocate, so that they will not take offence. I tend to begin with very broad-based questions relating to, for example, an overview of political events during the past year and the interviewees' reaction to certain events. I then move on to questions of a philosophical nature. This enables me to evaluate their political orientation and pursue a line of questioning that, for example, highlights which wing of the party they ally themselves with and what they think of intra-party factions. Finally I focus upon very specific questions in a bid to obtain information that is not necessarily in the public domain. The sorts of questions I have asked include:

- Do you understand why some members of the party feel uneasy with the way it has embraced the market?

- Could you ever foresee, or under what circumstances do you think it would be likely, that certain factions within the party or coalition would break away?

- Your critics are fond of using derogatory labels concerning your party's past; how would you respond to such accusations?

- What does it mean to be a social democrat in the latter part of the twentieth century?

From my own utilitarian perspective the benefits of undertaking such work remain with me to this day. I have a very impressive list of people with whom I have spoken, and this is always available and cited when I am writing to organizations in connection with the thesis, in the hope that they will view me not just as 'another' PhD student but as someone who has been involved in work that has some practical application. I have since found that using my political credentials, and a letter of recommendation from the International Office of the Labour Party, has been more successful in obtaining access to information than merely putting myself forward as a PhD student.[8]

The conference pyramid

Attendance at conferences has also led to considerable beneficial knock-on effects. It not only gives one the opportunity to 'network', but also to become part of someone else's network. At every stage the network of contacts widens. A conference on party politics in Manchester, for instance, resulted in a first meeting with many of the main players in East European studies from Britain and the region itself (it was during this conference that I made my first contacts with academics from Jagiellonian University, a chance encounter that was to have invaluable repercussions for the PhD). The panels were very stimulating and have since been instrumental in shaping my ideas. Many of the individuals were associated with the four-year ESRC programme 'Regime Change in East Central Europe', which was part of the wider East–West Initiative.[9] They offered friendly support and good company. It was during this conference that I handed over a manuscript on the Slovakian elections. Nine months later this piece of opportunism resulted in my first major publication (Day, 1995). Eight months later I was invited to attend the team's conference in Bulgaria. Once again, this was an invaluable experience. Four days with a group of approximately fifteen people was in complete contrast to life at my home institution. Again, this was not just a conference; it cultivated friendships with a number of people including Peter Pridhava from Comenius University, Bratislava. Together we decided to write a joint paper with a view to publication, which has slowly come to fruition via electronic mail. This sort of experience has been common. I have not needed to be pushy; rather, it is as though like-minded people have tended to gravitate towards one another.

Information technology

I am not an IT expert in any shape or form. My knowledge of the Internet stems from a couple of introductory classes and my own experimentation. It was not until my MA that I learned to use a word-processor, but once I found it could be mastered my curiosity was then opened to the world of the Internet.

It is perhaps ironic that an idea that was originally conceived via the Cold War (i.e., the United States hoped to be able to establish a network of computers that could maintain effective communications if any individual part was wiped out by a Soviet first strike) has now evolved into, among other things, a blossoming research and academic network. For academic purposes the Internet provides book reviews, articles, discussions on culture, history and politics, election statistics, newspapers, magazines, etc. It can also provide invaluable information, as the 1991 coup attempt against Gorbachev showed:

> *As the official television and radio stations broadcast opera, telephone lines and computer networks were clogged with messages about the events unfolding in Moscow, Leningrad and elsewhere. Hours before the release of any official 'news,' information about the coup had spread via computer throughout Russia and the outside world.*[10]

As of January 1996 there were more than 9,472,000 hosts, whereas ten years ago the figure was 2308.[11] Electronic mail, as well as providing instant communication with a colleague, also offers numerous discussion lists. The emphasis here should be on selectivity. Although many of the lists have appealing titles, their content, level of debate and abstraction is often very disappointing. Of course you are operating the system in isolation, but it is a system that offers the prospect of interaction and after a productive 'surf', if used selectively, you can come away invigorated and armed with new information.

The World Wide Web and Netscape

The World Wide Web (WWW) and Netscape (Ns), which operate through the Internet, offer a plethora of bulletin boards and discussion groups that stem from individuals, universities, community-based organizations, commercial organizations and transnationals. Both WWW and Ns are surpassing their previous incarnation, Gopher (although Gopher, with over 7000 servers, remains a valuable resource base, especially for those without a powerful computer system). WWW and Ns provide a forum for both text and, more excitingly, complex and moving images. When surfing the net, it is important to be aware of the following:

(a) Initially, it is common to feel that a lot of time can be wasted stuck in front of the screen. This is unavoidable. Despite the presence of a number of publications on different issues, you need to familiarize yourself with what exactly is out there. A time-saving function is the ability to be able to input a set of key words, via Yahoo, which can enable researchers to build up a picture of almost any topic. But even here you are often filled with false hope when, after peering into the entries selected, you realize they are often irrelevant and think, 'That's another hour I've wasted.' Or as Lynne Truss (1996, p. 3) writes:

> *I started dutifully scrolling through the A section until suddenly I was saved by a vision of my whole life drifting into a small black hole of pointlessness. Just seconds before it swallowed me up I pulled back and switched off. But it happens all the time,*

this. The search engine presents you with something irrelevant, then you spend hours of valuable time not learning anything, but just trying to work out why.

If at all possible, it is better to obtain a list already compiled as this can save a great deal of time. Nevertheless, when you are not feeling in the mood to write, surfing the net can prove to be a therapeutic exercise. It is also important to stress that before 12 a.m. or at the weekend is probably the best time to surf in the UK, as you will not be competing with the US, the business world or most students.

(b) Do not be put off by the nature of the host names (uniform resource locator – URL), for example:

http://www.engin.umich.edu/~zbigniew/periphery/periphery.html[12]

This is the language of the medium.

> *Http is a stateless client/server protocol, which means that a web server does not have a long attention span. It receives a request from a client (i.e. you) such as Mosiac, Netscape or Lynx and it processes that request and responds with either the information requested or an error message.* (Franks, 1995, p. 115)

(c) Although English seems to be the primary mode of communication, foreign-language sites offer additional and invaluable primary source material. Often they come in the form of daily newspapers (sometimes even in English) which, depending on the time zone, can often arrive on the net before they reach the news-stand. Examples include:

Name of Newspaper	Site Address
Polish Press Agency	http://www.pap.waw.pl/
Warsaw Voice	http://www.contact.waw.pl/voice
The Financial Times	http://www.ft.com/
Rzeczpospolita	http://www.rzeczpospolita.pl/
The Albanian Times	http://www.worldweb.net/~ww1054/times/times.html
Asahi	http://www.asahi.com/

(d) Remain wary of discussion lists. Although they can be informative, they can also prove to be misleading and manipulative. For many people the list is a forum for highly subjective comment, diatribe and often racist, sexist and classist views. In Internet language such material has become known as 'hate-speak'. During one surf I came across an enticing headline, 'Are you concerned about government censorship?' On closer inspection the site belonged to an anti-Semitic group that was attempting to deny the Holocaust through the use of academic respectability.

The growth of new technology in the guise of the Internet is still very much in its infancy, 'the spring-time of servers' to coin a phrase. And it is this almost transitional status that makes it an incredibly varied and valuable source of information. (See Appendix A for a list of interesting and useful sources consulted in my research.) How long this libertarian/anarchistic existence will continue remains to be seen, as governments attempt to limit its potential[13] or corporations, through advertising (burgers and cola!), want a site to send out specific images and hence limit what can be broadcast. At present it is still a tool that can be used by a wide range of people and groups, including 'extremists' of all shades. At the same time, one should consider the fact that over half of the world's population have never made a phone call, let alone had the opportunity to use a computer. Hence we should not forget the use of more conventional forms of communication.

Turn on, tune in and listen

The short-wave radio offers a source of information that may not immediately spring to mind. I first became interested in the use of radio during the mid-1980s when I used to tune into Radio Moscow during a time of unprecedented debate and openness (*glasnost*) for the Soviet media. Today I frequently tune into Radio Slovakia International, Radio Warsaw, the Voice of Russia, Voice of America and Radio Prague. It is also interesting to scan through various bands to discover what is being broadcast, for example Radio Tokyo, Australia and Bulgaria. (See Appendix B for a list of frequencies.) Short-wave radio enables international broadcasting to be picked up all over the globe. It works on the basis of bouncing electro-magnetic signals off the ionosphere. This means that seasonal and climatic conditions (including the activity of the sun) affect the signals, hence every station broadcasts on a number of different frequencies in a bid to improve reception. Stations are always pleased to receive reception reports from listeners and reply with free transmission schedules, etc.

Many of today's 'ghetto-blasters' (although not hi-fis) have short-wave capacity; alternatively, one could buy a dedicated short-wave radio which is capable of receiving all of the short-wave meter bands. This is probably a good investment if you intend to spend months learning another language or undertaking fieldwork, or if you want to stay in touch with international events via the English language. Most radios come with a short guide to the world of radio, which means you do not have to spend hours searching for stations that you think might exist but have no idea at which times they broadcast. It also tells you in which language they broadcast. Of course, many stations are part of the state-owned media, and hence operate with a particular slant, but none the less short-wave radio can provide a wealth of information as well as entertainment: with daily news bulletins, language tuition, and cultural, economic, political and social features.

Conclusion

A PhD can, at times, be a very frustrating process, hence the use of an eclectic array of methodological tools, the Internet, short-wave radio, networking, etc., can in many ways act as a remedy to many of the ills associated with its pursuit. Obviously there are some people whose commitment to their subject is so passionate that no matter what obstacles are thrown in their way, the intensity of that passion will carry them through. Even so, for students in this category as well as those whose passion is less intense, the ability to break free from the confines of an institution can be an invigorating experience whether in the guise of a domestic or international conference, a 'surf' of the Internet, or a scan of the airwaves. Academia is in a privileged position to be able to take advantage of these resources. The use of on-line resources is free, and there are always introductory courses for those unfamiliar with the Internet. From a preparatory angle, it is important to choose your institution wisely, based on whatever criteria one deems the most important – academic resources, financial resources, etc. Make sure that if you need to acquire another language you have the opportunity to learn, and that money is available for foreign and domestic trips. If you are like myself (I only ever attained a CSE Grade 2 in French), this can be a long, drawn out and often very frustrating experience. The only advice I can give is not to expect to be able to run before you have learned to walk. As your knowledge and confidence grow, it can be highly satisfying when you are able to make use of and cite primary source material. Find out exactly what you are entitled to, and exert your rights as a fee-paying customer. On a day-to-day level it's important to have confidence in both the ability and competence of your supervisor(s). Sometimes this comes instantaneously, but it may take a certain amount of time to develop. In the worst-case scenario, it may never develop at all. Create your own luck, by attending essential conferences, and leaving the confines of your institution to network and be networked.

Appendix A: Interesting and potentially useful sources

Here is a short list of sites that can be accessed directly and sites that act as a server for hundreds of others.

Name of site	Http address	Short description of site
Yahoo	http://www.yahoo.com/	A web searcher that offers a comprehensive guide to webs on specific countries.
UK Academic Sites	http://src.doc.ic.ac.uk/uk academic.html	A web searcher to all of the academic sites within the UK.
Political Science	http://www.keele.ac.uk/depts/po/psr.html	Definitely the best political science web page that I have come across. A wealth of information.
European Home Page	http://s700.uminho.pt/europa.html	This will display a map of Europe. Just click on any country map and start to surf.
Socialist International	http://www.dsausa.org/SL.html	An indispensable guide to Socialist parties worldwide.
Radio Free Europe/ Radio Liberty	http://www.rferl.org	A specialist site that covers many aspects of the transition in Eastern Europe and the former Soviet Union.
Slovak Store	http://www.eunet.sk/	Probably one of the best sites that I have come across, covering almost everything you need to know about Slovakia.
NATO	http://www.nato.int/	Provides information on many aspects of NATO.
World Bank EU UN	http://www.worldbank.org http://www.cec.lu/Welcome.html http://www.undcp.org/unlinks.html	A huge resource that can access information on all aspects of these organizations.
CNN	http://www.cnn.com/	Provides all the latest news from CNN, with numerous updates throughout the day.
Japanese Political Parties	http://www.kanzaki.com/jinfo/Political Parties.html	A fascinating insight into Japanese party politics. The Communist Party and the New Frontier Party provide the most comprehensive English language sites.

Appendix B: Short-wave radio frequency international broadcasts (English language service)

This is not a comprehensive list, but rather one that corresponds to my listening habits, and hence stations that have been obtained in the UK.

Name of radio station	Frequency (kHz)	Calling sign, time of broadcast* and comments
BBC World Service	5975, 9412	'This is London calling.' Can be picked up all day at various frequencies. Coverage continues on FM after Radio Four closes.
Voice of America	6040, 9760, 15445	'This is the Voice of America.' 0600–2200.
Radio Warsaw	7285, 7270, 6095, 6135, 7250	'This is Polish Radio Warsaw.' 1300–1400, 1800–1900, 2030–2130. A full array of news, culture and reviews. I often experience difficulties getting a clear signal, especially at lunch-time.
Radio Slovakia	6055, 7345, 6145	'This is Radio Slovakia International.' 1930–2000. News, views and features. A very clear signal.
Radio Prague**	7345	'Radio Prague, the external service of Czech Radio.' 0800–0830. Always a clear signal, with interesting content.
Radio Japan	7230, 11865, 5965, 6155	'This is Radio Japan, the overseas service of NHK in Tokyo.' 2200–2300, 0000–0100, 0700–0800. Often difficult to get a signal, but an interesting insight into Japan.
Germany *Deutsche Welle*	7235	'This is Radio Deutsche Welle, the voice of Germany.' 2400–0050. A very extensive news programme on European and Asian-Pacific events. Probably my favourite.

Appendix B cont.

Name of radio station	Frequency (kHz)	Calling sign, time of broadcast* and comments
Radio Bulgaria (Sofia)	7480, 9700	'This is Radio Bulgaria.' 2200-2300. Always a clear signal. An interesting insight into a country that gets little media coverage.
Radio Moscow	7125	'This is the Voice of Russia.' All day, various frequencies. I tend to find reception much better at night after 2200.
Radio Budapest	5935, 7250, 6140	'This is Radio Budapest, Hungary.' 2200-2230. An excellent opportunity to compensate for not being able to read or understand Hungarian.
Radio Romania	9690, 7195	'This is Bucharest calling.' 2200-2300. Always a clear signal. A lot of culture-related programmes.

* The times given are those for British Summer Time. Subtract an hour during the winter.

** A transcript of the day's news can also be obtained via e-mail. Send a message to robot@radio.cz and in the subject line write <subscribe>.

Notes

1. Alfred Stepan, Central European University Rector, quoted in Woodard (1995, p. 87).
2. Journals such as *Postcommunist and Transition Studies, The Journal of Communist and Transition Studies,* and *Europe-Asia Studies.*
3. Journals such as *Party Politics, Comparative Politics, Journal of Democracy.*
4. *Neues Forum* was the East German dissident organization (primarily artisans and intellectuals) that co-ordinated many of the momentous demonstrations throughout the GDR prior to the fall of the Berlin Wall. They advocated a policy of democratic socialism, wanted the GDR to remain a sovereign nation and build upon the positive aspects of the regime's achievements, while casting aside the negative aspects. But this was against a background of unification and the figure of Helmut Kohl, who, opening his hands to the people of eastern Germany, promised that they would soon benefit from the success of the West.
5. Much of this was related to the question of finances. I had already borrowed £2000 to pay for the tuition fees, but I still needed to live. I obtained a post within the residential system which entitled me to free board and lodging, and I was told I would be able to do some teaching within the department.
6. Upon arrival I arranged for the department to pay for me to attend a language course in Birmingham (two hours per week), for which I was very thankful. Unfortunately, it was full of Russian language graduates or finalists who within a few weeks were far ahead of me. Reluctantly I had to withdraw due to lack of ability, but the summer school in Krakow, two years later, provided me with the firm foundation that I so badly needed. I feel that if I want to establish myself as an East and Central European specialist then, as a minimum, I should be able to read a Polish newspaper!
7. The Westminster Foundation for Democracy is an all-party group that finances projects for the spread of 'democracy' in many parts of the world including the former Eastern Bloc, Soviet Union and Anglophone Africa. Since 1989 the three main parties have been keen to establish links with 'sister' groups within Eastern Europe. From the Labour Party's perspective, the first step would be to send someone on a fact-finding mission. That person would then deliver a written report from which future plans would be made. In my case, after indicating the potential benefits of organizing links with the opposition Social Democrats and the Democratic Party, a number of follow-up events have already taken place, including workshops on dealing with the media, organizational development, fund-raising, and local government workshops.
8. Many of the organizations that I contact claim to be of a social-democratic orientation and look upon membership of the Socialist International (SI), for example, as a seal of international approval which could be cultivated for domestic purposes. The Labour Party remains an important force within the SI, hence the importance of establishing contacts with it. Therefore it would seem apparent that as a mere PhD student I do not really have a great deal to offer, but as a member of the Labour Party (and someone who has worked for the International Department) I could possibly be of some benefit to them.
9. A four-year project that focused on Poland, Slovakia, Bulgaria, Hungary, and the Czech Republic. The British team consisted of Michael Waller, Bill Lomax, Paul G. Lewis and Gordan Wightman, who are regional specialists, and Geoffrey Pridham, who provided a Western European and theoretical component. The group have organized a number of international conferences and have published both individually in major journals and collectively in edited collections such as Wightman (1995), and Pridham and Lewis (1996).
10. Bob Travica and Matthew Hogan quoted in Woodard (1995, p. 86).
11. See 'On-line' – The *Guardian,* 29 February 1996, p. 3.
12. html stands for hypertext mark-up language, and indicates the ability to move from one document to another via the use of a mouse.
13. China and Iran are rumoured to be attempting to establish a register as a way of maintaining control of what is written and read by domestic users. In September 1996 Singapore brought in specific legislation to ban certain sites related to child pornography. Legislation, however, also included the control of material critical of the government.

17

Surviving the Viva[1]

PETER BURNHAM

It is generally acknowledged that, while the viva is the ultimate test of quality that must be faced by students, there is a serious dearth of research on the nature of the oral examination (Phillips, 1994, p. 133). To all but the initiated, what occurs in the lengthy 'judgely huddle' from which nervous postgraduates emerge either victorious or distraught is a mystery. 'Is the viva crucial to the award of the PhD?' 'Is it an exam?' 'If so, what do I have to do to pass?' No use reaching for a trusty methodology text or a PhD handbook.[2] The rules which govern the oral examination are rarely stated, and examination procedures can be highly context specific. Furthermore, until recently in Britain neither supervisors nor examiners had the opportunity to attend training sessions in supervisory practice and examination procedure.

Secrecy surrounding the viva both humiliates the examinee and diminishes the credibility of those who examine. As a contribution to a more enlightened practice, this chapter offers a 'student's guide' to the process, drawing upon my own experience[3] and that of supervisors and examiners as revealed at recently convened ESRC-backed training sessions.

Choosing an external examiner

In a recent issue of the PSA-sponsored publication *Gradnews*,[4] Dave Walker presented a caricature of 'the model research student' who would have identified an external examiner by the end of the second year and in all probability made his/her acquaintance, leaving a good impression, at an annual conference of a professional association. In reality, however, most doctoral students struggling to complete in their final year are simply bewildered by the thought of being involved, in however minor a capacity, in the process of choosing examiners. Phillips (1994, p. 133), for instance, conducting research on preparation for the viva, found that the majority of students did not even know the composition of their panel of examiners prior to the event. Many UK universities still follow this traditional practice whereby supervisors alone decide on examiners. Nevertheless, it is important for doctoral candidates to be aware that they have a legitimate right to be included in discussions concerning the choice of examiners.[5] Most regulations indicate that an external examiner must not have been involved in any substantial way in the development of a candidate's thesis. This does not rule out individuals who may have responded to particular queries as long as they have not seen draft chapters of the thesis-in-progress. Although it may be tempting to use the opportunity of the viva to try to capture a leading light in your field, the sanest solution for students is to solicit opinion on potential examiners from trusted members of staff. There are two golden rules. First, do not accept your supervisor's choice without researching in as much depth as possible other staff and student dealings with the named individual. Phillips and Pugh (1994, p. 138) suggest that one rule of thumb is to give first consideration to the British academic whose work is referenced most frequently in the thesis bibliography. But if it turns out that writers quoted in the bibliography are not appropriate, then you must study the works of those who are going to be appointed to see where they can be relevantly quoted. This piece of advice mars Phillips and Pugh's otherwise even-handed discussion of the viva. Attempting to second-guess the thoughts of an external on the basis of published work will not aid your preparation for the examination, and the inclusion of quotes designed to impress an external will more likely leave an air of sycophancy than scholarship. Your aim is to help to choose an external who will not be swayed by such affectation and who will, moreover, be sensitive to the process of research and the limits of a doctoral thesis. Second, pay particular attention to the choice and wishes of your internal examiner, since in most institutions your supervisor will have no part to play in the examination itself. In the viva it is the external who calls the shots and has the final word on the fate of the thesis. While few supervisors would be naive enough to choose a politically or methodologically incompatible examiner, student involvement in the choice of an external is more important than most postgraduates believe (although it is usual practice that suggestions will have to be ratified by a university-wide committee). In addition to acting as an examiner, your external will also, if you are successful, act as your publicist. The examination is therefore an opportunity to strike up a good working relationship on which you can later draw for references and in particular for recommendations when approaching academic publishers.

The organization of the viva

Most vivas are awkward affairs. The candidate is ushered into the internal's office to shake hands with the external he/she may have cited (even revered) but in all probability has never met. This is followed by approximately two/three hours of fitful conversation in which the candidate makes numerous nervous gaffes and the examiners mechanically take turns probing areas that are often peripheral to the thesis but reflect their area specialisms. To slightly redress the power differential, it is useful for candidates to be aware of the circumstances in which recommendations are made.

Having accepted the onerous task of agreeing to examine an unknown candidate's thesis, the external will receive in addition to the cherished volume, a copy of university regulations and an individual report sheet upon which he/she is asked to make a recommendation. Although university calendars are not usually high-priority reading, it is imperative that all research students are familiar with the requirements for the award of the MPhil/PhD and that they are aware of the recommendations that can be made. In most universities in Britain the internal and external examiners write individual 'independent' reports which are then exchanged on the day of the viva. This practice indicates that the decision on whether the thesis is up to the required standard is usually taken before the examination. However, it would be misleading to suggest that the viva itself is unimportant. Phillips (1994, p. 138) indicates that there is wide variation in the expectations of examiners in this matter, with many suggesting that the 'person' being examined is as important as the 'product'. In general, while a poor performance in the viva may well lead the examiners to question their earlier sentiments when compiling their joint report, it is unlikely that a good showing could affect the outcome if the written work is seriously flawed. More common, and more interesting, are cases where examiners leave open the recommendations made on their individual reports until they have been able to probe candidates in specific areas. For this reason, knowledge of the criteria used in assessment is extremely important.

Criteria used in assessment

A glance through most university calendars will reveal the minimum conditions which must be met for the award. However, few final-year researchers have their fears allayed by reading the officialese pumped out by university administrators. Only by looking behind the declared criteria can doctoral candidates begin to assess whether their creation is likely to succeed. There are four issues in particular that call for attention.

First, how seriously should you take stipulations concerning thesis length and presentation? The ESRC recommends that social science PhD dissertations should not exceed 70,000–80,000 words, inclusive of footnotes, bibliography and appendices (ESRC, 1991, p. 8). While it is unlikely that a thesis will be referred if it exceeds the recommended total by 10–15,000 words, a work totalling 120,000 words may well be deemed a suitable case for resubmission. A more common reason for referral is poor attention to the style and formatting of the thesis. In the frantic month leading up to the final submission date, it all too easy to continue correcting the text, leaving insufficient time to experiment with subheadings and create a professionally laid out bibliography. By far the best (and safest) way of ensuring high quality presentation is to read through PhD theses lodged in your university library with an eye solely to style and formatting. Pay particular attention to the abstract, the introduction and the conclusion. The most common criteria used in assessment are whether the candidate has clearly laid out the problem to be addressed, consistently developed this theme throughout the chapters, and skilfully stated the relevance of the conclusion for the discipline. Attention to presentation will not mask substantive deficiencies, but it can rescue a mediocre thesis from the clutches of referral. The acid test is to present a friend (preferably one versed in social science lore) with the abstract, introduction and conclusion and ask them faithfully to answer the following questions: What problem does this thesis address? Is a plausible argument developed consistently? Is the conclusion of significance to the discipline?

Secondly, a favourite focus of examiners is whether a thesis shows a satisfactory knowledge of primary and secondary sources, and in particular whether it contains an adequate literature review. All researchers fear that in the viva they will be politely told they have not consulted the work which constitutes the magisterial account in their field. The basic message here is that you cannot trust your supervisor! A sufficiently dense literature review in which you pay particular attention to cross-referencing should reveal what are considered to be the authoritative texts. Furthermore, your fall-back position can always be that you are not providing an exhaustive account of your topic, but only considering it from a viewpoint related, for instance, to the discipline of politics (that is, you are not providing 'a sociology of, an economics of, a psychology of', etc.). The literature review often presents difficulties when preparing for final submission. If the thesis is primarily empirical, a theoretical literature review can appear incongruous. Nevertheless, its absence constitutes a serious omission for many examiners and will almost certainly guarantee referral. The traditional PhD 'sandwich' (theory, empirical research, theory revisited) may be unadventurous, but for many examiners it is unfortunately one of the hallmarks of this particular academic exercise.

A third area to consider, and one which is increasingly important, is whether a thesis shows an appreciation of questions of methodology, and the candidate a knowledge of cognate fields. One of the ironies of PhD research is that, even after three years of 'fieldwork', most students pay scant regard to questions of methodology. However, if you cannot justify your choice of research technique and its underlying philosophy, the examiners may well feel that the thesis should be resubmitted with due attention given to a discussion of methodology. What price a PhD based on elite interviewing if you cannot respond to the question of how you attempted to corroborate the material collected in the transcripts? A sure-fire way of avoiding this embarrassment is to append to your thesis a 5000-word essay entitled 'Methodology and the Research Process'. In addition to charting the pros and cons of your particular research strategy, include an account of how your central themes were developed and how you overcame specific obstacles. This sort of appendix – or stand-alone chapter if your university regulations permit – not only side-steps difficult methodological questions, it also enables the examiners to be sure that the thesis is yours (and not a copy of a doctorate submitted to, say, the University of Göteborg in 1972). Few students can avoid panic attacks when told that the viva will also test their knowledge of cognate fields. The message here is that it is not necessary to rush out and digest the latest textbook offering an overview of your discipline. Examiners simply wish to see that candidates are able to discuss what implications the thesis in question may have for their broader discipline.

Finally, there is the all-important question of when is a thesis a PhD and not an MPhil? Most university calendars are decidedly unhelpful on this issue, baldly stating that an MPhil falls short of a PhD by approximately 20,000 words and that while the former is an original contribution to knowledge the doctorate is a *substantial* original contribution. Beyond this pretentious verbiage there are usually two criteria in play. First, that a PhD is the product of extensive primary research and not simply an extended literature review which has dabbled selectively with some primary material. Second, that a successful PhD thesis has rigorously scrutinized existing secondary accounts and in the light of the candidate's primary research these accounts have been found wanting. This is not to over-emphasize the concept of originality. If a thesis plausibly shows some degree of novelty (maybe by simplifying a previous ambiguity or complicating a truism) while engaging with a substantial body of literature, then it is certainly on the PhD track. In many ways the Chicago sociologist Louis Wirth (quoted in Becker, 1985, p. 136) bent the stick too far in arguing that originality was the product of a faulty memory. Nevertheless, Wirth's sentiment is a useful corrective to the bland statements on originality contained in regulations governing higher degrees. Moreover, examiners are now often asked to consider whether the thesis is publishable, and if so (given the above provisos), then it is more than likely a PhD. Although this stipulation regarding publishability is not meant literally (too few theses now find their way to publishers), it is an indication that examiners increasingly pay attention to thesis presentation and the overall coherence of the candidate's argument.

Surviving (even enjoying) the final test

The PhD process is as much about professional socialization as it is about producing an original contribution to knowledge. The knack for all research students, regardless of discipline, is to pinpoint what is required and model your work accordingly. If you fashion your thesis to meet the criteria outlined above, then, with a modicum of preparation on the day, the viva can be less of an ordeal and more of a chance to parade your hard-earned expertise (don't be bashful, after three years full-time research you are, however unwittingly, an 'expert' in your field).

The role of the viva is to test your understanding, and the general adequacy, of the material contained in the thesis. Since the date of the viva can often be two or three months after final submission, candidates must be prepared, a few days before the event, to undertake the Herculean task of rereading the thesis in full to avoid memory lapses. Supine candidates never impress, so prepare a series of searching questions for the examiners. In particular, this is a rare chance for students to gather free, and hopefully informed, advice on how the thesis can best be publicized and published (at what conferences, what kinds of journal, what revisions will be required, can I state you recommend the manuscript when approaching publishers?). On the day a robust performance is required, but be careful to avoid dogmatism. Examiners are impressed by thoughtful, reflective candidates who give consideration to constructive criticism and are able to modify their arguments accordingly. Nevertheless, it is crucial to remember that in most instances you, as a doctoral candidate, have more knowledge of the topic under discussion than either of the examiners present. Make this knowledge tell by drawing in detail on the empirical material gathered to support your central arguments.

Although there are slight variations between institutions, there are four main recommendations that can be made by examiners following the viva. Firstly, and exceptionally, the thesis can be accepted as it stands and approved for the degree of PhD without alteration. Even with the widespread use of word-processors this recommendation is extremely rare, and most successful theses are approved for the degree in question subject to making minor corrections/ amendments. This second recommendation usually entails attending to typographical errors, renumbering footnotes and/or making slight revisions to paragraphs to include material specified by the examiners. More serious is the recommendation that the candidate be permitted to submit a revised thesis for the degree of PhD within a prescribed period. This process of 'referral' of a thesis is usually allowed on one occasion only, and it indicates that significant revisions are necessary. Referral (often termed 'revise and resubmit') is becoming an increasingly common recommendation as students struggle to complete within three years. The resubmission period can be as long as one year, and in this way referral gains students more time while guaranteeing that institutions meet ESRC submission deadlines. Nevertheless, with only one resubmission allowed, students should think twice before knowingly presenting a half-baked thesis. Finally, examiners can approve the thesis for a degree of lower status (at Master's level) or ask for the thesis to be resubmitted for consideration for a Master's degree or even decide to award no degree (in these cases many institutions allow students to appeal, usually on grounds of either mitigating circumstances unknown to the examiners or incompetent supervision).

Surviving the viva depends fundamentally on preparation and on students' ability to demystify the examination procedure. In his excellent account of how to write a thesis, Howard Becker (1986, p. 167) suggests that doctoral candidates apply sociology's great liberating message to their own scholarly situation. Understand, he argues, that the troubles you may have are not entirely your own doing, nor the result of some terrible personal defect, but something built into the organizations of academic life. This insight applies with equal force to the organization of the viva. Identifying problems caused by social organization is the first step towards their solution. If, therefore, as it is often claimed, examiners do not wish to inflict the pain of referral (or worse) on candidates, then more open public debate among students, supervisors and examiners on the role of the PhD oral will benefit us all.

Notes

1. An earlier version of this paper was published in *Journal of Graduate Education*, **1**, 1(1994), 30–4.
2. It is understandable that, given their wide scope, textbooks on social research methods typically stop short at discussing the viva. More surprising is the failure of most 'PhD handbooks' to discuss the oral examination in any detail (see, for example, Salmon, 1992). Phillips and Pugh (1994) offer some sound general advice, and Phillips (1994) is extremely useful. Rudestam and Newton (1992) have a short description of 'dissertation orals', but much of the discussion centres on the American system.
3. A much broader discussion of how I tackled the research process can be found in Burnham (1992).
4. See Walker (1993). *Gradnews* is published three times a year by the Graduate Network of the Political Studies Association.
5. For a guide to good supervisory practice, see Walker (1992).

References

Ackoff, L. (1953) *The Design of Social Research*. Chicago: University of Chicago Press.

Advisory Board for the Research Councils (ABRC). (1982) *Report of the Working Party on Postgraduate Education*. Cmnd 8537. London: HMSO.

Bahry, D. L. (1981) 'Crossing borders: the practice of comparative research', in J. Mannheim and R. Rich, *Empirical Political Analysis*. (1st edn). Englewood Cliffs, New Jersey: Prentice-Hall.

Barnes, B. (1982) *T. S. Kuhn and Social Science*. London: Macmillan.

Becker, H. S. (1986) *Writing for Social Scientists: How to Start and Finish Your Thesis, Book or Article*. Chicago: University of Chicago Press.

Bell, C. and Encel, S. (eds) (1978) *Inside the Whale*. Oxford: Pergamon.

Bell, C. and Newby, H. (eds) (1977) *Doing Sociological Research*. London: Allen and Unwin.

Bell, J. (1992) *Doing Your Research Project: A Guide to First Time Researchers in Education and Social Science*. Milton Keynes: Open University Press.

Borg, W. R. (1963) *Educational Research: An Introduction*. London: Longman.

Brannen, J. (1988) 'Research note: the study of sensitive subjects', *The Sociological Review*, **36**(3), 552–63.

Broers, A., Follett, B., Roberts, D. and Sutherland, S. (1996) 'We are the champions', *The Observer*, 22 December.

Burgess, R. G. (1984) *The Research Process in Educational Settings: Ten Case Studies*. London: Falmer.

Burgess, R. G. (1993) *Research Methods*. Surrey: Thomas Nelson and Sons.

Burgess, R. G. (ed.) (1982) *Field Research: A Sourcebook and a Field Manual*. London: Unwin Hyman.

Burgess, R. G. (ed.) (1994) *Postgraduate Education and Training in the Social Sciences: Processes and Products*. London: Jessica Kingsley.

Burnham, P. (1992) 'Method and myth in political research: a practical guide for research students', *Politics*, **12**(1).

Carew, A. (1987) *Labour Under the Marshall Plan*. Manchester: Manchester University Press.

Cohen, R. (1987) 'Theorising international labour', in R. Boyd, R. Cohen and P. Gutkind (eds) *International Labour and the Third World*. Aldershot: Gower.

Dahl, R. (1966) *Political Opposition in Western Democracies*. New Haven: Yale University Press.

Day, S. (1995) 'Slovakia – the end of the beginning or the beginning of the end?', *Coexistence*, **32**(4), 261–74.

Denzin, N. K. (1970) 'The sociological interview', in N. Denzin (ed.) *Sociological Methods: A Sourcebook*. Chicago: Aldine Publishing Co.

Dexter, L. A. (1970) *Elite and Specialised Interviewing*. Evanston, Illinois: North Western University Press.

Dogan, M. (1988) 'Introduction: strains on democracy', in M. Dogan (ed.) *Comparing Pluralist Democracies*. Boulder, Colorado: Westview.

Dogan, M. and Pellassy, D. (eds) (1980) *La Comparaison Internationale en Sociologie Politique*. Paris: Librairie Technique.

Dogan, M. and Pellassy, D. (eds) (1984) *How to Compare Nations: Strategies in Comparative Politics*. Chatham, New Jersey: Chatham House.

Duncker, P. (1996) *Hallucinating Foucault*. London: Serpent's Tail.

Dunleavy, P. and Rhodes, R. (1990) 'Core executive studies in Britain', *Public Administration*, **68** (Spring), 3–28.

ESRC (1991) *Postgraduate Training Guidelines*. Swindon: ESRC.

ESRC (1996) *Postgraduate Training Guidelines*. (2nd edn). Swindon: ESRC.

Finch, J. (1984) '"It's great to have someone to talk to": ethics and politics of interviewing women', in C. Bell and H. Roberts (eds) *Social Researching: Politics, Problems, Practice*. London: Routledge and Kegan Paul.

Fowler, H. W. (1960) *A Dictionary of Modern English Usage*. Oxford: Clarendon Press.

Franks, M. (1995) *The Internet Publishing Handbook*. London: Addison-Wesley.

Fukuyama, F. (1989) 'The end of history', *The Independent*, 20 September.

Garfinkel, H. (1967) *Studies in Ethnomethodology*. Englewood Cliffs, New Jersey: Prentice-Hall.

Giddens, A. (1976) *New Rules of Sociological Method*. London: Hutchinson.

Goodin, R. E. (1982) *Political Theory and Public Policy*. Chicago: University of Chicago Press.

Goodin, R. E. (1988) *Reasons for Welfare: The Political Theory of the Welfare State*. New Jersey: Princeton University Press.

Griffin, J. (1993) 'How we do ethics now', *Supplementary Volume of the Royal Institute of Philosophy* 35.

Hammond, P. (ed.) (1964) *Sociologists at Work*. New York: Basic Books.

Hedrick, T. E., Bickman, L. and Rog, D. (1993) *Applied Research Design: A Practical Guide*. London: Sage.

Heritage, J. (1984) *Garfinkel and Ethnomethodology*. Cambridge: Polity.

Heyd, D. (1992) *Genethics: Moral Issues in the Creation of People*. Los Angeles: University of California Press.

Hobbs, D. and May, T. (eds) (1993) *Interpreting the Field*. Oxford: Oxford University Press.

Hoggett, P., Jeffers, S. and Harrison, L. (1994) 'Reflexivity and uncertainty in the research process', *Policy and Politics*, **22**(1), 59–70.

House of Commons (1980) *Thirty-Fourth Report from the Committee of Public Accounts* (Session 1979–1980). London: HMSO.

House of Commons (1988) *Seventeenth Report from the Committee of Public Accounts* (Session 1987–1988). London: HMSO.

Humphreys, C. (1981) *Zen, a Way of Life*. Sevenoaks: Hodder and Stoughton.

Judd, C., Smith, E. and Kidder, L. (1991) *Research Methods in Social Relations*. (6th edn). Florida: Holt, Reinhart and Winston.

Kavanagh, D. (1991) 'Why political science needs history', *Political Studies*, **39**.

Kiely, R. (1991) *The Politics of Labour and Development in Trinidad and Tobago, 1937–90*. PhD Diss. University of Warwick, Department of Sociology.

Kiely, R. (1996) *The Politics of Labour and Development in Trinidad*. Kingston: University of West Indies Press.

Knorr-Cetina, K. (1991) 'Social scientific method', *Philosophy of the Social Sciences*, **11**, 335–59.

Lazarsfeld, P. (ed.) (1967) *The Uses of Sociology*. New York: Basic Books.

Lichtman, A. and French, V. (1978) *Historians and the Living Past*. London: Haarlan Davidson.

MacIntyre, A. (1985) *After Virtue*. London: Duckworth.

Maier, C. (1987) *In Search of Stability*. Cambridge: Cambridge University Press.

Mannheim, J. and Rich, R. (1991) *Empirical Political Analysis: Research Methods in Political Science*. (3rd edn). London: Longman.

Marsh, C. (1982) *The Survey Method*. London: Allen and Unwin.

Medawar, P. (1963) 'Is the scientific paper a fraud?', *The Listener*, 12 September.

Middlemas, K. (1979) *Politics in Industrial Society*. London: André Deutsch.

Miller, D. C. (1991) *Handbook of Research Design and Social Measurement*. London: Sage.

Moon, J. D. (ed.) (1986) *Responsibility, Rights and Welfare: Essays in the Welfare State*. Westport, Connecticut: Greenwood Press.

Munck, R. (1988) *The New International Labour Studies*. London: Zed.

Oakley, A. (1981) 'Interviewing women: a contradiction in terms', in H. Roberts (ed.) *Doing Feminist Research*. London: Routledge and Kegan Paul.

Oxford Dictionary for Writers and Editors. (1981) Oxford: Clarendon Press.

Parfit, D. (1984) *Reasons and Persons*. Oxford: Oxford University Press.

Phillips, E. (1994) 'Quality in the PhD: points at which quality may be assessed', in R. Burgess (ed.) *Postgraduate Education and Training in the Social Sciences: Processes and Products*. London: Jessica Kingsley.

Phillips, E. and Pugh, D. (1994) *How to Get a PhD: A Handbook for Students and Their Supervisors*. (2nd edition). Milton Keynes: Open University Press.

Plant, R., Lesser, H. and Taylor-Gooby, P. (1980) *Political Philosophy and Social Welfare*. London: Routledge and Kegan Paul.

Platt, J. (1976) *The Realities of Social Research*. Brighton: Sussex University Press.

Pridham, G. and Lewis, P. (eds) (1996) *Stabilising Fragile Democracies: Comparing New Party Systems in Southern and Eastern Europe*. London: Routledge.

Reese, A. (1996) 'Misfits, misprints, mistakes', *Times Higher Education Supplement*, 17 May.

Rose, R. (1988) 'Comparative policy analysis: the program approach', in M. Dogan (ed.) *Comparing Pluralist Democracies*. Boulder, Colorado: Westview.

Rudestam, K. and Newton, R. (1992) *Surviving Your Dissertation*. London: Sage.

Salmon, P. (1992) *Achieving a PhD – Ten Students' Experience*. Stoke-on-Trent: Trentham.

Sartori, G. (1970) 'Concept misinformation in comparative politics', *American Political Science Review*, **54**(4), 1033–53.

Sjoberg, G. (ed.) (1967) *Ethics, Politics and Social Research*. London: Routledge.

Stainton, T. (1994) *Autonomy and Social Policy: Rights and Mental Handicap*. Aldershot: Avebury Press.

Stanley, L. (ed.) (1990) *Feminist Praxis*. London: Routledge.

Thody, P. (1992) 'The exclusion of eccentricity', *Times Higher Education Supplement*, 28 February.

Truss, L. (1996) 'Pigging out in the babe zone', *The Times*, 28 February.

Turabian, K. (1992) *A Manual for Writers*. (5th edn). Chicago: University of Chicago Press.

Vidich, A., Bensman, J. and Stein, M. (eds) (1964) *Reflections on Community Studies*. New York: Harper Row.

Walker, D. (1992) 'Is your supervisor a superhero?', *Gradnews*, **2**.

Walker, D. (1993) 'Are you a model postgraduate?', *Gradnews*, **4**.

Ward, R. E. (1964) *Studying Politics Abroad: Field Research in the Developing Areas*. Toronto: Little, Brown and Co.

Watson, G. (1987) *Writing a Thesis*. London: Longman.

Weale, A. (1978) *Equality and Social Policy*. London: Routledge and Kegan Paul.

Weale, A. (1983) *Political Theory and Public Policy*. University of York: Social Policy Research Unit.

Weber, M. (1975) *Roscher and Knies: The Logical Problems of Historical Economics*. London: Free Press.

Wightman, G. (ed.) (1995) *Party Formation in East Central Europe*. Aldershot: Edward Elgar.

Winfield, G. (1987) *The Social Science PhD*. London: ESRC.

Woodard, C. (1995) 'The Internet's explosive expansion', *Transition*, **1**(18).

Woodward, J. (1986) 'The non-identity problem', *Ethics*, July.

Youngman, M. (1994) 'Supervisors' and students' experiences of supervision', in R. Burgess (ed.) *Postgraduate Education and Training in the Social Sciences: Processes and Products*. London: Jessica Kingsley.

Name Index

Subject Index